Mutual, Cooperative and Employee-Owned Businesses in the Asia Pacific

The 25 years leading up to the international financial crisis have been depicted as 'capitalism unleashed', containing deregulation, privatization, demutualization and financialization. Yet remarkably, given this economic and political context, co-operatives and mutuals appear to have been gaining ground in many countries, albeit modestly, even before the international financial crisis and the resulting global recession, from which the global economy is still only slowly recovering.

The 2007–2008 international financial crisis called into question how appropriate the shareholder-owned model is, certainly if it is allowed to dominate the financial services sector. However, the International Co-operative Alliance is determined to make the mutual and co-operative sector of the economy a dynamic, sustainable and increasingly important sector of the global economy. This book looks at the contribution of co-operative, mutual and employee-owned firms to the Asia Pacific economy – both currently and prospectively – and the challenges the standard 'Western' model faces regarding employment and output. It also looks at the role of governments, the nature of co-operatives in China and the role of the state, and the future prospects for cross-border growth of co-operative and mutual business within the Asia Pacific, and more widely.

This book was originally published as a special issue of *Asia Pacific Business Review*.

Chris Rowley, Cass Business School, City University, London, UK; HEAD Foundation, Singapore; Griffith Business School, Griffith University, Australia. He has published widely in the field of HRM and Asian business and management in leading journals and books. He is co-editor of the *Asia Pacific Business Review*.

Jonathan Michie is Professor of Innovation & Knowledge Exchange at the University of Oxford, UK, where he is President of Kellogg College, Director of the Department for Continuing Education and Director of the Oxford Centre for Mutual & Employee-owned Business.

Mutual, Cooperative and Employee-Owned Businesses in the Asia Pacific

Diversity, resilience and sustainable growth

Edited by
Chris Rowley and Jonathan Michie

Routledge
Taylor & Francis Group

LONDON AND NEW YORK

First published 2015
by Routledge

2 Park Square, Milton Park, Abingdon, Oxon OX14 4RN
711 Third Avenue, New York, NY 10017, USA

Routledge is an imprint of the Taylor & Francis Group, an informa business

First issued in paperback 2017

British Library Cataloguing in Publication Data
A catalogue record for this book is available from the British Library

ISBN 13: 978-1-138-84953-2 (hbk)
ISBN 13: 978-1-138-05979-5 (pbk)

Typeset in Times New Roman
by RefineCatch Limited, Bungay, Suffolk

Publisher's Note
The publisher accepts responsibility for any inconsistencies that may have
arisen during the conversion of this book from journal articles to book chapters,
namely the possible inclusion of journal terminology.

Disclaimer
Every effort has been made to contact copyright holders for their permission to
reprint material in this book. The publishers would be grateful to hear from any
copyright holder who is not here acknowledged and will undertake to rectify
any errors or omissions in future editions of this book.

Contents

CONTENTS

Citation Information

The chapters in this book were originally published in *Asia Pacific Business Review*, volume 20, issue 3 (July 2014). When citing this material, please use the original page numbering for each article, as follows:

Foreword

Foreword
Charles Gould
Asia Pacific Business Review, volume 20, issue 3 (July 2014) p. 321

Chapter 1

Differing forms of capital: setting the scene for mutuality and co-operation in the Asia Pacific Region
Chris Rowley and Jonathan Michie
Asia Pacific Business Review, volume 20, issue 3 (July 2014) pp. 322–329

Chapter 2

The long march of Chinese co-operatives: towards market economy, participation and sustainable development
Andrea Bernardi and Mattia Miani
Asia Pacific Business Review, volume 20, issue 3 (July 2014) pp. 330–355

Chapter 3

Old and new Rural Co-operative Medical Scheme in China: the usefulness of a historical comparative perspective
Andrea Bernardi and Anna Greenwood
Asia Pacific Business Review, volume 20, issue 3 (July 2014) pp. 356–378

Chapter 4

The role and characteristics of social entrepreneurs in contemporary rural cooperative development in China: case studies of rural social entrepreneurship
Hong Lan, Ying Zhu, David Ness, Ke Xing and Kris Schneider
Asia Pacific Business Review, volume 20, issue 3 (July 2014) pp. 379–400

Chapter 5

Governmental influences on the evolution of agricultural cooperatives in Vietnam: an institutional perspective with case studies

Anne Cox and Viet Le

Asia Pacific Business Review, volume 20, issue 3 (July 2014) pp. 401–418

Chapter 6

Development and challenges of cocoa cooperatives in Papua New Guinea: case of Manus province

Elena Garnevska, Harold Joseph and Tanira Kingi

Asia Pacific Business Review, volume 20, issue 3 (July 2014) pp. 419–438

Chapter 7

Growth pattern of an employee-owned business: a narrative inquiry concerning the new venture creation experience of Wowprime in Taiwan

Li-Chung Chang, Chao-Tung Wen, Yeg-Ming Chang and Pei-How Huang

Asia Pacific Business Review, volume 20, issue 3 (July 2014) pp. 439–460

Chapter 8

From corporate social responsibility to creating shared value with suppliers through mutual firm foundation in the Korean bakery industry: a case study of the SPC Group

Dongmin Lee, Junghoon Moon, Jongpyo Cho, Hyoung-Goo Kang and Jaeseok Jeong

Asia Pacific Business Review, volume 20, issue 3 (July 2014) pp. 461–483

Chapter 9

Assessing the performance of co-operatives in Malaysia: an analysis of co-operative groups using a data envelopment analysis approach

Azmah Othman, Norma Mansor and Fatimah Kari

Asia Pacific Business Review, volume 20, issue 3 (July 2014) pp. 484–505

Chapter 10

Mutuality in the Asia Pacific region

Jonathan Michie and Chris Rowley

Asia Pacific Business Review, volume 20, issue 3 (July 2014) pp. 506–511

Please direct any queries you may have about the citations to
clsuk.permissions@cengage.com

Notes on Contributors

Andrea Bernardi has been Senior Lecturer in Organizational Behaviour at Manchester Metropolitan University, UK, since 2012. Prior to that he was Assistant Professor at Nottingham University Business School (China) and Lecturer in Organization Studies at the University of Rome (Roma Tre). His main research interests have included the diversity of the co-operative firm, industrial relations, and occupational health and safety. He is currently working on Chinese co-operatives and on the historical perspective in Organization Studies.

Dr Li-Chung Chang (Brian) is an Associate Professor at the Department of Management, Guangzhou Vocational College of Science and Technology and at the University of Electronic Science and Technology of China, Zhongshan Institute. He received his PhD in Business Administration from National Chengchi University (Taiwan). He received his MBA (Master of Business Administration) and bachelor degree in Business Administration from National Sun Yat-Sen University (Taiwan). He was a Director Research Fellow at Topology Technology, an Associate Research Fellow at TIER (Taiwan Institute of Economic Research) and an Analyst at TECO Group and OSE (Orient Semiconductor Electronics).

Dr Yeg-Ming Chang is a Professor in the Department of Business Administration, National Chengchi University (Taiwan). He received his PhD in Business Administration from the University of Illinois at Urbana Champaign (USA), MBA from National Chengchi University (Taiwan) and a bachelor degree in Electrical Engineering from National Taiwan University (Taiwan).

Jongpyo Cho is a Researcher of Program in Regional Information at Seoul National University. His research interests include consumer behaviour for food industry.

Dr Anne Cox is a Senior Lecturer at the University of Wollongong, Australia. She researches and publishes in three main areas, namely the transfer of multinational companies' IR/HRM policies and practices across borders, the transformation of HRM/IR systems in developing countries and gender equity. Her book *The transformation of HRM and industrial relations in Vietnam* was published by Oxford Chandos Publishing in 2009.

Dr Elena Garnevska is a Senior Lecturer in Agribusiness Management at Massey University, New Zealand. Her research interests include agricultural cooperatives, international agribusiness and strategies for environmental sustainability in the agri-food sector. She has authored and co-authored publications in various agribusiness journals.

Charles Gould is Director-General of the International Co-operative Alliance.

Anna Greenwood is Assistant Professor in British Colonial History at the University of Nottingham, UK. Previously she was Associate Professor of European Colonial History at the University of Nottingham Ningbo, China (2010–2014), Lecturer in Medical History at the University of Exeter, UK (2009–2010) and Lecturer in Imperial History at the University of Strathclyde, UK (2005–2009). She has published widely on the history of medicine in British imperial possessions, particularly on the social and cultural aspects of colonial interchange. Her new empirical research focuses on Indian migration to colonial Africa, while her recent theoretical interests lie in the inter-disciplinary utilization of historical methods.

Dr Pei-How Huang is an Associate Professor in the Department of Business Administration, National Sun Yat-Sen University. He received his PhD and master degree in Business Economics from the University of Mannheim (Germany), and bachelor degree in Philosophy from Chinese Culture University (Taiwan).

Jaeseok Jeong is an Associate Professor of Marketing in International Business at the Graduate School of Pan-Pacific International Studies at Kyung Hee University. His research interests include marketing metrics and strategic marketing management.

Harold Joseph was a graduate student at Massey University, New Zealand. He currently works in the cooperative sector in PNG.

Hyoung-Goo Kang is an Assistant Professor in the Department of Finance at Hanyang University Business School. His research focuses on financial innovations, innovative institutions, and non-technological innovation. He is also a non-resident Research Fellow in the Edmond J. Safra Center for Ethics at Harvard University.

Fatimah Kari is formerly the Director of the Centre for Poverty and Development Studies (CPDS), University of Malaya and Associate Professor in the Department of Economics, Faculty of Economics and Administration, University of Malaya. She has published and presented many scholarly papers in the area of environment and poverty, Poverty Indexing, and environment and growth. She has been a consultant for several consultancy projects sponsored by the Ministry of Energy, Green Technology and Water (KeTTHA), Ministry of Natural Resources and Environment (MNRE) and Economic Planning Unit, Prime Minister's Department, Malaysia.

Tanira Kingi has worked at AgResearch since 2010. He has a BBS in Agribusiness, a M.App.Sc (Hons) in Agricultural Systems from Massey University, and a PhD in Agricultural Economics and Development from the Australian National University.

Hong Lan is an Associate Professor at the Renmin University of China, School of Environment and Natural Resources. Her research focuses on carbon finance and community development.

Dr Viet Le is a Lecturer at the Faculty of Business and Enterprise, Swinburne University of Technology, Australia. He has work and research experience in several countries in the Asia-Pacific. His research interests include economic development, business management, and business performance with a focus in Asia Pacific region.

Dongmin Lee is a Researcher of Program in Regional Information at Seoul National University. Her research interests include food marketing for food industry.

Norma Mansor is currently a Professor in the Department of Administrative Studies and Politics and Director of Social Security Research Centre, University of Malaya. She has written nearly 100 academic reports, articles and chapters in book on topics ranging from public policy, public administration and governance. She serves as reviewer and editorial board member of several journals.

Mattia Miani is a Manager of Enterprise and Executive Education at the Vietnam campus of RMIT University. He leads executive programmes for corporate and government clients. His interests include creativity training, corporate social responsibility and marketing. Prior to moving to Vietnam he was an advisor to the Italian cooperative movement and a Lecturer and Academic Director at Alma Graduate School – University of Bologna.

Jonathan Michie is Professor of Innovation & Knowledge Exchange at the University of Oxford, where he is President of Kellogg College, Director of the Department for Continuing Education and Director of the Oxford Centre for Mutual & Employee-owned Business.

Junghoon Moon is an Associate Professor of Program in Regional Information at Seoul National University. His research interests include food marketing and strategies, and information management for food industry. One of his studies was awarded best paper of the year at AMCIS (Americas Conference on Information Systems) 2006.

David Ness is an Adjunct Associate Professor at the Barbara Hardy Institute and Australian Centre for Asian Business, the University of South Australia. His research focuses on infrastructure and community development.

Azmah Othman is currently a Senior Lecturer in the Department of Development Studies, Faculty of Economics and Administration, University of Malaya. She has been involved in teaching, research, writing and publishing on topics related to co-operative, development, agriculture and poverty. She serves as a member of the National Co-operative Consultative Council under the Malaysia Cooperative Societies Commission.

Chris Rowley, Cass Business School, City University, London, UK; HEAD Foundation, Singapore; Griffith Business School, Griffith Unviersity, Australia. He has published widely in the field of HRM and Asian business and management in leading journals and books. He is co-editor of the *Asia Pacific Business Review*.

Kris Schneider is an academic member of the Faculty of Business, Economics and Statistics, University of Vienna. Her research focuses on alternative energy and community development.

Dr Chao-Tung Wen is a Professor at the Graduate Institute of Technology, Innovation and Intellectual Property Management. He received his PhD in Environmental Engineering from Rensselaer Polytechnic Institute (USA), a master degree in Business Administration from the University of Rochester (USA) and a bachelor degree in Industrial Engineering from Tunghai University (Taiwan).

Ke Xing is a Senior Lecturer in the School of Advanced Manufacturing & Mechanical Engineering and Barbara Hardy Institute, the University of South Australia. His research centres on information technology and infrastructure development.

Ying Zhu is a Professor and Director of the Australian Centre for Asian Business, the University of South Australia. His research centres on human resource management, leadership, employment relations and economic development.

Foreword

When states consider how best to shield their economies from the financial turbulence witnessed in recent years, how best to empower individuals to lift their own livelihoods, how best to incentivize decision-making that is sustainable for the environment, for communities, and for the economy, co-operatives should figure large in their planning. The International Co-operative Alliance, which has studied and supported the co-operative model of enterprise since 1895, has evidence to show that it is, by design, a sustainable model, in good times and bad, less buffeted by recessions, in part due to its lower risk profile, a natural result of being created to serve specific needs of its member–owners, rather than to pursue profit for itself.

Co-operatives are not new to the Asia-Pacific region. Asian countries were among those that established the International Co-operative Alliance, and Asian countries feature in the Alliance's World Co-operative Monitor, an annual report on the world's largest co-operatives. Japan, South Korea, New Zealand, and Australia are all in the top 20 list of co-operatives with annual turnovers exceeding USD 100 million. When the list is organized by turnover relative to the country's per capita GDP, the inclusion is dramatically increased, and in fact the five largest co-operatives in the world, by that measure, are from the region (in India, Japan, and South Korea).

As a percentage of these overall economies, however, the co-operative sector remains under-represented today. Rectifying this requires a legal and policy framework that supports co-operative establishment and growth. This is one of five critical strategic areas that the International Co-operative Alliance identified in its Blueprint for a Co-operative Decade, adopted by its members in 100 countries at the conclusion of the United Nations International Year of Co-operatives in 2012. Too often, co-operatives are forced to try to work within legislation that was drafted for a different and dominant model and which does not allow for the unique needs of a distinctive owner–member model; or they are prohibited from operating in certain business sectors, largely due to outdated thinking or misunderstandings about the co-operative model.

Ministers in the Asia-Pacific Region have recognized this need for a supportive policy environment, recently at the 9th Asia-Pacific Co-operative Ministers' Conference on Co-operative Legislation and Policy, organized by the International Co-operative Alliance in Bangkok in February 2012. As a result of this commitment to a larger and more durable space for co-operatives, we have seen significant legislative improvements in the Philippines, Bhutan, Sri Lanka, and India, to name a few.

Continued government backing will require fresh, contemporary, relevant data on the ongoing impact of co-operative enterprises today. Studies and assessments such as those represented in this special issue are essential to keeping the co-operative agenda front and centre. All of us in the co-operative movement express our appreciation for the work of the authors and editors of this Review.

Charles Gould
Director-General
International Co-operative Alliance

1

Differing forms of capital: setting the scene for mutuality and co-operation in the Asia Pacific Region

Chris Rowley and Jonathan Michie[1]

The post-2008 global financial crisis rekindled the spotlight on alternative forms of corporate organization, including mutuals and co-operatives. These are the focus for this collection. We explain and cover such organizational forms across north-east Asia (China, Taiwan, South Korea) and south-east Asia (Vietnam, Papua New Guinea, Malaysia) and a range of sectors, from agriculture to bakeries to health. We also provide a tabular overview of the collection's content and proffer some implications and pointers to the future for both research and theory.

Introduction

The 'standard' business organizational model or pattern has generally been regarded to be private ownership, either directly by an individual or family or by external shareholders, often as 'at all costs' profit-maximizers and aggressively competitive. This narrow, blinkered and ethnocentric perspective has too often been blindly followed in academia and research. Yet, there are alternatives to this. These include mutuals and co-operatives, organizations that are generally owned and run by and for members. Indeed, following the 2008 global financial crisis, such organizational forms and structures have received renewed interest, especially by some politicians who have belatedly come to see the 'standard' or 'typical' private sector organization, especially in finance, as having no social responsibility, being rapacious and overly paying for non-performance due in part to moral hazard. There are clearly alternatives to this.

The rest of this introduction takes the following structure. We provide a background to mutuals and co-operatives, consider some examples and discuss their links to corporate social responsibility (CSR). We then provide an outline of the collection's content by themes, sectors, theories and methods in tabular form and note the content. Finally, we provide a brief discussion and some implications for the future.

Background and examples

Mutuals and cooperatives have a long history and stories of their success in terms of contributions to economic and social development can be found across sectors and around the world. The roots of modern co-operation can be traced back to a variety of forms of collective or communitarian work, such as those within the Roman Empire, ancient Egypt, ancient Asian societies or the Latin American pre-Columbian peoples. In 1844, the first modern co-operative organized around a formal business model was established in Rochdale, near Manchester, UK. As a response to the side effects and social problems of the industrial revolution, Western societies developed the co-operative model. In the following years, the co-operative became a worldwide model of economic organization across production, retail, manufacturing, services and banking sectors (Bernardi and Miani[2]).

The co-operative movement involves share ownership, but it is not monolithic, with four categories (Bounds 2013). These are (1) consumer-owned, where members are the customers, who could have an account with a credit union or live in a housing co-operative; (2) worker-owned, where members are employees, represented at board level, but professionals often run enterprises; (3) enterprise-owned, where members are businesses that trade with the co-operative, with common ones being farmers' co-operatives selling crops centrally and sharing costs, some have been set up by independent retailers to pool buying power and share distribution; (4) mixed, where members are customers, staff and producers, which include football clubs, local pubs and village shops.

For the UK, the term 'mutual' covers several different ownership models which are organizations ' . . . owned by, and run for, the benefits of its members, who are actively and directly involved in the business – whether its employees, suppliers, or the community or consumers it serves, rather than being owned and controlled by outside investors' (BIS 2011, 2). Mutuals can be based on a variety of legal structures. There is also an incorporated legal structure which is specifically mutual: the industrial and provident society, with two types: co-operative societies and community benefit societies (BIS 2011). Co-operative societies operate for the benefit of their members and distribute any surplus to them. Co-operative is defined by the International Co-operative Alliance as 'an autonomous association of persons united voluntarily to meet their common economic, social cultural needs and aspirations through jointly owned and democratically controlled enterprise' (in BIS 2011). Co-operatives must also reflect four ethical values: honesty, openness, social responsibility (see our later link to CSR) and caring for others, while subscribing to a set of principles: voluntary and open membership; democratic member control; member economic participation; autonomy and independence; provision of education, training and information; and co-operation among co-operatives.

The advantages of mutuals and co-operatives include managing in the best interests of customers; focus on long-term horizons and minimizing principal-agent problems. However, weaknesses and problems of employee governance are noted (Nam 2003). These include risk aversion, lacking information required for strategic decision-making; monitoring difficulties in capital-intensive firms and heterogeneity of interests and objectives. There are also problems of difficulties in financing investments and making sustained growth as well as poor incentives for more productive employees and managers (Nam 2003).

We now note one of the most famous workers co-operatives, Mondragon, founded by a Catholic priest in Spain's Basque country in 1956. One of the world's largest collectively owned companies and one of Spain's top 10 companies by turnover, it is a conglomerate stretching from banking to supermarkets with revenue of E14 billion (2014), 83,000 employees, with about 50% collective members. However, Spain's post-2008 global financial crisis finally caught up with its oldest member – Fagor – Europe's 5th biggest white goods manufacturer, employing 5600 and generating 8% of the group's sales in 2012, as it filed for protection against creditors (Johnson 2013).

Indeed, mutuals have also come under increasing external threats from the 1980s. In the USA, legislative changes boosted trends to de-mutualise, as had happened in the UK and also Australia. This has reduced the capacity for new mutuals to form with ' . . . confidence that they will retain their proper function of enabling their members to engage in self-help' – at the cost of excluding sections of society whose interests mutuals served, and public trust (Mathews 2000, 3).

Might Asia be different when it comes to mutuality and co-operation? We might think so for a number of reasons. An important reason is the context – socio-economic and cultural – which leads us to expect there may be more fertile ground because of cultures of Confucianism and collectivism (see Rowley 2013). Then there is the potentially greater 'agency problem' in Asia because of the long-term and continuing dominance of families in business organization across a range of economies. Therefore, the origin and role of co-operation in Asia, particularly in countries characterized by Confucianism, collectivism and community values, are important. However, in reality the situation is more complicated, not only because of other conflicting values, but also as values have to engage with economic and political regimes, which have evolved from colonial regimes and centrally planned economies under state control to more open free markets.

Co-operatives did operate in Asian countries, although data are hard to come by. Some of the best known are Singaporean co-operatives, established by the National Trade Union Congress (NTUC) with government support, such as taxi and mini-bus services (Nam 2003). However, here the goals are not only to provide low-priced goods and services, but to allow union leaders to gain management experience in a way that is expected to contribute to better labour-management relations. Such attempts at integration are typical of this economy. This model was replicated in Indonesia with its transportation co-operative, but which is closer to a consumer co-operative (Nam 2003). In the Philippines, worker co-operatives are relatively new but legislation was introduced to boost them (Villegas 2012). Another possible example is China's Huawei, founded in 1887 and now one of the world's largest telecom companies. It has been argued that it is almost 99% 'owned' by 80,000 of its 150,000 employees under an 'employee stock option plan' introduced in 1997. However, in reality it is not controlled by such common shareholders, but rather by an elite subset of its management (Serastopulo 2014).

This leads us to issues of governance. Since ownership is a prime source of governance, worker-ownership provides another channel for workers to participate in corporate governance (Nam 2003). Indeed, the idea of greater 'industrial democracy' and 'employee directors' was an area of policy and practical reform in Europe and even the UK up to the 1980s with widespread academic interest. Also, as we saw, one of the 'ethical values' for co-operatives was 'social responsibility'. Thus, another strand to the area of mutuals and co-operatives concerns CSR.

CSR

Meanings and definitions of CSR have proliferated since the 1950s and it remains a contested concept. In contrast to traditional views that an organization's primary (if not sole) responsibility is to shareholders earning a return for investors and complying with laws, others see further 'higher' (albeit profitability remains primary) responsibilities – ethical and philanthropic. This also includes other constituencies, such as employees, suppliers, customers, local communities, governments, environmental groups and other special interest groups or 'stakeholders'. This extension of economic responsibilities to non-economic (or social) domains with morals and values was popularized by Carroll (1979).

Carroll's (1979) conceptualization of CSR has been durable and widely cited. Its pyramid of four 'layers' of organizational responsibilities suggests a sequential order, weighting and evolution of importance and development. Thus, early company emphasis on the economic (profitability), then legal (law abiding) is followed by others – ethical (conducting affairs in a fair and just way, to more than just comply, but to also make proactive efforts to anticipate and meet society norms) and finally discretionary (to be socially supportive and 'good citizens', with such things as philanthropic support for communities, donating employee expertise and time to causes, etc.) responsibilities in business conduct (Carroll 1983). Carroll (2004) also incorporated the notion of stakeholders into CSR. This moved it closer to earlier stakeholder theory that organizations be responsive to the competing demands of multiple stakeholders (Freeman 1984).

CSR has developed some convergence towards sustainability, with ideas that company success requires consideration of both the natural and the social environment. This movement has led corporations to take a more strategic perspective as an approach to non-market strategies to benefit from the creation of 'social value', or creating shared value (CSV). Thus, CSV expands CSR by adding in the total pool of economic and social value, rather than redistributing values already created by firms (Lee et al.).

Content

We now provide an overview of the content of the rest of this volume. Its spatial range goes from north-east Asia (China, Taiwan, South Korea) to south-east Asia (Vietnam, Papua New Guinea, Malaysia). It also has broad sectoral and organizational coverage, from rural, agriculture, cocoa to restaurants, bakery to health. The themes range from co-operative history, socio-economic and political contexts, rural social entrepreneurship and leadership, evolutionary ownership patterns to measuring performance. To help organize our content, we use a structure that moves from a focus on the more macro, broader and historical to the more micro, narrower and contemporary. We provide an overview of content by country, theme, sector, theory and methods in simple tabular form in Table 1.

First, 'The long march of Chinese co-operatives: towards market economy, participation and sustainable development' provides a useful and important history of co-operative firms in China from their origins. It describes how the co-operative movement diverged from the Western notions. To understand the similarities and differences, it considers a number of economic and cultural factors, including the etymology of the Chinese and English words for 'co-operative', Confucian culture and the influence of political contingencies.

Second, 'Old and new rural co-operative medical scheme in China: the usefulness of a historical comparative perspective' compares the 1960s health co-operatives to the post-2002 New Rural Medical Cooperative System. China's challenge has been an affordable and effective means of providing equitable medical care to the rural millions. So, the 2002 Scheme provides basic medical insurance in return for annual membership payments, underpinning the development of a sustainable health framework. However, to understand the present, we first need to understand the past context from which this health scheme evolved Therefore, this work maps the continuities and discontinuities in the way the co-operative model has been deployed under these different contexts.

Third, 'The role and characteristics of social entrepreneurs in contemporary rural cooperative development in China: case studies of rural social entrepreneurship' notes that rural communities have experienced rapid changes as social entrepreneurship led by village leaders and entrepreneurial individuals increased. It explores the key issues related to the role of social entrepreneurship and leadership in developing co-operatives. Economic reform led to large societal changes in particular rural communities experienced rapid transformation in three stages. First, the 1980s reform was based on replacing the 'commune system' with a 'household responsibility system' which allocated land to

Table 1. Content coverage by country, theme, sector, theory and methods.

Paper	Country(s)	Theme(s)	Sector(s)	Theory(s)	Method(s)
1	China	Co-operative history Content: political, economic and cultural	All	Civil society Human development	Etymological Historical and conceptual analysis
2	China	Rural health care Historical context	Health	History + organization	Archive work Historical analysis
3	China	Rural social entrepreneurship Village leadership	Rural	Social constructivism	Interviews (6)
4	Vietnam	State Legal environment	Agriculture	Institutional approach	Case studies (2) Interviews (17)
5	PNG	Cooperative development State	Agriculture, Coca	Cooperative	Case studies (4) Interviews (22)
6	Taiwan	Ownership pattern stages Succession planning	Restaurants	Dynamic circles	Narrative inquiry Interviews (7)
7	South Korea	Strategy transformation process CSR and CSV	Bakery	Activity Triple helix	Case study: Focus group and interviews
8	Malaysia	Performance: productivity and efficiency State	All	Mutual incentive	Data envelopment analysis

individual households for agri-production and business. Second, from the early 2000s, reform was based on 'voluntary co-operatives' emphasizing new business co-operation among villagers through village enterprises and their connection with markets. Third, the more recent reform with the slogan of 'new countryside development' encouraged rural communities not only for economic growth, but also well-being in education, healthcare, infrastructure and services and ecological sustainability. Given the challenging political, social and economic environments, the role and characteristics of rural social entrepreneurs are examined.

Fourth, 'Governmental influences on the evolution on agricultural co-operatives in Vietnam: an institutional perspective with case studies' examines the development and government roles in agricultural co-operatives. Agricultural collectivization remains a significant issue in Vietnamese political and economic history. Co-operative development went through four phases: voluntary collectivization, 1954–1975; compulsory collectivization, 1975–1981, de-collectivization, 1981–1997; neo-collectivization, since 1997. The sector remains important not only in gross domestic product terms, but especially for employment.

Fifth, 'Development and challenges of Cocoa cooperatives in Papua New Guinea: the case of Manus Province' covers the co-operative movement in PNG. Co-operatives have had a significant contribution to development and the cocoa industry was PNG's second most important in terms of export earnings. The industry had been contracting and the local government tried to revitalize it by promoting co-operative development. The government in 2000 implemented policy reform for economic recovery and growth; empowerment of people; poverty alleviation and infrastructure development. Agricultural-based co-operatives were promoted to increase farm production and income, employment opportunities and self-reliance and contribute to communities and national development.

Sixth, 'Growth pattern of an employee-owned business: a narrative inquiry concerning the new venture creation experience of wowprime in Taiwan' explores patterns of growth in employee-owned business. It outlines four stages: (1) 'family-owned', (2) 'family- and manager-owned', (3) 'family-, manager- and staff-owned' and (4) 'family-, manager-, staff- and franchisee-owned'. It seeks to explain why mutual ownership can better grasp opportunities and turn environmental threats into new opportunities.

Seventh, 'From corporate social responsibility to creating shared value with suppliers through mutual firm foundation in the Korean bakery industry: a case study of the SPC Group' analyses the transformation process of non-market strategy from CSR to CSV. Important reasons for establishing co-operatives were: economies of scale, responding to government policy and seeking government support, overcoming market constraints (i.e. transport costs), increasing efficiency in processing, employment opportunities and household incomes. The framework depicts cases of supplier relationship management (SRM), through the activity of a bakery franchise using non-market strategies as a tool for SRM. The analysis explains the backgrounds of the change and their ramifications on SRM actions, such as mutual firm foundations, long-term contracts and temporal relations. A mutual firm is suggested as the representative form of CSV activity.

Eight, 'Assessing the performance of co-operatives in Malaysia: an analysis of co-operative groups using a data envelopment analysis approach' looks at the productivity and efficiency of co-operative groups. Although co-operatives were first introduced to Malaysia by the British colonial administration, they were not considered significant for economic growth in national development plans. The primary objective of co-operatives was to assist people in rural areas to combat rural and urban indebtedness. Despite greater state involvement in the economy through the New Economic Policy (1970–1990), with its twin objectives of eradicating poverty and restructuring of society with very strong identification of race with economic activities (see Rowley and Bhopal 2006), co-operatives were still not viewed as mechanisms for growth. The focus was on private sector enterprise and foreign direct investment to propel economic growth. Finally, the role of the co-operative movement was recognized as a 'third sector' in contributing to the economy, but no serious effort was made to develop them. However, post-1997 Asian Financial Crisis the government did begin to consider the option of co-operatives, although it still took a decade to reform institutional support to ensure stability and soundness of financial and management operations of co-operatives.

Discussion and implications

Our overview of the themes and contents of this collection produces several implications for further discussion. First, it shows the importance of mutual and co-operative forms of organization in Asia, despite the all-too-common academic focus on large, 'blue chip' and 'successful' private sector companies.

Second, the collection has implications for research. It indicates the wealth of indigenous research coming from the Asia Pacific. This is often undertaken by local teams of collaborators. It also shows the useful diversity of research methods being used in such research.

Third, in turn this leads to issues in business and management research and theory, not only internationally, but across contexts. This includes the issues of conceptual and measurement equivalence and possible ways to address these (see Shapiro et al. 2007 and Cascio 2012 for explanations and details) in research and also relevant theorizing.

Conclusion

In this overview, we have outlined the background to alternative organizational forms – mutuals and co-operatives – and given examples of their operation. We have detailed the content of the collection and also noted some implications for future research and theory development for this topic as situated in the Asian Pacific area, and for Asia more generally.

Notes

1. Email: jonathan.michie@kellogg.ox.ac.uk
2. Where listed without year the reference refers to authors in this collection.

References

BIS. 2011. "A Guide to Mutual Ownership Models." Department of Business, Innovation and Skills, November.

Bounds, A. 2013. "A Model That Covers Farms and Footballers." *Financial Times*, November 19, p. 3.

Carroll, A. B. 1979. "A Three-Dimensional Conceptual Model of Corporate Performance." *Academy of Management Review* 4 (4): 497–505.

Carroll, A. B. 1983. "Corporate Social Responsibility: Will Industry Respond to Cut-Backs in Social Program Funding?" *Vital Speeches of the Day* 49: 604–608.

Carroll, A. B. 2004. "Managing Ethically with Global Stakeholders: A Present and Future Challenge." *Academy of Management Executive* 18 (2): 114–120.

Cascio, W. 2012. "Methodological Issues in International HR Management Research." *International Journal of Human Resource Management* 23 (12): 2532–2545.

Freeman, R. E. 1984. *Strategic Management: A Stakeholder Approach*. Boston, MA: Pitman Publishing.

Johnson, M. 2013. "Mondragon Cooperative Reels After Loss of Oldest Member." *Financial Times*, December 10, p. 22.

Mathews, R. 2000. "Co-Operatives: The Growing Threat to Credit Unions, Mutuals." *News Weekly*, October 21.

Nam, S. W. 2003. "Employees in Asian Enterprises: Their Potential Role in Corporate Governance." *Asia Development Bank Institute*, Research Paper 52.

Rowley, C. 2013. "The Changing Nature of Management and Culture in South Korea." In *Managing Across Diverse Cultures in East Asia*, edited by M. Warner, 122–150. London: Routledge.

Rowley, C., and M. Bhopal. 2006. "The Ethnic Factor in State-Labour Relations: The Case of Malaysia." *Capital and Class* 88: 87–116.

Serastopulo, D. 2014. "Huawei Starts to Open Doors Over Ownership." *Financial Times*, February 28, p. 19.

Shapiro, D., M. A. Von Glinow, and Z. Xiao. 2007. "Toward Polycontexually Sensitive Research Methods." *Management and Organization Review* 3 (1): 129–152.

Villegas, B. 2012. "Worker Cooperatives." *Changing World, Manila Bulletin*, July 13.

The long march of Chinese co-operatives: towards market economy, participation and sustainable development

Andrea Bernardi[a,b1] and Mattia Miani[c2]

aDepartment of Management, Manchester Metropolitan University, Manchester, UK; bNottingham University Business School China, Ningbo, P.R. China; cRMIT International University, Ho Chi Minh City, Vietnam

This work presents a history of the co-operative firm in China from its origins in the early twenth century. The aim is to describe how in its evolution, the Chinese Co-operative Movement has diverged from the western notion of a co-operative. To understand the similarities and the divergence, we will consider a number of economic and cultural factors, including the etymology of the Chinese and English words for 'co-operative', the Confucian culture and the influence of the political contingencies. We argue that contemporary Chinese economic transition would benefit from the presence of a strong, western style, co-operative sector but that the contribution of the co-operative sector towards sustainability cannot take place unless a civil society develops as well.

1. Introduction

The co-operative firm is an institution with a very long history. The roots of modern co-operation can be traced back to a variety of forms of collective or communitarian work, such as those that existed within the Roman Empire, ancient Egypt, ancient Asian societies, or the Latin American pre-Columbian peoples (Douglas 1986).

In 1844, the first modern co-operative organized around a formal business model was established in Rochdale, near Manchester, UK. At the end of the industrial revolution, and as a response to its side effects and social problems, western societies developed the co-operative model; co-operatives emerged from the same context that generated the Workers' and Democratic Movements of the 1800s, trade unions, the Communist Manifesto and later the *Rerum Novarum* encyclical. In the following 150 years, the modern co-operative became a worldwide model of economic organization in agriculture, retail, manufacturing, services and banking sectors (Birchall 1997).

The origin and the role of co-operation in Asia, and particularly in China and other countries with a Confucian culture, have received relatively little attention in scholarly research (Taimni 2000). It is particularly important to study the role of the co-operative firm in countries with a culture characterized by a high propensity for collectivism and community values (Hofstede 2001; Lockett 1988; Hofstede and dan Bond 1988; Littrell 2002). It might be expected that countries which embrace such collective values would provide fertile ground for co-operation to take root and grow. In reality, the situation is much more complicated, not only because the propensity for collectivism coexists with other conflicting values (Laaksonen 1984), but above all because these values have to engage with the economic and political regimes that have developed in these countries. Despite their success and diffusion, to measure national cultures remains a controversial methodological challenge (McSweeney 2002; Williamson 2002).

Studying co-operation in Asian countries such as China (Taimni 1994), and also Vietnam (Kornai and Yingyi 2009; Taimni 2000) and Cambodia, it is vital to address how this form of enterprise has evolved in a period of transition (Hongyi 2000) from centrally planned economies which are under the strict control of the state to economies open to the dynamics of the free market (Smith 1994).

The modern form of co-operative arrived in China at the beginning of the twentieth century. This work argues that the model has proved to fit with Chinese institutions and local historical contingencies and that it might prove especially useful to the transformations that contemporary China is undergoing, particularly in dealing with social and economic inequalities and sustainable development. The Chinese Government and Legislature have recently (in the 12th Five-Year Plan and in the 2013 meetings of the National People's Congress) defined such challenges and, in some cases, have explicitly mentioned the co-operative firm as a tool that might help to address them.

This work has its foundations in a literature review of international literature on the Co-operative Movement. But the authors' experiences of teaching and doing research in academic institutions in Asia (China and Vietnam) also played a role in its genesis. In particular, one author was able to visit a number of co-operatives and to engage with co-operative leaders in the following areas: Beijing, Shanghai, Hong Kong, Zhejiang and Guangxi. The research questions that triggered this investigation are:

(1) Does the western notion of the co-operative fit the Chinese case?
(2) Has Maoism contributed to the flourishing of the Co-operative Movement?
(3) How has the co-operative model evolved alongside political and institutional transition?
(4) Can the Co-operative Movement contribute to contemporary China's development and sustainability challenges?

We have not followed the traditional order (literature review–data analysis). This is because the four research questions investigate very different issues and hence will be addressed with varied methods of analysis. Individual sections are devoted to answering each research question following the relative literature review and analysis. The first analysis is etymological. The second and third questions are answered through theoretical and historical analysis. The fourth question is addressed through a theoretical analysis and by adopting the Human Development Index (HDI).

In Section 2, *Co-operatives and China*, we will answer the first research question after the etymological analysis of the Chinese word 'co-operative', the analysis of western and Chinese notions of co-operation and its history. In Section 3, *Co-operatives and Mao*, we will answer the second research question with a literature review and an historical analysis that will highlight how Maoism has dramatically changed the evolutionary path of the Chinese Co-operative Movement. In Section 4, *A long institutional transition*, we will answer the third research question by providing a historical account of the main forms of collective and co-operative organizations in the People's Republic of China. In Section 5, after identifying the *Challenges of contemporary China*, we will answer the fourth research question with a policy approach. Section 6 will present the implications for theory, practice and policy. Brief conclusions will follow.

2. Co-operatives and China

Enquiry into Chinese co-operatives begins with a linguistic and epistemological difficulty: do we mean the same thing in China and in the West when we talk about a co-operative? To answer this, we will turn to the etymology of key terms, to the values promulgated by the International Co-operative Movement and to the dominant Chinese cultural values.

2.1 Etymology

To start with etymology, according to the Merriam-Webster dictionary, the use of the adjective 'co-operative' dates back to at least 1603, when it meant 'willingness or ability' to work with others. As a substantive, it was already established enough in the late 1820s for William King to publish a series of papers entitled 'The Co-operator'. The word 'co-operation' in English means 'working together', using the prefix 'co-' from the Latin 'cum' ('be with'). The Chinese definition is more complex. It brings in a number of related concepts that in English have found expression through other formulations, such as 'mutual aid', 'mutual help' and so on. The Oxford English Dictionary provides a definition of the co-operative firm:

> The combination of a number of persons, or of a community, for purposes of economic production or distribution, so as to save, for the benefit of the whole body of producers or customers, that which otherwise becomes the profit of the individual capitalist. As originally used by Owen the name contemplated the co-operation of the whole community for all economic purposes, i.e. communism. In practice, the principle has been carried out in production, when a body of workmen corporately own the capital by which their concern is carried on, and thus unite within themselves the interests of capital and labour, of employer and employed; and in distribution, when an association of purchasers contribute the capital of a store by which they are supplied with goods, and thus combine in themselves the interests of trader and customers.

In Mandarin Chinese, the characters used for co-operative are 合作社; the Pinyin transliteration is *He Zuo She*.

He (合): a pictographic character. The character is reminiscent of a container, the lower rectangle (口), with a lid, the upper triangle (△). This originally meant 'close or shut the lid'. Subsequently, it has come to mean assemble, unite, ally, combine, and even to merge, amalgamate, marry and make friends (Zuo 2006; Xie 2000).

Zuo (作): an ideographic character. In ancient bronze-age inscriptions, the lower part resembled a knife and the top represented divination. The overall image is that of an oracle engaged in divination through the use of the knife on plants or animals. The range of meanings of the character has included making, embarking on, cutting and setting up. Later the meaning of the character was extended to doing, arising, building, performing, playing and reaching (Gu 2008).

She (社): an ideographic and pictographic character. In the ancient scriptures of the Bronze Age, it represented veneration of the god of the earth. The character is composed of two parts: on the right, a stone altar, a place for offerings and sacrifices, and on the left worship combined with the character for wood. In ancient times, these traits take on the complex meaning of a place of sacrifice to the god of the earth, municipality and agency (Gu 2008). Today, the immediate meaning is work unit or social structure. The place of worship of deities or ancestors in Chinese villages was located at the centre of the family home or the village itself. For this reason, the image of the place of worship takes us to the idea of social structure.

While *He* stands for an attitude (coherence, no conflict, harmony), *Zuo* stands for a form of behaviour (to act, to do, to start) and, finally, *She* stands for a place where the action takes place (the team, the group, the community, the small firm). Thus, the etymology of the Chinese word for co-operation invokes images of union, mutual help, realization, society and community. Such images are fully compatible with the western conception of the idea of co-operation (Cheng-Chung 1988). In this model of a firm, it is the workers and members of the co-operative who own it. As such, this type of firm tends to take an especial interest in sustainable and responsible development.

2.2 *International values*

The leading co-operative organization, the International Co-operative Alliance (ICA), has helped to define a set of common values among the national Co-operative Movements. In defining a co-operative firm, the ICA in 1995 drafted a statement of co-operative identity: 'A co-operative is an autonomous association of persons united voluntarily to meet their common economic, social, and cultural needs and aspirations through a jointly-owned and democratically-controlled enterprise.' This definition is especially useful in understanding the co-operative phenomenon because it is the result of the combined work of delegates of national co-operative associations from all over the world.

In defining the essence of a co-operative firm, one might be tempted to adopt a legal definition. While co-operative enterprises exist in most jurisdictions around the world, each country provides a different, sometimes deeply different, legal definition of a co-operative enterprise. Clearly, it is not the legal form to differentiate co-operative firms from other forms of enterprise. The ICA definition helps us overcome this challenge of identifying similarities across a number of different manifestations of the phenomenon.

To qualify as a co-operative, the definition suggests that the following criteria need to be met:

(a) Autonomy from other organizations: A co-operative cannot be owned by another enterprise, but it can control other entities for instrumental purposes.
(b) Persons united voluntarily: Again, if people are forced to join, the organization ceases to be a genuine co-operative. This element does not rule out co-operative consortia, but only if they are built ultimately to serve the individual.
(c) Economic, social and cultural needs. This element of the definition is crucial to expanding the notion of the co-operative firm beyond the realm of mere economic exchange and hence taking into account organizations focused on solving social problems or promoting cultural production and consumption.
(d) Jointly-owned: Members must also be shareholders of the organization.
(e) Democratically controlled: There must be a competitive governance system, in which people can contribute effectively to steering the organization.

In its 1995 statement, the ICA moves beyond a simple working definition to spell out seven universal values to be embraced by co-operative enterprises (they have subsequently become part of co-operative founding charters in several countries). Some of these values are a direct consequence of the principles embedded in the definition we are using: *Voluntary and open membership*; *Democratic member control*; *Autonomy and independence*; *Member economic participation*. However, three further value statements are worthy of note, adding some flavour to the overall definition of a co-operative enterprise: education, training and information; co-operation among co-operatives and concern for community.

The idea of education, training, and information as a founding value can be linked to the idea of democratic control: it is hard to imagine members being an effective part of the organizational governance if they are not properly informed of and trained in their role.

The last principle is of great interest in order to fully comprehend the nature of a co-operative firm: that a co-operative is concerned for community is not a truism, as it might appear at first sight. Rather, it means that it should go beyond its members' interests to embrace the interest of the wider community. In other words, according to this principle, co-operatives should be socially responsible entities taking into account all of their stakeholders' interests (Bernardi 2007; MacPherson 2008).

The principle of co-operation among co-operatives can be seen as the founding principle of the Co-operative Movement in its contemporary sense (Birchall 1997). The principle is well illustrated by the existence of a myriad of co-operative business associations and consortia representing the interests of co-operatives at the local and national level. At the international level, the ICA is technically an association of associations and this principle is connected to the notion of an International Co-operative Movement (Birchall 1997). Through the ICA and national associations, co-operative enterprises can be seen as 'activists', promoting co-operative firms as a potential solution for a number of economic and social issues (Nilsson 1996). A number of individuals in the early nineteenth century played a role in the birth of the Co-operative Movement, most significantly, Robert Owen and William King, but the history of the Movement dates back to 1844, with the institution of the first successful co-operative: The Rochdale Society of Equitable Pioneers. By no accident, their rulebook shares a great deal in common with the ICA's current definition.

Applying these definitions to the Chinese context may be challenging because some of the components of the definition could be called in question when it comes to the development of co-operative institutions in the history of the People's Republic of China. Chinese co-operatives meet the basic conditions; however, the level of autonomy and democratic control exercised by members has varied across time.

The voluntary and open membership principle is no longer violated by the collectivist policies, although democratic control and independence principles are certainly lacking in most cases. As will be described in detail in Section 4, the 2007 law on Farmers' Specialized Co-operatives is a telling example because it was purposefully introduced to improve the economic initiative and participation of members, but ended up giving too much power to higher-level co-operatives and organizations. As we will argue in Section 5, intrusions from external actors and organizations to the detriment of true member participation are not only due to the pressures coming from national and local political authorities, but are also the result of the lack of a civil society able to sustain participation and control (Brook and Frolic 1997; Franceschini 2014; Fulda, Yanyan, and Quinghua 2012; Wakeman 1993; White, Howell, and Xiaoyuan 1996). The Chinese Co-operative Movement has not been fully integrated into broader civil society (Hall 1995), unlike its counterparts in the western world. Democracy exists in China only at a very local level; where the citizenship is not used to democracy, it naturally follows that the growth of democratic participation of workers and members on the co-operative model is not likely to flourish. Not by chance, the Co-operative Movement in England took hold at the very same time as social battles for labour and political rights were being fought. Democratic and Co-operative Movements have longstanding ties in many nations.

2.3 Confucianism

A final argument about how well, or not, the Co-operative Movement fits with China's social and institutional environment is the cultural one. The main cultural pillar of Chinese society is Confucianism (Weber 1951), a complex philosophical system that extends beyond the original writings of Confucius (Hofstede and dan Bond 1988; Wah 2010). While it is beyond the scope of this work to attempt to provide a description of this complex system, there is no question that striving for harmony is one of the basic values of a society with a Confucian legacy (Bell and dan Chaibong 2003). Social harmony is a value *per se* and everything that undermines social unity is considered evil (Hill 2006). This principle notably carries two almost opposite implications for the understanding of co-operative firms within the context of Chinese culture. On the one hand, as Weber was already noting in her seminal 1951 work on the sociology of religion in China, the value of social harmony tends to reaffirm the *status quo* and undermine performance and merit. This is potentially detrimental to the idea of independent and democratically controlled entrepreneurial activities. On the other hand, the principle of social harmony seems to be calling for economic and social organizations that can promote the value of mutual help and working together, values that are inherent to an agricultural society, as China has been for millennia (Cheng-Chung 1988).

The need for social harmony and co-operation was formalized in the 2011–2015 Five-Year Plan by the former political leadership of China. The ex-president Hu Jintao and ex-premier Wen Jiabao left incomplete the challenge of the Harmonious Society, *héxié shèhuì* (Wong and Lai 2006). It is striking that one of the characters of 'Harmonious Society' in Chinese is the same as 'Co-operative' in Chinese. Cheng-Chung (1988) explicitly addresses the compatibility of Chinese culture and co-operative principles in describing how western theories came to China.

We are thus in a position to answer the first research question. The western notion of co-operative and co-operation fits well with China. The etymological analysis has revealed that the meaning historically embedded in the words 'co-operation' and 'co-operative' in China and in the West is broadly the same. Furthermore, China is a full and active member of the international Co-operative Movement and has played a part in elaborating the co-operative values, most of which are compatible with the unique nature of the Chinese institutional system today. Finally, as a Confucian society, China might provide a good cultural environment that allows co-operative organizations and behaviour to develop, if supported by national and local policies.

In the next section, we will argue that despite the fact that all the conditions for the development of a true Co-operative Movement have been present since the beginning of the last century, the influence of Maoism meant that the developments made from 1912 fell into abeyance for a long period. As will be explained later, from the 1980s China has been back on track and moving towards the development and progression of a strong and genuine co-operative sector, as testified in the Government initiatives of 2002 (New rural co-operative scheme), 2007 (Farmers' specialized co-operatives law) and 2009 (Farmers connected to supermarket projects).

3. Co-operatives and Mao

In answering the second research question, we turn to history, asking if Maoism contributed to the flourishing of the Co-operative Movement.

It is possible to divide the modern history of the Chinese Co-operative Movement into three phases: the Republican period (1912–1948), the Maoist period (1949–1976) and the Contemporary China period (after Mao's death in 1976). In this section, we argue that Maoism has represented a deviation from the western, or, indeed, international notion of co-operation. The Republican period and the Contemporary China period see a gradual convergence with the international notion of the co-operative. The Maoist version of co-operation, even more than the Soviet one, has represented a discontinuity from the idea of co-operation as shared in the West and in contemporary China (MacFarquhar and Fairbank 1987, 1992).

The history of Chinese co-operation, excluding the primordial forms of informal co-operation widely present in ancient civilizations worldwide (in China connected to the management of water for agricultural purposes), seems to date from the first decade of the twentieth century. For a long time, the Empire of Japan controlled Manchuria (1931–1945) and the island of Taiwan (1895–1945), and during this period successfully introduced the co-operative model in agriculture. However, an autochthonc Chinese Co-operative Movement emerged, at the time of the establishment of the Republic of China in 1912. In the early decades of the twentieth century, some Chinese political and social reformers, such as Sun Yat-sen, the founding father of the Republic, introduced the co-operative model encountered abroad. This idea met with repression out of fear that co-operation came hand in hand with socialism. In 1921, the Chinese Communist Party was founded.

Some co-operative milestones, in those politically dramatic years, are well documented, others less so. We know that the first co-operatives appeared in 1912 and the first co-operative bank was founded in 1923 in Hebei Province. We also know that in 1937, there were over 12,000 co-operatives across 191 counties (Fairbank and Feuerwerker 1986). The European co-operative ideals and practices, once they had arrived in China, were elaborated by local intellectuals; for instance, Xue Xian-Zhou, who theorized a utopian 'Project of National Co-operativisation' (Cheng Chung 1988).

Between 1928 and 1949, following a financial crisis, the Nationalist Government of Chiang Kai Shek decided to support the introduction of a system of credit co-operatives along the German Raffaisen model. During the era of Chiang Kai-Shek's Republic of China, Chinese organizations for the promotion of co-operative firms were established with the financial and intellectual support of the West. This is the case with the intervention of the Rockefeller Program and of the missionary devotion of a Christian philanthropist and social reformer, John Bernard Tayler (Trescott 1993).

3.1 Gung Ho

The oldest co-operative society was founded in wartime, with a set of values including mutual assistance and the defence of national identity. This organization, named the Gung Ho, or ICCIC (International Committee for the Promotion of Chinese Industrial Co-operatives), was founded in 1938 in Hong Kong, thanks to the inspiration of the New Zealander Rewi Alley and some other foreigners (intellectuals, journalists, western diplomats, adventurers, bankers, Christian missionaries and British politicians) and western educated Chinese (engineers, intellectuals and the wife of Dr Sun Yatsen). Their aim was to organize the unemployed and refugees to take part in productive activities in support of the war of resistance against the Japanese invaders. Gung Ho spread throughout the unoccupied Chinese territories from 1939 and reached its peak in 1941. Approximately 3000 co-operatives were active, with 30,000 members, and produced essential goods for the population, as well as supplying the front with blankets, uniforms and other goods for the Chinese army (Cook and Clegg 2012). The Gung Ho became the place for the cultivation of ideas and the mobilization of patriotism and independence. Something very similar occurred in Finland. There, the Pellervo Society and its co-operatives, during the Russian rule of Finland, were the only associations not prohibited by law. The society was then a place for the elaboration of co-operative and patriotic ideals.

The Statute of the ICCIC says that the spirit of Gung Ho is to 'work hard and work together, helping one another to achieve common prosperity'. The organization's principles are:

> voluntary organization, self-financing, self-government, independent accounting, taking responsibility for gains and losses, democratic management, with distribution to each in proportion to their work and dividends in proportion to shares.

These resemble modern western principles of co-operation and recall many aspects of the ICA Manchester Statement in 1995 (*Voluntary and open membership*; *Democratic member control; Member economic participation*; *Autonomy and independence; Education, training and information*; *Co-operation among c-operatives and Concern for community*).

The Gung Ho was supported by western individuals, organizations and government bodies because of its strategic role during the Japanese invasion and the Second World War (Barnett 1940). The British Empire and the USA decided to fund and support the Gung Ho because they recognized in it a social democratic political and economic alternative to the increasingly powerful Chinese Communist Party (Wales 1941; Barnett 1940). The Gung Ho originally operated in the areas under the control of both the Communist and the Nationalist armies and was supported by both Mao and Chang Kai Scheck, though this support was accompanied by a certain suspicion and they both soon started to express misgivings about its foreign-influenced nature (Cook and Clegg 2012).

When Mao gained full control in Mainland China, he managed to have the activities of ICCIC suspended. Mao's ideology did not fit well with the Gung Ho which was an advocate of democracy, bottom-up participation and industrial rather than agricultural development (Fairbank 1998; Vermeer, Pieke, and Lien 1998).

Despite formal support by Mao Zedong, Zhou Enlai, Soong Ching Ling, Ye Ting and other revolutionary leaders for its contribution to the cause of Chinese liberation, the ICCIC activities were suspended in 1949. Other associations of co-operatives, more in line with party ideology and the institutional developments of China, were established. Among those, for instance, the All China Federation of Handicraft and Industrial Co-operatives was established to serve the national planning started in 1950. Such federations still exist and they kept a very strong relationship with the Government.

3.2 Maoism

A very different period begins when Mao enters the stage of Chinese history (Osinsky 2010). Even before the establishment of the People's Republic of China in 1949, Mao had recognized that it would be necessary to organize production, consumption and credit along co-operative lines in order to develop a collectivized economy (Keating 1997). Maoism took shape during the Civil War and the 1933–1935 Long March and was put to the test, drawing from Marxism-Leninism and from the Soviet example, in the remote base of the Red Army in the middle of China, near the city of Yan'an, where Mao's revolutionary army was headquartered. Mao quickly focused his strategy on agriculture rather than industry (Teiwes and Sun 1993) or the intellectual class. Between 1943 and 1944, rural co-operativization was started in areas under the steady control of Mao's army. In the case of Yan'an, the model seems to have worked and was soon idealized and used as an example to be replicated everywhere. Thus was born the myth of the 'Yan'an Way' (Keating 1994; Stettner and Oram 1987). It is not easy to say whether Mao's co-operatives were co-operatives in all respects; if, for example, they respected the principle of voluntary membershi' It might be that over the years, the ideological aspect of sharing gave way to party bureaucracy and to disillusionment. It can also be supposed that the size of the villages, co-operatives or land may have sometimes facilitated the participation of members and social control (Keating 1997).

Du (2002) provides estimates that show the number of Chinese co-operatives leaps from 722 in 1928 to almost 169,000 in 1948. With the establishment of the People's Republic of China, Mao would progressively collectivize the organization of economic production based on the Soviet model, but going further still (Teiwes and Sun 1993). From 1952, rural co-operation started to develop across the Chinese mainland (Vermeer, Pieke, and Lien 1998). In rural areas – a large part of Chinese territory even today, and especially at that time – three main types of co-operatives developed: production co-operatives, distribution and marketing co-operatives, and rural credit co-operatives (Cheng 2006; Lynette Ong 2012; Xie 2003).

The escalation of the collectivist ideology began in 1958, with the launch of the Great Leap Forward. In that long period, several forms of collective work were deployed in agriculture, industry and services. The co-operative model was involved in that huge economic, political and social experiment that peaked in the 1970s but which, as it turned out, proved dramatically ineffective and inefficient when it came to fulfilling Mao's projected goals.

An example of how the co-operative model was used by Mao, beside Soviet-style collectivization, is the so-called Rural Co-operative Medical Scheme. This was the main provider of health care in rural China until the late 1970s (Bernardi and Greenwood 2011). It was a vast undertaking, but by no means equated to the western system of mutual health because of the ideological use that the national and local authorities made of it. Similarly, most of the other forms of collective economic production, dealt with in the next section, were not a business initiative with bottom-up participation and control.

The concept of People's Communes originated in 1958. By the end of that year, more than 740,000 rural production co-operatives had been reorganized into 26,000 People's Communes, with almost all farmers absorbed into this system. The system would remain fairly stable until the decade of opening-up policies and reform when new forms of co-operative arose under such names as 'specialized co-operatives' and 'stock-holding co-operatives' (MacFarquhar and Fairbank 1992; Vermeer, Pieke, and Lien 1998).

The relationship between collectivist values and Maoism has been explored in scholarship. A study by Ho (1978) shows that Mao Zedong wanted an anti-individualistic, pro-collectivist spirit to penetrate traditional Chinese culture so that a national collectivist culture could be established (Harrison 2000). For Mao, individualism represented absolute evil and individualists were selfish, putting their personal interests first. Collectivism, by contrast, was seen to have a purer and higher purpose: its adherents place importance on duty and harmony, recognizing that their individual interests are subordinate to those of the group to which they belong. International studies on individualism, national cultures and work-related values have consistently confirmed the Chinese collectivist nature (Hofstede and dan Bond 1988; Hofstede 2001; Littrell 2002).

The second research question can be answered as following. Mao used the co-operative model ideologically in a bid partially to disguise his plans of forced collectivization and propaganda. During his long rule of China, collectivized work and production were confused with the notion of the co-operative firm that had appeared in China long before Mao gained power. While some types of co-operatives, such as the Rural Co-operative Medical Scheme, peaked under Maoism, when it comes to quality and adherence to the original model, this period was not a remarkable moment for the Chinese Co-operative Movement.

The contribution of this section is a clear statement about the ambiguous relationship between Mao and the Chinese Co-operative Movement. Maoism represented a deviation from original co-operative ideals and practices as imported to China by foreigners and western-educated Chinese people who, together, developed a local Co-operative Movement. That long experience is now very distant and neglected by contemporary political elites. Consequently, the Chinese Co-operative Movement could develop a better and freer relationship with the political authorities, though we will argue in section 6 that a civil society (Franceschini 2014; Fulda, Yanyan, and Quinghua 2012; Mercer 2002; Shieh and Guosheng 2011) is a requirement for the flourishing of such a genuine Co-operative Movement.

4. A long institutional transition

Mapping the transformation of the forms of collective work, we will answer the third research question: how has the co-operative model evolved alongside political and institutional transition?

Over the years, very different organizational forms and structures have been given the label co-operative or collective (see Table 1). The dramatic institutional transition that

Table 1. Evolution of main co-operative business forms.

Institution	Sector	Period	Characteristics
Gung Ho Co-operatives	Manufacture	1938–1949	Small scale, voluntary membership, individual investment in the equity and individual incentives
Mutual Aid Team	Agriculture	1949–1955	Up to five families, voluntary membership, individual ownership of land
Elementary Co-operative	Agriculture	1955–1979	Up to 30 families, voluntary membership at the beginning
Advanced Co-operative	Agriculture	1955	No individual ownership of means of production, no voluntary membership
People's Commune	Agriculture	1958–1978	Up to 5000 households originally, than 30 families, no voluntary
Supply and Marketing Co-operatives	Agriculture and distribution	From 1954, reformed in 1982	No voluntary membership until reform. Also, 15 and then 30 years lease of land to farmers, individual responsibility on productivity and revenues
Technology Association	Agroindustry and distribution	From 1980s	Focused on technological improvements
Household Responsibility System	Agriculture	From 1981	Voluntary membership. Individual responsibility and rewards
New Rural Co-operative Medical Scheme	Health-care	From 2002	Voluntary membership
Specialized Farmer Consortia and Co-operatives	Agroindustry	From 2007	Individual lease of the land for a medium to long period. Small and multi-business

transformed the nation at the founding of the Republic and later of the People's Republic, through Maoism, the Cultural Revolution, the opening-up policies, to the most contemporary reforms, has entirely altered the legal framework and the very notion of the co-operative in China (MacFarquhar and Fairbank 1987, 1992).

Table 1 summarizes the main forms of collective work that through time, in different ways, have been juxtaposed, rightly or wrongly, with the notion of the co-operative in China. Maoist variants are examples of deviation from western principles. In general, over time, efficiency, responsibility and incentives that were originally individual became collective. The average dimension of the collective grew and voluntary membership disappeared. The most recent forms represent a return to the original characteristics: small scale, individual participation and incentives (Keating 1994, 1997; Hongyi 2000; Perotti, Sun, and Zou 1998; Xiangyu, Schmit, and Henehan 2008).

4.1 Gung Ho co-operatives

The co-operatives established in the 1910s and 1920s, as well as those in the 1930s and 1940s (properly members of the Gung Ho Movement), were fully western style co-operatives with voluntary organization, self-financing, individual responsibility for gains and losses, democratic management and distribution of profits to each member in proportion to their work or their economic interaction with the co-operative.

4.2 Mutual aid team

Among the various forms of co-operatives, the mutual aid team has enjoyed great popularity. In this model, based on voluntary participation, four or five households from a neighbourhood put together their agricultural equipment and their farm animals. The collaboration went as far as exchanging working hours on temporary or long-term agreements, while the land remained the property of individual families. Between 1949 and 1955, the mutual aid team was promoted as the principal method of increasing production in the countryside.

4.3 Elementary co-operative

From 1955 to 1979, co-operatives became a tool of the Chinese Government in controlling agricultural production and making it a collective effort. The Elementary Co-operative emerged in 1954 and expanded rapidly in its early years. A greater number of families participated in the elementary co-operative compared to the mutual aid team (usually 20–30), and members shared land in addition to animals and equipment. The co-operative's profit was distributed according to two principles: payment for the contribution of land, animals and equipment made by each member, and a second payment in relation to the amount of work done by each member. During this period, the attitude towards the development of co-operatives was cautious and peasants were encouraged to participate in different types of co-operative organization on a voluntary basis (Chinn 1980).

4.4 Advanced co-operative

Among the various forms of co-operatives, the Advanced Co-operative emerged around 1955 with a number of distinctive features. All means of production including the land were collective property; members worked under centralized management and remuneration was based solely on the number of hours worked. In 1955, the central

Government decided to accelerate the process of collectivization. As a result, the principle of voluntary participation was deliberately forgotten and peasants were persuaded, if not forced, to participate in the advanced co-operative system. The number of advanced co-operatives increased from 500 in 1955 to 753,000 in 1957, involving around 119 million households.

4.5 People's commune

In 1958, a new type of collective work was introduced on a vast scale, the so-called People's Commune, which was to play a decisive role in rural areas until 1978. A People's Commune consisted of about 30 advanced co-operatives, combining an average of 5000 households and 10,000 acres of cultivable land. Initially, payments in the commune were based in part on subsistence needs and partly in relation to work accomplished. Later, in 1962, when production and management were delegated to smaller units, with production teams consisting of about 20–30 families, the system changed. The production team became the basic unit for work and accounting. Under the new system, members of the team received 'work points' for their performance, and at the end of the year income was distributed to individuals on the basis of work points accumulated. The system of collective agriculture remained until 1979 (Powell 1992; Hu et al. 2007).

4.6 Supply and marketing co-operatives

In the collectivized agricultural system, the supply of goods required for agriculture, and the processing and marketing of products were centrally planned by the government. Supply and marketing co-operatives were government organizations that provided farmers with inputs and work materials. Agricultural products were harvested and distributed by the government and farmers did not have the freedom to sell their production in a free market (Hendrikse and Veerman 1997). Until the 1980s, this method was known as the Unified Purchasing and Supply System (UPSS, or 'tonggou-tong-xiao' in Chinese). A study has argued that the majority of Supply and Marketing Co-operatives were still not effectively controlled by their farmer-members (Xiangyu, Schmit, and Henehan 2008). Still today, All China Federation of Supply and Marketing Co-operatives, ACFSMC, the biggest organization of its kind in the world, is formally tied with the national government.

4.7 Technology association

New forms of co-operatives emerged in the transition simply to deal with inefficiencies concerning access to inputs, technology, information and markets by small farmers. In the 1980s, new co-operative organizations called 'Technology Associations' were formed by farmers to promote the use of new technologies, for the supply of farming materials, and to encourage commercialization. The 'Technology Association' was adopted not only by the farmers but also by large processing companies, local authorities in rural areas and by the state itself in organizing farming supply and commercialization (Deng et al. 2010). Data up to 2004 bear witness to the success of the new model, with more than 150,000 active co-operatives (The Rural Development Institute 2004, 157).

4.8 Household responsibility system

As is well known, China began a political and economic transition in 1978 (Naughton 1996). The central planning of economic activities was gradually transformed into a market-oriented system. In the new system, with the support of Deng Xiaoping from 1981, agriculture based on collective structures was replaced by a system based on the family. A system of family responsibility was adopted experimentally in 1978 by farmers in the province of An'hui. It gave the peasants temporary control of land ownership and any related income. The system was characterized by collective ownership of land, although farmers and their families were independent production units. Ownership of the land belongs collectively to the villages (Perotti, Sun, and Zou 1998) and these loan it to nuclear families based on the number of people and workers in each family. Initially, the length of the loan ranged from one to three years, eventually being renewed for 15 years. In 2002, contract renewal was extended to 30 years. The contract specified the family's obligations to the state for dues, taxes and related charges. The family had the right freely to dispose of anything in excess of these obligations. The system introduced incentives for farmers who invested in order to increase productivity. In the first six years of the reform, agricultural production increased by 30%. As the reform progressed, the UPSS was phased out to make room for a free market in agricultural products. By 1982, the Government was starting to encourage farmers to sell their products in the markets. In 1985, the UPSS was officially abolished and from then on the Government bought wheat and cotton based on negotiated contracts, while pork, fish, vegetables and other products were open to free trade. The transition (Hongyi 2000) brought new challenges for farmers who, instead of producing the quantities and types of products required by the state, were obliged to deal with the dynamics of market demand.

4.9   New rural co-operative medical scheme

Chinese co-operatives are not only found in the agricultural sector. Since 2002, the national government has been re-launching the rural health co-operative scheme, essentially similar to the model of the western 'health mutual insurances' (Bernardi and Greenwood 2014). The Chinese version is also directly involved in the management of basic health services and it is connected with the experience of the 'barefoot doctors' (Brown and Theoharides 2009; Bernardi and Greenwood 2011). The central government, aware of the rural-urban divide of opportunities and living conditions, has been giving great emphasis to rural health care reform through the New Rural Medical Co-operatives (Brown, de Brauw, and Du 2009; Zhao 2011).

4.10   Specialized farmer consortia and co-operatives

The new co-operatives that arose, starting in the 1980s, take two different forms: consortia (or associations) on the one hand and pure co-operatives on the other. Specialist agricultural consortia represent 65% of the 150,000 organizations in a 2004 census, while specialized agricultural co-operatives constitute the other 35% (The Rural Development Institute 2004, 157). The main difference between the two models lies in the ownership of assets and the way they carry out such functions as production, marketing and processing. In general, specialized co-operatives are registered with the Industry and Commerce Administration; they have invested capital and resemble western co-operatives in the functions they perform. The specialized agricultural associations, however, are registered with the Office of Civil Affairs, have no capital invested, do not require the payment of a social contribution and are primarily concerned with providing technical assistance and training. The Farmer Professional Co-operatives Law, 2006, proclaims in one of its first articles principles perfectly in line with those of the international Co-operative Movement:

The farmer co-operative shall comply with the following principles: (a) farmers play the dominant role among its members; (b) the key purpose is to serve members and act in the common interests of all members; (c) the members shall join and exit voluntarily; (d) all members are equal and Co-operatives are democratically controlled; (e) surplus should be redistributed based on the volume of members' patronage.

The deployment of this law has been somehow controversial. It raised high expectations for its emphasis on bottom-up economic initiative and participation and because of the possibility for farmers' co-operatives to diversify with a plurality of businesses such as farming, energy production or recreation. Unfortunately, higher-level co-operatives are allowed to join the capital and to use voting rights to up the 20%. This has proved to be problematic in many cases. A small group of farmers can hardly handle the power imbalance between them and the huge organizations now authorized to take active initiative in the life of the co-operative. Additionally, there is a conflict of interests between the individual members and the corporate members who trade services and goods with the specialized farmers' co-operatives.

Notwithstanding the experience of township villages (Hongyi 2000), cases of industrial co-operatives are rare. There are, however, numerous co-operative banks (Wang 2005). Yet, after the many scandals of the past decade, the sector has undergone a drastic restructuring that has included the bailout performed by the National Bank of Agriculture (Lynette Ong 2009; Yuk-Shing 2006).

The adoption of the co-operative model for emerging problems is an on-going process. For instance, a very recent case is connected to the rising pressure from urbanization policies and the growth of conflicts at village level. The government has incentivized the creation of village co-operatives in charge of controlling the collective land, deciding about its use, and sharing the revenues of infrastructures or real estate developments, if agreed in the community (OECD 2013).

As Figure 1 shows, over the last 10 years, collective forms of business ownership have been declining in importance, whereas private enterprises have increased substantially. The size and role of the state are also being readjusted dramatically though a strong hold remains on regulation, planning and ownership of strategic corporations. Unfortunately, the OECD and the national statistics data do not identify specific forms of co-operative, but we assume these to be mostly part of the 'collective' area.

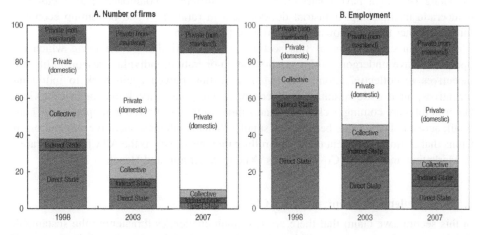

Figure 1.   Relative economic weight by ownership type, number of firms and employment (OECD 2010).

At this point, it is difficult to see what proportion of these are proper co-operatives and which are local collective enterprises controlled by local authorities. It would be even more difficult to establish the proportion of the co-operatives in which the enterprises are genuinely owned and controlled by workers or users, rather than being nominal co-operatives under the control of the managers who in one way or another have assumed leadership. It can be argued that the Chinese transition from socialism to market economy has been much more effective than the Russian one and that this can be partly attributed to the role played by those forms of collective organization of production and ownership. The collective acted as a buffer between state and market during the transition and development of new institutions.

We can now address our third research question, namely 'How has the Co-operative model evolved together with the political and institutional transition'? The Chinese Co-operative Movement has undergone considerable alteration through its history, during which quite a few models and institutional forms have been developed, transformed or abandoned. This process of transformation was provoked by significant political, ideological, socio-economic and institutional changes (Stettner 1984; Stettner and Oram 1987).

Through time, responsibility and incentives that were previously collective became individual, raising participation, real co-operation and productivity. Workers were progressively given freedom to take individual responsibilities. We are not sure whether, though, the Chinese society, as it stands, permits a full membership and active participation, which might require the civil society to have developed (Franceschini 2014; Hall 1995; Salmenkari 2013; Shieh and Guosheng 2011; Spires 2012). In developing social entrepreneurship (Galera and Borzaga 2009) without active citizenship (Van de Ven, Sapienza, and Villanueva 2007; Short, Moss, and Lumpkin 2009), the risk here is that the outcome might be a hybrid organization with traditional managers and silent membership unwilling or incapable of exercising its rights in the assemblies. This is as well, sometimes, the case in Europe or in the Americas (Bernardi and Köppä 2011), where traditional entrepreneurship takes place in the guise of co-operative firms serving the interests of the few, while true social entrepreneurship should serve the community or a range of active stakeholders. Civil society is a requirement for the development of true social entrepreneurship. Nevertheless, the Gung Ho approach is alive again, at least as an ambition if not yet as a widespread practice. Had it been successful in the 1930s and 1940s, the Gung Ho might have contributed to a very different evolutionary path focused on democratic membership, industrial development in rural areas and bottom-up economic initiative rather than top-down organization of production.

The main contribution of this section is the description of the cycle which co-operatives have undergone: from small-scale co-operation, individual responsibility and incentives to collectivization. After Mao, transition moved again back to individual incentives, small-scale voluntary co-operation and responsibility. It may be that the Gung Ho principles are coming back. The organization itself was allowed to reopen in 1987 and is still active today, despite being much smaller than the other co-operative associations in China that claim to represent up to 160 million members, such as the All China Federation of Marketing and Supply Co-operatives (Xiangyu, Schmit, and Henehan 2008).

5. The challenges of contemporary China

In this section, we claim that there are two main challenges threatening the sustainable development of contemporary China. Answering our fourth research question, we argue that the Co-operative Movement can contribute to this.

The first challenge is the transition from state to private ownership and the consolidation of a non-capitalist market economy model. In the literature on the Chinese economic system (Nathan 1997; Arrighi 2007; Tsai 2007; Naughton 1996, 2007), a common focus is the so-called capitalism without democracy on the one hand, and the market without capitalism on the other. By its nature, the co-operative enterprise form is liable to remain excluded from such a dialectical model. One key element of co-operative diversity (Bernardi 2007) is the ownership right system, a non-capitalist one:

> the freedom of enterprise is a fundamental characteristic of the most advanced modern economies. Capitalism, on the contrary, is contingent; it is simply the particular form of ownership that most often, but certainly not always, proves most efficient with the given technology. (Hansmann 1996)

Arrighi (2007), in his compelling book *Adam Smith in Beijing*, challenges the neo-liberal interpretation of the economic success of China. On the contrary, in anticipation of a conflict between western and Asian models, he proposes a reinterpretation of Smith and Marx. In particular, according to Arrighi, in China today there are firm signs of a type of non-capitalist market economy described by Smith in his *Wealth of Nations*. At that time, Adam Smith was aware of the leading role of China, but was not able to predict how the industrial revolution would enable the great leap forward of the western nations.

Only 30 years ago, the Chinese economy was almost entirely controlled by the various levels of government. At the peak of their development, state businesses were responsible for the vast majority of industrial production and they employed the majority of the non-agricultural workforce. Collective enterprises accounted for the rest, with no other type of business allowed. Since the authorization of private enterprises in 1979, the proportion of production resulting from enterprises, whether state or collective, has continued to decrease exponentially. The international literature in recent years on China's transition is very rich. However, the analyses focus on the dialectic of state versus private and, if anything, allude to the 'collective' sector; reference to co-operatives is conspicuously absent.

The second challenge is the sustainability of growth. The economic policies of the last two decades have favoured economic growth and the nation's modernization. Every year, millions of Chinese have crossed the threshold out of poverty and the prospects of well-being and living conditions have improved sharply between generations and within the same generation. However, social problems and the growth of inequality have begun to alarm the Chinese Communist Party. A useful tool to measure successes and failures of contemporary Chinese policies is the HDI inspired by Amartya Sen and developed by Fukuda-Parr and Kumar in 2003. The HDI is an attempt to take account of other factors, not just the usual GDP, which determine the well-being of individuals and the development of a nation: longevity (as measured by life expectancy at birth), educational level (measured by the literacy rate of adults) and GDP *per capita* expressed through purchasing-power parity. This index ranges from 0 to 1. An HDI level below 0.5 represents low development, and according to the 2013 report, there are about 30 countries in this band, all located in Africa bar four Asian nations. A level above 0.8 HDI is highly developed and in this band, comprising 70 countries, we find all the developed countries of North America, Western Europe, Oceania, East Asia and some developing countries. Figures 2 and 3 show success measured by the HDI at national level, comparing China's performance with the world-average trend and with other nations' trends.

An HDI of between 0.5 and 0.8 represents the medium development, and in this group we find all countries with intermediate development and developing countries, including India and China (Rowley 2012). In the case of India, performance in terms of HDI is much

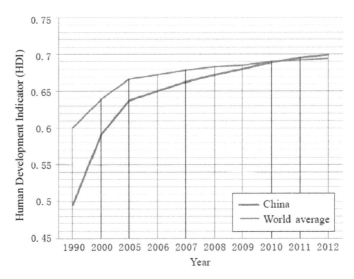

Figure 2. HDI of China and the world average, 1990–2012 (UNDP 2013).

higher than that measured by GDP *per capita*. The Chinese HD scores are encouraging, particularly when compared with those of other developing nations (see Figures 2 and 3). Yet China is a country of great contradictions and striking regional disparities (Clegg 2006). Figure 4 presents an indicator of Human Development at provincial level. Even within these same (and vast) provinces, there are large differences, primarily between rural and urban areas. Particularly noteworthy are the distinctions between the north-western interior of Mainland China and its southern and eastern coastal regions.

Given those two sustainability challenges, human development and smooth economic transition, can the Co-operative Movement contribute to the needs of contemporary China?

With regard to the economic transition from state to private market, the collective and co-operative sector made possible in China what did not happen in Russia. Several buffer institutions (Table 1) have assisted collective organization of production and collective ownership during the slow transition away from state ownership and state planning. If the institutional evolution of the co-operative sector and the relevant legislation moves towards democratic participation and bottom-up entrepreneurial initiatives, this process will provide considerable support to Chinese transition more broadly and will help with sustainability. The co-operative sector and the third sector could contribute in the case of market failures (Salamon 2010; Stiglitz 2009). Moreover, the co-operative sector worldwide has proved notably resilient, especially during periods of crisis, whether in the past or in more recent times (Birchall and Ketilson 2009; Michie and Llewellyn 2010; Stiglitz 2009).

The growth of the Chinese economy is continuous, showing great intelligence in economic policy as well as in international strategy (Zou 1994). However, despite significant progress in the indexes of well-being and of absolute poverty, there is an evident and growing inequality of income. There is growth, there is a market economy and there is a modern and very ambitious financial market. But despite claiming to be socialist (Zhang 2009), the Chinese nation lacks many of the institutions of social protection. China cannot continue to prosper for very much longer without proper health-care insurance and

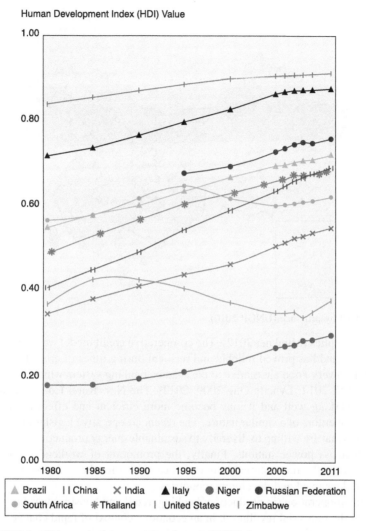

Figure 3. HDI for China and other countries. *Source*: UNDP data.

social security (Florence and Defraigne 2013). The vision of a harmonious and cohesive society cannot be realized without decent public health-care throughout the country, without a universal social-security system, without the protection of labour, without the enforcement of decent minimum wages, without occupational health and safety policies, or labour rights (Cooney, Biddulph, and Zhu 2013; Pringle 2011). Co-operatives may provide an answer to many of those issues (ILO 2002; Simmons and Birchall 2008; United Nations 2013). Key priorities are the fight against pollution and the contamination of natural resources, as well as the sustainability of urbanization and rural poverty. The period which was marked by an emphasis on growth at all costs has ended. The policy objectives for the latest five-year plans have put great emphasis, instead, on social security and the sustainability of development.

As far as growth and human development are concerned, the co-operative sector has longstanding worldwide experience of providing solutions (Vicari 2014). Farmers' co-operatives and consumers' co-operatives have served the cause of food security and

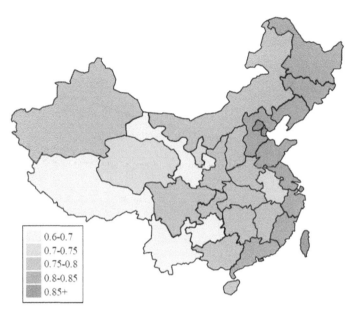

Figure 4.   HDI by province (UNDP 2010).

responsible supplies (Münkner 2012). The co-operative credit model was born to serve the working class and has proved reliable and resilient during times of crisis for centuries; it could also be a very good alternative to the shadow banking system which is ubiquitous in China (Birchall 2014; Lynette Ong 2009, 2012). The New Rural Co-operative Medical Scheme is working well and it may become more efficient and effective still with the arrival of competitors of a similar nature. The recent co-operative legislation also supports co-operatives that are willing to diversify to sustainable energy production, through micro-hydro or biomass power stations. Finally, the promotion of workers' co-operatives is recommended by the International Labour Office (2002) for the diffusion of decent work practices in developed and developing countries.

Modern co-operation (in production, banking, retail and housing) was born in Europe shortly after the industrial revolution, in an economic context of rapid change and serious social problems (urbanization, pollution, exploitation of labour, little social or union protection, poverty and inequality). This scenario in part describes China's boom of the last 20 years. But the more advanced forms of western co-operative enterprise (MacPherson 2008), such as the social co-operative, the green energy co-operatives and the peer-to-peer banking co-operatives, would also fit well with China's contemporary needs (Florence and Defraigne 2013). Both traditional and new models of co-operation have the potential to improve the living and working conditions of Chinese people (Cooney, Biddulph, and Zhu 2013). The Chinese Government and Legislature have recently (in the 12th Five-Year Plan and in the 2013 meetings of the National People's Congress) defined such challenges and, in some cases, have explicitly mentioned the co-operative firm as a tool which has the capacity to address them.

6.   Implications

In this section, implications for theory, for practice and for policy are presented. They are connected with our four research questions but are also interconnected. These will be followed by short comments on the limitations of this study and on the need for future research.

The main implication for theory is that it is essential in studying co-operation in China to use the construct of civil society (Salmenkari 2013). Studies on co-operation and civil society are now available in the scientific literature of most western countries (Birchall 2011). In the case of China, those studies are lacking, despite the fact that they would be indispensable, we argue. A theoretical advance in the knowledge and understanding of the Co-operative and mutuals phenomena in China must be coupled with the issue of members' participation and bottom-up social entrepreneurship. Therefore, we argue, scholarship must consider and use the theoretical construct of civil society. We have argued that the new Chinese economic environment seems favourable to the co-operative enterprise. While this remains marginal compared to both state and private companies, there is room for co-operative initiatives. However, an active co-operative economy requires an active civil society (Fulda, Yanyan, and Quinghua 2012), and this is still an under-developed concept in China (Franceschini 2014; Shieh and Guosheng 2011; Spires 2012). The idea of civil society includes all those formal and informal organizations that act as a bridge between government and business, such as charities, voluntary organizations, political parties and so on (Hall 1995). In these spaces, people can self-organize and take responsibility for their problems, sometimes superseding Government intervention. Given this premise, it is not surprising that in contemporary China a strong civil society does not exist (Fulda, Yanyan, and Quinghua 2012), since it would quite clearly pose a threat to governmental power (Franceschini 2014; Mercer 2002; Salmenkari 2013; Shieh and Guosheng 2011; Spires 2012). At the beginning of its history, the Chinese Co-operative Movement complied with this requirement, as the Gung Ho experience flourished because it had its roots in participation, sustainability and democracy (Cook and Clegg 2012). Today this is not at all widely the case. For those reasons, the scholarly research on Chinese mutuals and co-operatives must investigate the presence of democracy and autonomy at organizational level and of civil society as a trigger and catalyst of true social entrepreneurship initiatives.

From a theoretical point of view, we have shown how useful and appropriate the ICA's statement on co-operative identity is as a tool in describing and evaluating the co-operative phenomenon. This paper has also made clear, however, that Chinese co-operatives do not always possess the essential characteristics of the co-operative as outlined by ICA's definition. In some cases, what a government or a social group calls a co-operative might not be a real co-operative. While we are aware that ICA's statement was not born as a theory-based tool, the fact that it distils views and opinions on co-operative enterprises from member associations based in all Continents and over 100 counties makes it a powerful instrument to describe and evaluate the co-operative phenomenon worldwide beyond the Chinese case.

The main implication for practice is that the interactions between Chinese and international Co-operative Movements need to be established on the basis of a sincere agreement of common values. The International Co-operative Alliance shall make sure that its Chinese members are not agencies of the Government working to implement its directives but rather associations or federations of true co-operatives The Chinese Co-operative movement should gain autonomy from politics. It is now too late to hope for the growth of the Gung Ho, only a minor organization compared to the giant federations, which are deeply involved with government bodies and supposedly represent millions of members and hundreds of thousands of Chinese co-operatives, such as in the case of the All China Federation of Supply and Marketing Co-operatives. Nevertheless, ICA can still support the heritage of the Gung Ho and state that its values and principles are the same as the international Co-operative Movement and ICA itself. Clarity on the nature of Chinese co-operatives and their second and third level organizations would make it easier for Chinese members of the ICA to participate actively, but would also improve the likelihood of business collaboration between western and Chinese co-operatives.

The implications for policy are connected with what we have argued about theory and practice. This study has explained how the co-operative business model may contribute to sustainability: providing opportunities for human development and smoothing the transition of the economic system from state planning and ownership towards market and private ownership. If moving beyond market fundamentalism to a more balanced economy is a worldwide necessity (Stiglitz 2009), this is all the more true for China, and co-operatives can contribute to this. But this contribution is provided only by true co-operatives; because, for instance, a fake co-operative is not necessarily more environmentally sustainable than a capitalist firm, or a fake co-operative bank is not necessarily reliable. Furthermore, a fake co-operative would not help to empower farmers and villagers and would not protect them in the interactions with much bigger organizations (see the case of the Farmers' Specialized Co-operatives). For that reason, the Chinese Government has to facilitate the emergence of a true co-operative model, and, as we have argued, a civil society is needed to support the flourishing of participation in true co-operatives. NGOs, associations and other civil-society organizations are today again on the increase in China (see Table 2), yet this is without the concerted support of the government and it is happening very slowly when compared to usual Chinese trends.

Indeed, such organizations must have formal authorization to operate, so that any undesirable organization has no chance of success. The central government's attitude towards associations remains cautious; support is granted only to those kinds of associations that are entirely economic in nature, and will not become even slightly involved in political issues. Even when it comes to economic issues, a true civil-society organization might pose a risk for the political establishment because collective organizations might express interests in conflict with those supported by local or national authorities:

> Non-governmental organization (NGO) can contribute to urban management in a number of ways, serving as a channel for participation, and playing important roles in aiding vulnerable people, increasing social tolerance and safeguarding social stability. They help reduce the misuse of market mechanisms and government interventions. Legislation to encourage NGO participation lags behind, however, even as the number of these groups is increasing rapidly. (UNDP 2013, 42)

Table 2. Growing number of NGOs.

Year	Mass organizations (10.000)	Private non-enterprise organizations (10.000)	Foundations
2001	12.9	8.2	–
2002	13.3	11.1	–
2003	14.2	12.4	954
2004	15.3	13.5	892
2005	17.1	14.8	975
2006	19.2	16.1	1144
2007	21.2	17.4	1340
2008	23.0	18.2	1597
2009	23.5	18.8	1780
2010	24.3	19.5	2168
2011	25.3	20.2	2510

Source: Ministry of Civil Affairs and UNDP (2013).

Civil society could also play also a role as a watchdog of the policy makers and the private firms when sustainability and fairness are at stake. There are opportunities for the Chinese Co-operative sector, but it must converge with the western model, or better go back to its origins, when, between 1912 and 1949, Chinese intellectuals and practitioners developed an autochthone Chinese co-operative model incorporating foreign experiences. If the Chinese authorities are truly concerned with the sustainability of their growth model, and if they are genuinely interested in the co-operative sector as one of the possible answers to this, they must aim for the development of a true Co-operative Movement and not of a hybrid characterized by strong ties with Government bodies and lack of democracy and bottom-up entrepreneurship.

There are two limitations to this study. We had to rely on oral and written translation of the Chinese Mandarin language. This does not necessarily compromise the results of such a study, but must nonetheless be taken into account. Furthermore, we started the research taking for granted the validity of the assumptions of the collectivist nature of Chinese culture. We had to consequently challenge those assumptions, which nevertheless, with some precaution, remain an interesting device for management research, teaching and practice (Hofstede 2002).

Further research is needed. First of all, the evolution of Chinese culture and business practices needs to be monitored as the exchanges between Asia and the western world grows (Warner 2013; Nankervis et al. 2013). The evolution of the Chinese co-operative legislation and relevant national and local Government policies needs to be observed further. Finally, the interactions between the ICA, its western members and its Chinese components require investigation. We do not know yet whether and how an institutional process of mutual influence is taking place, nor else in which direction any such influence is working, i.e. if China is influencing the ICA or rather the ICA is shaping the Chinese Co-operative sector.

7. Conclusions

In this work, we have shown that the western notion of the co-operative fits well with the Chinese case and that we are in fact dealing with the same phenomenon, one which has a long history. We have described how Maoism has represented a deviation to the evolutionary path of the Chinese Co-operative Movement that otherwise, earlier and after that experience, has been converging to the western model. Its original development itself was indeed shaped by western direct influence. We have told the story of how the co-operative model has evolved hand in hand with political and institutional transition. We have finally argued that in contemporary China, the Co-operative Movement has the potential to make really quite dramatic contributions to the sustainable and prosperous development of China. The memory of forced collectivization and limits placed on the growth of a proper civil society are far from helpful to the revival of co-operation in China. However, despite a very heavy historical legacy and some contemporary institutional constraints, a bright future is not only desirable but possible for the Chinese Co-operative Movement.

Notes

1. I am now at Manchester Metropolitan but I started this research at the University of Nottingham in China.
2. Email: mattia.miani@rmit.edu.vn

References

Arrighi, G. 2007. *Adam Smith in Beijing, Lineages of the Twenty-First Century.* London: Verso.
Barnett, R. W. 1940. "China's Industrial Cooperatives on Trial." *Far Eastern Survey* 9 (5): 51–56.
Bell, D. A., and H. dan Chaibong. 2003. *Confucianism for the Modern World.* Cambridge: Cambridge University Press.
Bernardi, A. 2007. "The Co-operative Difference, Economic, Organisational and Policy Issues." *International Journal of Co-Operative Management.* 3 (2): 11–23.
Bernardi, A., and A. Greenwood. 2011. "Rural Health Co-operatives in China. History and Contemporary Organisational Models." 27th EGOS Colloquium, University of Gothenburg.
Bernardi, A., and A. Greenwood. 2014. "Old and New Rural Co-operative Medical Scheme in China: The Usefulness of a Historical Comparative Perspective." *Asia Pacific Business Review.* doi:10.1080/13602381.2014.922820.
Bernardi, A., and T. Köppä. 2011. "Co-operatives as Better Working Place. The Finnish Case in a Comparative Organisational Climate Analysis." *The International Journal of Co-operative Management* 5 (2), 40 pp. special issue on Finland.
Birchall, J. 1997. *The International Co-Operative Movement.* Manchester: Manchester University Press.
Birchall, J. 2011. *People-Centred Businesses: Cooperatives, Mutuals and the Idea of Membership.* London, New York: Palgrave MacMillan.
Birchall, J. 2014. *Finance in an Age of Austerity, The Power of Customer-owned Banks.* Cheltenham: Edward Elgar Publishing.
Birchall, J., and L. H. Ketilson. 2009. *Resilience of the Co-Operative Business Model in Times of Crisis.* Geneva: International Labour Office.
Brook, T., and B. M. Frolic, eds. 1997. *Civil Society in China.* Armonk, NY: Sharpe.
Brown, P. H., A. de Brauw, and . Du Y. 2009. "Understanding Variation in the Design of China's New Co-Operative Medical System." *The China Quarterly* 198: 304–329.
Brown, P. H., and C. Theoharides. 2009. "Health-Seeking Behavior and Hospital Choice in China's New Co-Operative Medical System." *Health Economics* 18: 47–64.
Cheng, Y. S. 2006. "China's Reform of Rural Credit Co-operatives Progress and Limitations." *The Chinese Economy* 39 (4): 25–40.
Cheng-Chung, L. 1988. "European Cooperativism in Chinese Perspective." *Annals of Public and Co-Operative Economics* 59 (3): 369–377.
Chinn, D. L. 1980. "Co-Operative Farming in North China." *The Quarterly Journal of Economics* 94 (2): 279–297.
Clegg, J. 2006. "Rural Co-Operatives in China: Policy and Practice." *Journal of Small Business and Enterprise Development, Bradford* 13 (2): 219–234.
Cook, I., and J. Clegg. 2012. "Shared Visions of Co-Operation at a Time of Crisis: The Gung Ho Story in China's Anti- Japanese Resistance." In *The Hidden Alternative: Co-Operative Values, Past, Present and Future*, edited by A. Webster, A. Brown, D. Stewart, J. K. Walton, and L. Shaw, 327–346. Helsinki: United Nations University Press.
Cooney, S., S. Biddulph, and Ying Zhu. 2013. *Law and Fair Work in China.* Abingdon: Routledge.
Deng, H., J. Huang, Z. Xu, and R. Scott. 2010. "Policy Support and Emerging Farmer Professional Co-Operatives in Rural China." *China Economic Review* 21 (4): 495–507.

Douglas, M. 1986. *How Institutions Think*. New York: Syracuse University Press.

Du, Y. 2002. *Co-Operatives: Modern Enterprise Institutions in Agriculture*. Nanhang: Jiangxi People Press.

Fairbank, J. K. 1998. *China: A New History*. Cambridge, MA: Belknap Press of Harvard University Press.

Fairbank, J. K., and A. Feuerwerker, eds. 1986. *The Cambridge History of China*, Part 2. Vol. 13. Cambridge: Cambridge University Press.

Florence, E., and P. Defraigne, eds. 2013. *Towards a New Development Paradigm in Twenty-First Century China, Economy, Society and Politics*. Abingdon: Routledge.

Franceschini, I. 2014. "Labour NGOs in China: A Real Force for Political Change?" *The China Quarterly* 218: 474–492.

Fulda, A., L. Yanyan, and S. Quinghua. 2012. "New Strategies of Civil Society in China: A Case Study of the Network Governance Approach." *Journal of Contemporary China* 21 (76): 675–693.

Galera, G., and C. Borzaga. 2009. "Social Enterprise, An International Overview of its Conceptual Evolution and Legal Implementation." *Social Enterprise Journal* 5 (3): 210–228.

Gu, Y. K. 2008. *Chinese Characters Etymology Dictionary*. Beijing: Chinese Language Press.

Hall, J. 1995. *Civil Society: Theory, History, Comparison*. Cambridge: Polity Press.

Hansmann, H. 1996. *The Ownership of Enterprise*. Cambridge, MA: The Belknap Press.

Harrison, H. 2000. *The Making of the Republican Citizen: Political Ceremonies and Symbols in China, 1911–1929*. Oxford: Oxford University Press.

Hendrikse, G. W. J., and C. P. Veerman. 1997. "Marketing Co-Operatives as a System of Attributes." In *Strategies and Structures in the Agrofood Industries*, edited by J. Nilsson, and G. Van Dijk, 111–129. Assen, The Netherlands: Van Gorcum & Comp.

Hill, J. S. 2006. "Confucianism and the Art of Chinese Management." *Journal of Asia Business Studies* 1 (1): 1–9.

Ho, D. Y. F. 1978. "The Concept of Man in Mao-Tse Tung's Thought." *Psychiatry* 41: 391–402.

Hofstede, G. 2001. *Culture's Consequences: Comparing Values, Behaviors, Institutions, and Organizations Across Nations*. Thousand Oaks, CA: Sage.

Hofstede, G. 2002. "Dimensions Do Not Exist, a Reply to Brendan McSweeney." *Human Relations* 5 (11): 1355–1361.

Hofstede, G., and M. H. dan Bond. 1988. "The Confucius Connection: From Cultural Roots to Economic Growth." *Organizational Dynamics* 16 (4): 4–21.

Hongyi, C. 2000. *The Institutional Transition of China's Township and Village Enterprises: Market Liberalization, Contractual form Innovation and Privatization*. Aldershot: Ashgate.

Hu, Y., Z. Huang, G. Hendrikse, and X. Xu. 2007. "Organization and Strategy of Farmer Specialized Cooperatives in China." In *Economics and Management of Networks, Franchising, Strategic Alliances, and Cooperatives*, edited by G. Cliquet, M. Tuunanen, G. Hendrikse, and J. Windsperger, 437–462. Heidelberg, New York: Physica-Verlag.

ILO. 2002. *R193, Promotion of Cooperatives Recommendation*. Geneva: International Labour Organisation.

Keating, P. B. 1994. "The Yan'an Way of Co-Operativization." *The China Quarterly* 140: 1025–1051.

Keating, P. B. 1997. *Two Revolutions: Village Reconstruction and the Cooperative Movement in Northern Shaanxi, 1934–1945*. Stanford, CA: Stanford University Press.

Kornai, J., and Q. Yingyi, eds. 2009. *Market and Socialism: In the Light of the Experiences of China and Vietnam*. IEA. New York: Palgrave Macmillan.

Laaksonen, O. 1984. "The Management and Power Structure of Chinese Enterprises During and after the Cultural Revolution." *Organization Studies* 5 (1): 1–21.

Littrell, R. F. 2002. "Desirable Leadership Behaviours of Multi-cultural Managers in China." *Journal of Management Development* 21 (1): 5–74.

Lockett, M. 1988. "Culture and the Problems of Chinese Management." *Organization Studies* 9: 475–496.

Lynette Ong, H. 2009. "The Communist Party and Financial Institutions: Institutional Design of China's Post-Reform Rural Credit Co-Operatives." *Pacific Affairs* 82 (2): 251–278.

Lynette Ong, H. 2012. *Prosper or Perish: Credit and Financial Systems in Rural China*. Ithaca, NY: Cornell University Press.

MacFarquhar, R., and J. K. Fairbank, eds. 1987. *The Cambridge History of China, 1987, Vol. 14, Part 1, The Emergence of Revolutionary China, 1949–1965*. Cambridge: Cambridge University Press.

MacFarquhar, R., and J. K. Fairbank, eds. 1992. *The Cambridge History of China, 1992, Vol. 15, Part 2, Revolutions Within the Chinese Revolution, 1966–1982*. Cambridge: Cambridge University Press.

MacPherson, I. 2008. "The Co-Operative Movement and the Social Economy Traditions: Reflections on the Mingling of Broad Visions." *Annals of Public and Co-Operative Economics* 79 (3/4): 625–642.

McSweeney, B. 2002. "Hofstede's Model of National Cultural Differences and Their Consequences: A Triumph of Faith – A Failure Of Analysis." *Human Relations* 55 (1): 89–118.

Mercer, C. 2002. "NGOs, Civil Society and Democratization: A Critical Review of the Literature." *Progress in Development Studies* 2 (1): 5–22.

Michie, J., and D. T. Llewellyn. 2010. "Converting Failed Financial Institutions into Mutual Organisations." *Journal of Social Entrepreneurship* 1 (1): 146–170.

Münkner, H. H. 2012. "Cooperation as a Remedy in Times of Crisis. Agricultural Cooperatives in the World. Their Roles for Rural Development and Poverty Reduction." *Marburg Studies on Cooperation and Cooperatives Nr 58*.

Nankervis, A. R., Fang Lee Cooke, S. R. Chatterjee, and M. Warner. 2013. *New Models of Human Resource Management in China and India*. Abingdon: Routledge.

Nathan, A. J. 1997. *China's Transition; with Contributions by Tianjian Shi and Helena V.S. Ho*. New York: Columbia University Press.

Naughton, B. 1996. *Growing Out of the Plan: Chinese Economic Reform 1978–1993*. Cambridge: Cambridge University Press.

Naughton, B. 2007. *The Chinese Economy: Transitions and Growth*. Cambridge, MA: MIT Press.

Nilsson, J. 1996. "The Nature of Co-Operative Values and Principles, Transaction Cost Theoretical Explanations." *Annals of Public and Co-Operative Economics* 67 (4): 633–653.

OECD. 2010. *China Economic Survey*, Volume 2010/6, February 2010. Paris: OECD.

OECD. 2013. *Economic Surveys, China*, March 2013. Paris: OECD.

Osinsky, P. 2010. "Modernisation Interrupted? Total War, State Breakdown, and the Communist Conquest of China." *The Sociological Quarterly* 51 (4): 576–599.

Perotti, E. C., Laixiang Sun, and Liang Zou. 1998. *State-Owned Versus Township and Village Enterprises in China*. Helsinki: UNU World Institute for Development Economics Research.

Powell, S. 1992. *Agricultural Reform in China: From Communes to Commodity Economy 1978–1990*. Studies on East Asia. Manchester: Manchester University Press.

Pringle, T. 2011. *Trade Unions in China the Challenge of Labour Unrest*. Abingdon: Routledge.

Rowley, C. 2012. "Development in China: Position and Nationhood in Asia and the World." *Asia Pacific Business Review* 18 (1): 1–6.

The Rural Development Institute. 2004. *Chinese Academy of Social Sciences, Green Book of China's Rural Economy*, 157. Beijing: Foreign Languages Press.

Salamon, L. M. 2010. "Putting the Civil Society Sector on the Economic Map of the World." *Annals of Public and Co-Operative Economics* 81 (2): 167–210.

Salmenkari, T. 2013. "Theoretical Poverty in the Research on Chinese Civil Society." *Modern Asia Studies* 47 (2): 682–711.

Short, J. C., T. W. Moss, and G. T. Lumpkin. 2009. "Research in Social Entrepreneurship: Past Contributions and Future Opportunities." *Strategic Entrepreneurship Journal* 3: 161–194.

Shieh, S., and D. Guosheng. 2011. "An Emerging Civil Society: The Impact of the 2008 Sichuan Earthquake on Grass-Roots Associations in China." *The China Journal* 65: 181–194.

Smith, S. C. 1994. "On the Law and Economics of Employee Ownership in Privatization in Developing and Transition Economies." *Annals of Public and Co-Operative Economics* 65 (3): 437–468.

Simmons, R., and J. Birchall. 2008. "The Role of Cooperatives in Poverty Reduction: Network Perspectives." *Journal of Socio-Economics* 37 (6): 2131–2140.

Spires, A. 2012. "Lessons from Abroad: Foreign Influences on China's Emerging Civil Society." *The China Journal* 68: 125–146.

Stettner, L. 1984. *Chinese Co-Operatives: Their Role in a Mixed Economy*. Oxford: Plunkett Foundation for Co-Operative Studies.

Stettner, N., and B. Oram. 1987. *The Role of Co-Operatives in the New Socialism*. Manchester: Holyoake Books, 115 pp.

Stiglitz, D. J. 2009. "Moving Beyond Market Fundamentalism to a More Balanced Economy." *Annals of Public and Co-Operative Economics* 80 (3): 345–360.

Taimni, K. K. 1994. "Asia's Rural Co-Operatives Origin, Evolution and Emerging Challenges." *Annals of Public and Co-Operative Economics* 65 (3): 469–488.

Taimni, K. K. 2000. *Cooperatives in Asia*. Geneva: International Labour Office.

Teiwes, F. C., and W. Sun, eds. 1993. *The Politics of Agricultural Cooperativization in China: Mao, Deng Zihui, and the 'high tide' of 1955*. Armonk, NY: M. E. Sharpe.

Trescott, P. B. 1993. "John Bernard Tayler and the Development of Co-Operatives in China, 1917–1945." *Annals of Public and Co-operative Economics* 64 (2): 209–226.

Tsai, K. S. 2007. *Capitalism Without Democracy: The Private Sector in Contemporary China*. Ithaca, NY: Cornell University Press.

UNDP. 2010. *China Human Development Report 2009–2010*. Beijing: China Translation and Publishing Corporation, United Nations Development Program.

UNDP. 2013. *China Human Development Report 2013*. Beijing: United Nations Development Program.

United Nations. 2013. "China's Progress Towards the Millennium Development Goals 2013 Report, with Ministry of Foreign Affairs of the People's Republic of China." Beijing.

Van de Ven, A. H., H. J. Sapienza, and J. Villanueva. 2007. "Entrepreneurial Pursuits of Self- and Collective Interests." *Strategic Entrepreneurship Journal* 1 (3–4): 353–370.

Vermeer, E. B., F. N. Pieke, and Woei Lien Chong, eds. 1998. *Cooperative and Collective in China's Rural Development: Between State and Private Interests*. New York: Armonk.

Vicari, S. 2014. "The Co-operative as Institution for Human Development: The Case Study of Coppalj, a Primary Co-operative in Brazil." *Journal of International Development*. doi:10.1002/jid.3003.

Wah, S. S. 2010. "Confucianism and Chinese Leadership." *Chinese Management Studies* 4 (3): 280–285.

Wakeman, F., Jr. 1993. "The Civil Society and Public Sphere Debate: Western Reflections on Chinese Political Culture." *Modern China* 19 (2): 108–138.

Wales, N. (pseudonym of Helen Foster Snow). 1941. *China Builds for Democracy: A Story of Cooperative Industry*. New York: Modern Age Books.

Wang, J. 2005. *Restructuring China's Rural Credit Co-operatives: Lessons Learned*. Washington, DC: East Asia Pacific Region, World Bank.

Warner, M. 2013. *Understanding Management in China, Past, Present and Future*. Abingdon: Routledge.

Weber, M. 1951. *The Religion of China: Confucianism and Taoism*. Clencoe, IL: The Free Press.

White, G., J. A. Howell, and S. Xiaoyuan. 1996. *In Search of Civil Society, Market Reform and Social Change in Contemporary China*. Broadbridge, Wotton-under-Edge: Clarendon Press.

Williamson, D. 2002. "Forward from a Critique of Hofstede's Model of National Culture." *Human Relations* 55 (11): 1373–1395.

Wong, J., and H. Lai, eds. 2006. "China into the Hu-Wen Era: Policy Initiatives and Challenges." Hackensack, NJ: World Scientific Publishing.

Xiangyu, G., T. M. Schmit, and B. M. Henehan. 2008. "Rural Supply and Marketing Cooperatives in China: Historical Development, Problems, and Reform." *Journal of Rural Cooperation* 36 (2): 157–174.

Xie, G. H. 2000. *Chinese Characters Etymology Dictionary*. Beijing: Peking University Press.

Xie, P. 2003. "Reforms of China's Rural Credit Co-Operatives and Policy Options." *China Economic Review* 14: 434–442.

Yuk-Shing, C. 2006. "China's Reform of Rural Credit Co-Operatives." *Chinese Economy* 39 (4): 25–40.

Zhang, L. 2009. *Socialism is Great! A Worker's Memoir of the New China*. New York: Anchor Books.

Zhao, L. 2011. "Understanding the New Rural Co-Operative Movement: Towards Rebuilding Civil Society in China." *Journal of Contemporary China* 20 (71): 679–698.

Zou, D. 1994. *Chinese Politics in 20th Century: View from Macro-History and Micro-Behaviour*. Hong Kong: Oxford University Press.

Zuo, M. A. 2006. *Details of Chinese Characters*. Beijing: Jiu Zhou Press.

Old and new Rural Co-operative Medical Scheme in China: the usefulness of a historical comparative perspective

Andrea Bernardi[a] and Anna Greenwood[b1]

[a]Department of Management, Faculty of Business and Law, Manchester Metropolitan University, Manchester, UK; [b]School of International Studies, University of Nottingham Ningbo, Administration Building, Ningbo, Zhejiang Province 315100, People's Republic of China

This work compares the health cooperatives fêted in Maoist China in the 1960s to the New Rural Medical Co-operative Scheme (NRCMS) that has been operating in China since 2002. Organizational and ideological similarities between the old and new co-operative medical schemes are described. By mapping continuities and discontinuities in the way the co-operative organizational model has been deployed under different contexts, we argue for the usefulness of blending historical method and organizational analysis as a means of understanding some of the challenges of contemporary Chinese social policies. Using this technique of historical comparison, this work concludes that the NRCMS, despite being different in orientation, is still affected by political influences, and organizational traits, evident within its former incarnation. This acknowledgement, we argue, has important implications for policy and practice today.

1. Introduction

One of the challenges of China's booming growth in the past few decades is the search to find an affordable and effective means of providing equitable medical care to the millions of rural inhabitants who constitute almost half of the total population of China. To this end since 2002, the Chinese government has sought to implement a New Rural Co-operative Medical Scheme (NRCMS), providing basic medical insurance to the majority poor in return for annual membership payments. This scheme was not entirely new and was broadly based on an older scheme of co-operative rural healthcare (Rural Co-operative Medical Scheme) formally inaugurated by Mao Zedong in 1965. Understandably given the large differentials, in terms of market and political contexts, which have evolved between 1965 and 2002, these two schemes demonstrate key differences. Perhaps most prominently, while in the past the health co-operative was given a degree of autonomy in terms of organizing its own local structures and medical services, today, the NRCMS is obviously more voluntary and centrally led comprising all broad intents and purposes an imitation of a western-style mutual scheme whereby individuals can invest in return for basic health insurance.

Today, the NRCMS initiative is proudly displayed by Chinese health policy makers as one of the cornerstones in the development of a sustainable health framework for contemporary China. This position has been most recently exemplified by the public announcements to introduce new pilot pension schemes in Shanghai and Beijing as a means to address the financial burdens on its rapidly ageing population (UNDP 2013). With huge challenges ahead of China with its large and unequal population, health care policies have been in the public eye as never before capturing the attention of not only academics, but also social and political commentators within both governmental and international organizations.

The motivation behind this study is to understand the differences and similarities between the two incarnations of this health scheme. For all of its claims for modern relevance, the NRCMS is, we believe, strongly historically rooted with Maoist policy. It is perhaps a surprising choice for the government of China to so obviously resurrect a scheme from a past that in many ways it chooses to forget, but what is even more surprising is that scholars have not studied the meanings and implications of these continuities and discontinuities (in ideology and organization) with the past. This presents a large gap in the literature of analysis of Chinese health provision and highlights the importance of the past as a tool to better understand both the present and the future. Despite inherent difficulties in comparing dissimilar contexts, particularly when the political and socio-economic landscapes have changed as much as they have in China, a glance historically backwards can, and regularly should, offer useful insights.

Additionally, we argue that the use of historical perspectives can have very tangible relevance for practice and research. To this end, our work extends non-comparative studies of the co-operative medical system in China (for example, Zhang 1982; Yip and Hsiao 2009; Babiarz et al. 2010; Qin et al. 2012; Dong et al. 2013) and also adds a new dimension to other academic works examining the modern health problems of China (Wagstaff and Lindelow 2005; Wang 2009; Wagstaff et al. 2009). Moreover, it will supplement understandings about the development of the co-operative ideal in China (Cheng-Chung 1988; Gao and Chi 1996). Two research questions are to be explored:

(1) To what extent can both the old and the new Rural Co-operative Medical Schemes (RCMS) be seen as ideologically similar?
(2) To what extent is the new organizational approach of the NRCMS similar to or different from western models of mutual insurance?

We stress from the outset that this research is firmly historical, offering new perspectives to contribute to and extend already existing work within the Chinese and international literature on health care, co-operatives, management, and economic policy in China. The method therefore is principally one of qualitative textual analysis of both primary and secondary literature on the topic. It is based on extensive archival research undertaken in both historical and contemporary Chinese and English source material, including research at the World Health Organization (WHO) archive, Geneva, and original documental research undertaken in China. The data collection took place between 2009 and 2013 when both authors were employed in an academic institution in China. This made it possible to visit a number of co-operatives and hold discussions with co-operative leaders and members in the Beijing, Shanghai, Hong Kong, Zhejiang, and Guangxi areas. It was conducted as part of a larger research project on Chinese co-operatives. The archive work has uncovered data never analysed before with this comparative historical perspective and has never been subjected to organizational analysis.

The co-operation of History and Organizational Studies to the understanding of contemporary Chinese policy presents something original in itself as although cross-disciplinary analysis has become more favoured in recent years (Wadwani and Bucheli 2013; Rowlinson, Hassard, and Decker 2014; Greenwood and Bernardi 2014), the need to look back at organizational developments historically is nevertheless still far from assumed behaviour. To this end, the techniques of analysis deployed are both historical and sociological with the joint authorship also reflecting the truly cross-disciplinary nature of this endeavour. Additional to the historical approach, Institutional Theory is also used as a secondary-level analytical tool to explain how Chinese co-operatives have been deeply shaped by the socio-economic transition and the political contingencies.

Given the predominantly historical nature of this work, it is necessary to separately outline the contextual circumstances and subsequent literature around each health co-operative scheme. Section 2 presents the literature review and the data on the old RCMS. Section 3 presents the literature review and the data on the NRCMS. Section 4 compares the old and the new systems, answering in turn our two central research questions. In Section 5 we argue for the usefulness of the historical method in organization studies. There, we also consider the limitations of this study and the need for further research. Section 6 presents the implications of this research for theory development, for practice and policy. Short conclusions follow in Section 7.

2. The rural co-operative medical system (1934–1981)

The modern co-operative model arrived in China (comparatively late compared to Europe) in the first decade of the twentieth century from England, Japan, and Germany based directly on their experiences of co-operative farming and banking (Fairbank and Feuerwerker 1986). Chinese intellectuals and practitioners with western education developed a local co-operative movement with the active support of western expatriates and missionaries (Cook and Clegg 2012).

Although small-scale singular examples existed in the early years of the twentieth century, the concept took some time to be established, with the first co-operatives in China, established in 1912. Despite this cautious start, however, during the first two decades of the century intellectuals, politicians and social reformers (Sun Yatsen had a Christian education) increasingly tried to disseminate the co-operative ideal in China, just as intellectuals and elites had disseminated it in Europe in the previous century. A particular turning point can be identified in 1939 when, stimulated by war-time exigencies, co-operatives were embraced as part of the 'Gung Ho' movement proposed in Shanghai two years before. Gung Ho's central principles were of voluntary organization, self-funding, self-governing, independent accounting, democratic management, and distribution to each according to his/her work and dividends according to shares. The accession of Mao and his now famous programme of collectivization (commenced 1958) meant that the Chinese co-operative movement suddenly changed and began to embody deviations from the original western notion of co-operative firm and co-operation. This is therefore not just a history of the development of co-operatives in China as an alternative business model, but rather is a story of how a model was adapted to suit a regime and to mesh with changing political intrigues.

In terms of health co-operatives specifically, it is notable that the idea (Scott 2003) of organizing healthcare in this way also had a pre-history. Indeed, it can be seen that for at least 30 years previous to the launch of Mao's scheme, health co-operatives were being seriously investigated as a sustainable possibility. In fact, the first call to reform rural healthcare provision system occurred during the early 1930s, with a regulation by the Department of Health coordinating and integrating rural public health passed in 1934 (Zhang 1982, 24). Although the chief objectives were agreed in principle at this early stage, it was not until 1937 that a national medical scheme of this type was formally enacted through legislature. It may seem ironic that the idea officially adopted in 1965 by the Communist Party originated within the nationalist Kuomintang (KMT, or Chinese Nationalist Party).

In 1945, Mao announced his intention to 'follow the co-operative route' in terms of his healthcare reforms (Mao 1991, 1078).[2] Correspondingly, by 1950, the then Deputy Minister of Health, He Cheng outlined at the first National Health conference that without serious attention paid to problems of disease and sanitation, the 'national production and construction and people's peaceful life cannot be ensured'.[3] Thus, in the political rhetoric, health became formally intertwined with nationalist discourses of strength and survival from early on.

In 1956, the Third Session of the National People's Congress adopted the document 'The Regulations of the Practice of Advanced Agricultural Production Co-operative Model'. Here it was stipulated that co-operatives should be responsible for the care of members who had become wounded or ill during work. This seems to have been the spur for further action as after this, medical units, based on either the collective economy or on the combination of collective and individual funding, began to develop in many rural areas. During the period from the foundation of PRC to the late 1950s, a coherent rural co-operative medical care plan was formed mainly out of the experiences of local areas. In November 1959 in Jishan County in Shanxi Province, the Ministry of Health held the National Rural Health Conference, in which the adoption of the system was formally affirmed (Cai 2009).

The final impetus to turn the rhetoric into action seems to have come from the broader political momentum to set up agricultural production co-operatives as the cornerstone of the People's Commune. To this end, through the Great Leap Forward, millions of Chinese peasants who moved into collective farms were said to move from an agrarian economy into a modern communist society. These communes needed healthcare services and it seemed logical to also organize these, like production, around the fundamental organizational model of the co-operative (Mao 1956, 1958). Before the scheme came to fruition, several trials were undertaken at a provincial level, notably, the Ding County Test and the Shaanxi–Gansu–Ningxia border drug agency. Stimulated by posted reports over the success of these trials, Mao took the issue further when in 1960 he published his *Instructions for Public Health* (Mao 1960). This began by emotively regretting the inattention made to date on public health issues and stated that people should 'rekindle the patriotic public health movement which has been left behind during the Great Leap Forward, and be sure that achievements are to be made within the period from 1960 to 1962'.[4] The solution proposed was to convert all existing health services into a collectively owned model. It was also partially a response to the severe criticisms the Department of Health had been under as the available health services had been largely confined to the elite urban-based population (Xu 1997).[5]

The scheme was launched on 26 June 1965 with Mao giving his famous speech 'Directive on Public Health' (Mao 1965). Within the next months, the Department of Health issued its supportive statement entitled 'Report Prioritizing Primary Level Medical Services to Rural Areas' strenuously pointing out that 'more than 80 per cent of China's population are farmers, if the medical and health problems of these farmers cannot be dealt with seriously, the socialist health policy will come to nothing' (Department of Health 1965).

In September 1965, the central committee of the Communist Party of China approved the document 'A Report Concerning Putting Emphasis on Medical Care in Rural Areas' and sent it to the party committee of the Ministry of Health. Following this lead, by the end of 1965, medical co-operative systems were initiated in Shanxi, Hubei, Jiangxi, Jiangsu,

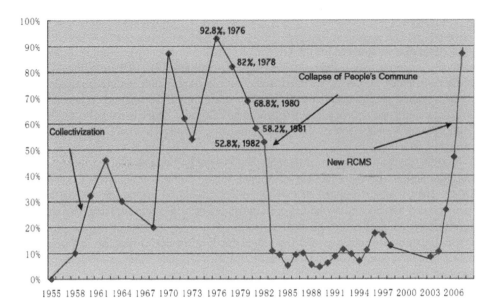

Figure 1.   Rise and fall of the Rural Co-operative Medical Scheme: percentage of participation among local level administrative units in rural China (Liu 2004).

Fujian, Guangdong, and Xinjiang provinces and shortly after were started all over China. The scheme was successfully propagandized nationwide via publications like the *People's Daily* and the *Newspaper of Health* (an official newspaper run by the Department of Health). By 1976, it was estimated (although this is an official, and therefore unreliable, estimate) that 90% of peasants participated in the co-operative medical care system nationwide. In Figure 1, it is possible to observe the fast rise and decline of membership to the RCMS.

Although coverage was extremely good during the 1970s (another estimate in 1975 estimating that 84.6% of the rural population of China was covered by this medical system) (Zhu et al. 1989, 431–441), official discussions at a conference of barefoot doctors in Shanghai still quietly acknowledged that more could still be done and 100% coverage was never achieved (Department of Health 1976). Nevertheless, in the middle of the 1970s, around 5 million staff participated in the RCMS, of which 1.8 million were barefoot doctors (Appendix E), 3.5 million other health personnel, and 0.7 million midwives, making it undoubtedly the centrally most important medical scheme of China (Zhang, Wen, and Liang 2002, 28). It was an army in dimension as well as in organizational design. Horn described the barefoot doctors as 'a million-strong army' (Horn 1975, 22). The system at its peak comprised a huge branching system of ambulatory, provincial, and local health management intertwined with the local organizational structures of the Chinese Communist Party (CCP). At its peak, in the mid-1970s, it involved millions of personnel and covered 90% of the country (Wang 2009, 14).

In December 1979, the Ministry of Health, Ministry of Agriculture, Ministry of Finance, and the State Pharmaceutical Administration of the National Federation jointly issued the document 'The Regulation of Rural Co-operative Medical Care Service'. This converted the majority of the co-operative medical care institutions into private clinics of village doctors. According to the survey of the 45 counties in 10 provinces in 1985, the peasants' participation rate in rural co-operative medical care had dropped dramatically to only 9.6%, while 81% of the peasants paid for medical care at their own expense. In 1986, only 5% of the villages nationwide supported the rural co-operative medical care system, including the suburbs of Shanghai, Zhaoyuan County in Shandong Province, Wuxue County in Hubei Province, Wu County in Jiangsu Province, Wuxi, and Changshu. Although some attempts were made to revive the model, it was to take until 2002 for it to return with any political force, revamped and revived.

But although the scheme died a fairly conclusive death in China by 1981, this did not mean that interest in the scheme diminished globally. Indeed, significant international interest can be identified during the 1970s and 1980s as other nations and health organizations looked for new ways to deliver healthcare to rural populations, a drive particularly motivated by the WHO's goal of *Health for All by the Year 2000*. Indeed, as one report suggested, 'the time was ripe for the Chinese model and method to be hailed as the ideal' (Skeet 1984, 292). Throughout the 1970s and 1980s, the WHO (1974, 1988, 1989) conducted a series of study missions to China publishing widely on the RCMS potential merits (Bryant 1978, 144–148; Li 1985; Prescott and Jamison 1984; Lambo 1980). It seemed that even though the system had flaws (usually pinpointed as the fact that it operated under an oppressive political regime), it contained within it a centrally viable kernel of an organization model to apply to rural healthcare provision in other national contexts.

Given this international interest and enthusiasm, the rapid decline of the RCMS needs brief mention. At first, the decline of the RCMS did not seem at all inevitable with the new Constitution of the Republic of China of 1978 specifically stipulating that provision should be made for the co-operative medical service (PRC 1978). Quite quickly, however, the tone changed from one that presumed continuity to one that advocated change. Particularly the experiences of one County, Xiangxiang, were widely cited as evidence that farmers were not able to shoulder their current burden (Central Political Bureau 1978). After this initial declaration, other provinces quickly followed the route, also stating that they found the economic burden of the RCMS too heavy (Zhang 1982, 31–33; Wang 2009). The decline was rapid – by 1985, only 39.9% of the rural population in China were covered by the scheme. A substantial drop since the 1970s, not least as the rural population had grown by nearly 14% between 1975 and 1985 (Zhu et al. 1989, 431–441).

The reasons for the decline have been the subject of much debate, with most scholars identifying political and economic changes as the root causes (Jamison et al. 1984; Huang 1988; Young 1989; Yu 1992; Bloom and Gu 1997a). After the 1980s, the restructuring of the Chinese rural economy individual production became prioritized over collective production, thereby increasing the pressure on peasants to devote themselves to farm work and de-incentivizing participation in the scheme (Zhu et al. 1989, 431–441, 433). Crucially, central support was perceived to have gone – thereby robbing the scheme of the 'political will, national commitment and community involvement' essential for its success (WHO 1988).

All three institutional pressures to conform (Scott 1995; Suchman 1995), *coercive*, *normative*, and *mimetic* isomorphism, had suddenly gone. Mao became very rapidly a controversial figure and the allegiance to him and the previous scheme disappeared (*normative*), the rigid central supervision on the system declined (*coercive*), along with the dramatic declination in the need to strictly correspond to the overall collectivist structure (*mimetic*). We would add to this the impact of Deng's reforms, particularly those that dealt with the ownership rights system that saw no place for this organizational model.

3. Modern visions of the new rural co-operative medical scheme

After many years of inaction on behalf of the Chinese government, finally the catastrophic implications of ignoring rural health were acknowledged and in October 2002 at the China National Rural Health Conference, the model for the NRCMS was announced (Klotzbücher et al. 2010). It is unsurprising that the way the new scheme was presented was one which stressed its progressive modernity and was keen to present it, despite its roots and its name, as far removed from the old Maoist model. The system was publicized as predominantly a mutual health insurance scheme (Brown, De Brauw, and Du 2009), such as frequently existed within the contemporary western context (the French case for instance, although this was not monopolistic as the Chinese one was going to be). Its Chinese predecessor, as explained in Section 2, was a huge structure in charge of health care operations such as the management of the medical practice, the organization of pre-emptive public medicine works in the villages, the production of herbs, and the training of barefoot doctors.

The impetus behind this urgency for change and reform is clear. Figures 2 and 3 show the gap of opportunities between members of the rural and urban populations in China. The economic success of the most privileged areas of development in coastal provinces and urban areas made this rural problem all the more visible. It must be noted though that Figure 2 also represents an improvement since 2009.

This scheme was to comprise nine new directions for national health policy, most importantly promising central subsidization of healthcare for all. As such, China declared its intention to work towards a social insurance model as opposed to other alternatives (such as private insurance or full direct government financing). In its current incarnation, the scheme is heavily subsidized at both central and county levels, essentially using tax revenues to supplement household contributions (payable by all members at a flat rate accept the very poor).

In October 2002, it was pointed out in the document 'The CPC Central Committee and the State Council's Decision on Further Strengthening Rural Health Work' that 'China aims to gradually establish a New Rural Co-operative Medical Scheme'. Here the plan for the scheme to unfold was outlined in detail, projecting the hope that 'by 2010, rural

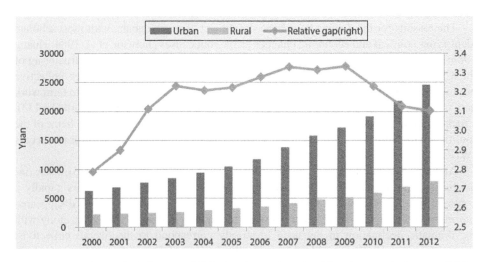

Figure 2.   Absolute and relative gap of China's urban and rural residents' per capita income, 2000–2012 (UNDP 2013).

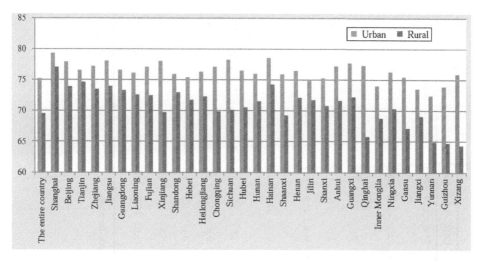

Figure 3.   Urban and rural life expectancy by province or metropolitan areas in 2000 (UNDP 2013).

residents should be involved in the new rural co-operative medical care system generally'. The scheme promised from 2003 that:

> the central finance department will provide RMB 10 per person annually for those farmers who participate in the new rural medical care system in the middle and western China. Local financial departments should provide at least RMB 10 financial subsidies for those farmers who participate in the new rural medical care system. (CPC Central Committee and State Council 2002)

By December 2004, a total of 310 counties nationwide participated in the New Rural Co-operative Medical Scheme. By March 2009, see Figure 1, the coverage of the new RCMS was said to have reached 830 million people. This seems impressive, even if we accept the unreliability of government statistics.

In accordance with the requirements of the '11th Five-Year Plan', at least 80% of rural areas were expected to participate in the New Rural Co-operative Medical Scheme in 2010. On 17 February 2011, the Chinese government released the document 'The Arrangement of Five Key Reforms Concerning Medical and Health Care System in 2011'. This document pointed out that the government would raise the financial subsidies for peasants' medical care from RMB120 per person annually in 2010 to RMB 200 per person annually in 2011. In 2012, government budget at all levels raised the financial subsidies for peasants' medical care from RMB 200 per person annually in 2011 to RMB 240 per person annually. In Table 1, it is possible to observe some key trends of wealth and well-being before and after the introduction of the NRCMS.

If we look at Table 1 considering the curve displayed in Figure 1, mapping the four stages of decline and growth of the RCMS, it is clear that from 2005 the private expenditure on health (as a percentage of total expenditure on health) declined. The public involvement had risen, though the total expenditure on health (as a percentage of gross domestic product) remained rather stable between 1999 and 2009. This information should be considered together with our knowledge that the per capita government expenditure on health had been raised much less than the per capita total expenditure on health. This suggests that other actors, different from individuals and the government, are now contributing to finance the system: for instance the local authorities or their agencies.

Table 1. Key indicators of wealth and well-being in China, 1990–2002–2009.

	2009	2008	2007	2006	2005	2004	2003	2002	2001	2000	1999	1998	1997	1996	1995	1994	1993	1992	1991	1990
Private expenditure on health as a percentage of total expenditure on health	49.9	52.7	54.7	59.3	61.2	62.0	63.8	**64.2**	**64.4**	61.7	59.1	58.2	55.8	53.4	49.5	–	–	–	–	–
General government expenditure on health as a percentage of total expenditure on health	**50.1**	47.3	45.3	40.7	38.8	38.0	36.2	35.8	35.6	38.3	40.9	41.8	44.2	46.6	**50.5**	–	–	–	–	–
Per capita total expenditure on health at average exchange rate (US$)	169	146	112	93	81	70	61	54	48	44	39	36	31	27	21	–	–	–	–	–
Total expenditure on health as a percentage of gross domestic product	4.6	4.3	4.2	4.6	4.7	4.7	**4.8**	**4.8**	4.6	4.6	4.5	4.4	4.0	3.8	3.5	–	–	–	–	–
Out-of-pocket expenditure as a percentage of private expenditure on health	82.6	82.6	82.6	83.1	85.3	86.5	87.6	90.0	93.1	95.6	94.5	94.3	94.8	94.8	93.7	–	–	–	–	–
Social security expenditure on health as a percentage of general government expenditure on health	**66.3**	**66.3**	**66.3**	57.3	54.1	55.2	53.4	54.8	55.1	57.2	54.2	55.8	60.4	62.1	64.2	–	–	–	–	–
Polio (Pol3) immunization coverage among 1-year-olds (%)	**99**	**99**	94	94	87	87	87	86	86	86	86	85	85	84	82	87	90	93	95	**98**
Private prepaid plans as a percentage of private expenditure on health	**6.2**	6.2	6.2	6.5	5.8	5.5	5.8	3.3	1.9	1.0	1.70	1.3	0.8	0	0	–	–	–	–	–
Per capita government expenditure on health at average exchange rate (US$)	**85**	69	51	38	31	27	22	19	17	17	16	15	14	12	11	–	–	–	–	–
Per capita total expenditure on health (PPP int. $)	309	265	234	215	191	170	152	135	117	107	95	85	73	62	52	–	–	–	–	–
Gross national income per capita (PPP int. $)	–	**6010**	5430	4700	4100	3590	3180	2830	2560	2330	2110	1950	1810	1640	1480	1340	1170	1020	890	800

Note: The grey area represents the introduction of the New Rural Co-operative Medical Scheme in 2002. The bold values mark the peaks.
Source: Authors' selection and elaboration from WHO data.

Nevertheless, the scheme has not been unequivocally successful (Qin et al. 2012; Dong et al. 2013). A study found that while the NRCMS reached more people (Wagstaff and Lindelow 2005; Wagstaff et al. 2009) and gave them access to better medical facilities and technologies, in fact the expense of medical care per visit tended to be higher than previously.

The increase in healthcare costs is a trend common to most nations, particularly those with ageing populations, the public regulation or intervention in health care insurances is a very current and complex topic (Gertler and Gruber 2002). In the Chinese case, some bad practices (for instance the excessive use of antibiotics and over referring as a means of making more profits) seem to have made the situation worse. Several studies have monitored the effectiveness and the efficiency of the scheme in contemporary China (Babiarz et al. 2010; Yip and Hsiao 2009; Dong et al. 2013). This situation meant that despite heavy government subsidization, people (especially the poorest groups of society) were actually more out of pocket than they had been under the old scheme. This meant that the poor, cognizant of this extra expense, were less likely to seek this sort of formal medical care (Wagstaff et al. 2009; Wang et al. 2005). Furthermore, Liu has argued that the leadership currently offered by the Chinese government for the scheme is still not strong enough; without this, he argues 'China will not be able to establish a sustainable rural health insurance system' (Liu 2004, 164). The assessment of the first decade of NRCMS is not yet clear. The United Nations, for instance, by way of contrast recently wrote that:

> Policies implemented in the new century, including the rural tax reform, the policy for rural compulsory education, the new rural co-operative medical care and medical assistance policy, and the new insurance policy for rural old people, have all played their roles in rural poverty reduction and provided policy support for China's achievements in poverty reduction. (United Nations 2013, 12)

4. Data analysis: comparing the past and the present

Turning now to our research questions: what insights does this historical analysis give us? To this end, we have considered it important to build from the archive work our organizational analysis of the past and present RCMS, as suggested recently by Decker (2013) and Wadwani and Bucheli (2013). It is instructive to map the differences and similarities between past and present models of health co-operatives in China. Broadly, these can be divided into two categories: first, the differences in the political climate in which both schemes variously operated and second, (but connected to the first point) the way the organizational remit and structure of the system has been altered to fit this changing context.

(1) To what extent can both the old and the new Rural Co-operative Medical Schemes be seen as ideologically similar?

The NRCMS clearly was different in some of its fundamental orientations and approaches. Most prominently it was now very much recast as a voluntarily participatory insurance scheme, which although clearly had funding and support from central government, nevertheless was far distanced from the old RCMS model that had been specifically tailored to fit the political ideals of collectivization and its associated needs for production. All studies of the RCMS in the 1960s have centrally acknowledged the strictures put upon it by the political context in which it operated. The first WHO study mission to China noted (Appendix E) that it felt there was 'no mystery' in the success of the RCMS that was based 'on the rational utilization of resources locally available and on the mobilization of the masses'.[6] As the first article of the *Code of Conduct* stated: 'RCMS is a socialist medical system built by the members of People's Commune on the basis of voluntary and mutual help. It is collective welfare services for commune members' (DAHF 1980, 62).[7] In short, the RCMS was fully integrated with the wider political organizational units of the state. This immediately raises questions of true freedom and autonomy. As scholars of socialist systems have already mentioned in other contexts (Kornai and Yingyi 2009; Tsoukas 1994, 33), when membership was obligatory and allegiance to the State essential (Shenkar 1996), to what extent can this be conceived as a true co-operative in the western conceptualization? Can the barefoot doctors within this structure be accurately seen as free agents working for the community when ultimately how they worked and where they worked needed to be within the constraints of party political acceptability? Is there a central problem in being both a disinterested doctor and an interested party member? What is clear is that the Maoist government clearly stated that their preference in terms of recruitment of barefoot doctors was for 'children of the poor and lower-middle peasants': in short stipulating that candidates needed to be loyalists to be selected for the role (Zhang, Wen, and Liang 2002, 25; Mao 1968).[8] In accord with this, the clearly-stated mission of the RCMS was to promote favoured party strategies, so for example, barefoot doctors were explicitly told to promote the one child policy, see Appendix B (DAHF 1980, article 3 points 1 and 6, 62). It must be noted that the largest federations of co-operatives in China, for instance All China Federation of Supply and Marketing Co-operatives, were (and still are) directly influenced by the state authorities.

When we examine the situation in which health co-operatives originally flourished in China, we find ourselves in an entangled web that integrates healthcare and CCP politics even at the most local level, despite the government rhetoric, which celebrated the way this scheme allowed considerable community self-management. The stated mission of the RCMS explicitly sustained the government's priority of supporting production (DAHF 1980). As Article 10 of the Code of Conduct of the RCMS stipulated in 1979: 'co-operative medical facilities at each level should be collective welfare units, they should not be run as enterprises or side-line business and should not be required to hand in profits' (DAHF 1980, 63).[9] In the simplest terms, the RCMS provided the first basic tier of healthcare provision available to rural Chinese people as part of their collective farming units. Significantly, the role of the barefoot doctor therefore was very publically interwoven with that of the regime it served. As a local observer was recorded as pointing out: barefoot doctors were referred to by their patients as 'tongzhi' (comrade) rather than as 'yisheng' (doctor) (WHO 1978, 94). They served as an interface between community and government and became a commanding socialist symbol of power and knowledge in the hands of the proletariat, of self-management and the collective ideas of community self-help.

A common organizational pathology, the means-end inversion (Crozier 1964; Merton 1936), can therefore be seen in the Chinese context as caused by this central problematic role of ideology and politics running through most organizational endeavours. This in turn brings to mind frequent examples of ineffectiveness and inefficiency that have characteristically plagued state-dominated institutions (Scott 1995; Shenkar 1996; Tsoukas 1994). There is no doubt that the original RCMS exemplified leadership patterns, managerial styles and decision-making processes primarily shaped by their explicit ties to the Maoist State but also because of Chinese ideals of man fundamentally differ from those in the West (Ho 1978).

We can answer the first question by concluding that the *explicit* ideological mission has disappeared from the NRCMS. Observing the posters in the rural clinics that we have visited, accessing the official documents and reading the national and international literature, it seems that this propaganda side is certainly less openly declared as part of the scheme's mission. During our fieldwork (Appendices C and D), visits to the clinics belonging to the NRCMS showed us that advertisements for the new system stressed the individual's responsibility to utilize health insurance, guided by state help and advice. This contrasts with the old-style health propaganda posters[10] for the RCMS, which emphasized the scheme as a cornerstone of the broader scheme of collectivization (Landsberger and van der Heijden 2009, 186). Here health provision was closely wound up with the necessity to have a population that could maintain production, with figurative depictions of barefoot doctors clearly keen to represent them as comrades and workers. Today, the tone has a subtler message of individualism, emphasizing that Chinese people need to have access to specialists and hospitals and medicines, a message underscored (although never explicitly stated) with the WHO/UN ideals of good health access as a basic human right.

Local authorities and local political leadership have more autonomy and flexibility in applying national policies or in finding innovative ways to meet national goals. It is still true that local doctors are supposed to work towards, sometimes controversial, national policies such as family planning, but today's rural doctors are a dim reflection of the centrally organized Maoist Barefoot Doctor.

(2) To what extent is the new organizational approach of the NRCMS similar to or different from western models of mutual insurance?

Perhaps the most dominating difference between the old and new incarnations of the scheme was that the NRCMS emphasized the responsibility of the central government for its funding in a way the earlier scheme never did. Investment from the governmental budget increased from 1.5 billion in 2004 to 3.5 billion in 2006 (Central Committee of the CCP and State Council 2002). Furthermore, NRCMS differed significantly in emphasis because it focused on paid contributions to join the scheme. This also protected the scheme from financial ruin. What makes the more recent scheme additionally distinctive, however, is that it was also put in place in some urban areas, though with a different infrastructural emphasis (since the cities are already provided with hospitals) and with a different financial contribution system, reflecting the higher cost of care (Brown and Theoharides 2009).

This modern focus upon centralization and reliance upon government funding is in contrast to, at least the rhetoric of, the original RCMS. Indeed, the RCMS that operated under Mao prided itself on its local flexibility and reliance upon self-management. Even if ultimately all services were rendered as part of the Maoist regime, the RCMS was locally able to organize the cultivation of natural plant remedies, the management of physical structures, the selection and training of staff, and the construction of public health facilities such as village draining systems (WHO 1973).

On one hand it can be seen that the way that the RCMS was conceived and organized reflected both the centrality of the state and the priorities given to local collective decision-making, one that seemingly affords precedence to the decisions of the local community above those of the remote central government. Perhaps this emphasis is most directly illustrated in Article 4 of the *Code of Conduct of the RCMS*: 'The form of the conduct of RMCS should be based on the local conditions and full discussion of the people's commune members' (DAHF 1980, 62).[11]

Similarly, although the state dictated what the code of conduct of barefoot doctors should be, and what the ideal ratio of barefoot doctors to population should be (normally 1 barefoot doctor for every 500 people was recommended), provision was also made for the local commune to decide the number of barefoot doctors according to local conditions (DAHF 1980, 63).[12] For example in more dispersed communes, it might be convenient to have more barefoot doctors for fewer people, simply because of the inconveniences of travel between the patients. Selection, training programmes, and re-training refresher courses were therefore organized according to local judgements (DAHF 1980, article 16, 63). Organizationally then, despite the power of the state ideology and state responsibility for 'broad policy, technical direction and financial support' at a county and provincial level, the original RCMS was publically promoted as being 'decentralized and flexible, in keeping with the principles of self-reliance' and providing 'full opportunities for peripheral units to solve their own problems' (WHO 1978). This can well be read with the lenses provided by Mintzberg (1993) to observe the role of ideology, power, decentralization, and flexibility in organizational design (Zeffane 1989).

Furthermore, if one looks at the way personnel actually operated, it is clear that there was no real autonomy. The barefoot doctor's role was more one 'of execution rather than of conception or supervision'.[13] Although simple decisions were in the hands of the individual to decide how to treat the patient, in fact these rarely went beyond the purview of the extremely limited immediacy of the doctor–patient relationship. Any wider decisions on when to conduct vaccination campaigns, when to perform public sanitation campaigns, the content of health education programmes were all determined at a commune level. These decisions were guided by government policy (the most obvious expression of which being the edict to promote the one child policy, see Appendix B) (DAHF 1980, article 3, points 1 and 6, 62). In terms of Institutional Theory (Powell and DiMaggio 1991; Jepperson 1991), the local branches of the RCMS were subject to organizational isomorphic pressures of all three kinds: *coercive*, *normative*, and *mimetic* (Scott 1995). Local officers and doctors were forced to follow the policies and the orders (*coercive*), many of them might truly believe in the system (*normative*), most of them wanted the organizational unit under their responsibility to look pretty much the same (Suchman 1995) to the other parts of the system (*mimetic*).

The differences however, between the old and the new schemes seem in this regard perhaps more slight than one might necessarily assume. Indeed, although the NRCMS emphasized the role central government had to play in funding subsidies, it nevertheless organized itself in a way surprisingly similar to that of the RCMS. For sure, the new scheme was organized around larger operational units at the county level (rather than at a village level as during Mao's time), but nevertheless the emphasis of the NRCMS is still on decentralization (Mintzberg 1993; Zeffane 1989). Local decision-making and experimentation are promoted above any single state policy (Wagstaff et al. 2009). In a sense, the distinctions are subtle – in the old RCMS, the state promoted local initiative, did not fund the scheme centrally, but ultimately dictated its policies. In the NRCMS, the state also talks of local responsibility, but this time funds the scheme centrally, and still dictates general policies, but in a way less ideologically heavy-handed than that experienced under Mao.

Finally, mention needs to be made of the way the schemes had different financial structures. The RCMS was a prepaid medical service but one that essentially conformed to structures typical of co-operatives in other national contexts in that it was based upon a co-financing, risk sharing approach to disease control (Bloom and Gu 1997b). Local people paid an annual membership fee – which varied slightly between regions, but was from 0.35 Yuan to 3.60 Yuan per year. This amount represented between less than 1% and 3% of a family's disposable income (Zhu et al. 1989, 431–441). Some other subsidy was available from brigade and commune funds, but the government itself made no payments to the RCMS, except exceptionally in the very poorest regions (Zhu et al. 1989, 432). Communes supplied the RCMS with housing, equipment, and essential drugs from commune-owned estate and public welfare funds. The financial contributions received from the peasants were used locally to pay healthcare costs and the costs of medicine. Their local commune considered the contribution of barefoot doctors voluntary, with them receiving no payment for their health work specifically, rather only for their agricultural work.

This is a big contrast to the way that the NRCMS is financed and funded in modern China. In the new voluntary system, contributions are paid at a flat-rate per household, and while all contributions are then in turn subsidized by government funds, both at a county and national level, the very poorest members of the community have their contributions *entirely* subsidized by the government (Wagstaff et al. 2009, 3).

Membership to the RCMS was not theoretically obligatory, but the political structures in place greatly encouraged it. Whereas in the 1960s membership was entirely voluntary on an individual basis, from 1971 once a brigade had voted to join the system, all members of that brigade found themselves to automatically be part of the scheme and their payments would be expected. Households were organized into teams, then teams formed brigades, and brigades formed the commune. This, essentially mandatory, necessity for enrolment in the scheme should be seen in marked contrast to the entirely voluntary membership promoted as an integral part of the NRCMS today. Mirroring the spread of market culture, perhaps even the slightly more democratic tendencies, starting to become acceptable in modern China today.

This tension between centralism and either apparent or true local initiative can be situated in the broader tradition of socialist organizations; 'This seemingly paradoxical leadership style was the translation of Leninist democratic centralism to the economic and organizational domains: a combination of centralized direction of the economy by the state with the democratic initiative of the people' (Tsoukas 1994, 35). But significantly, this also fits in with other scholarly work illuminating that China might not be as centralistic as it might appear to be in its institutional structures. Even within PRC, from the time of its very foundation, there appears to have been more space for innovation than the dominance of the State might suggest. Several bottom-up political innovations, protests, local bargaining, and competition (Whiting 2000) still now continue to shape Chinese policies, values, and organizations in ways unanticipated and unplanned from Beijing (Fairbank 1998).

While the very hierarchical nature of the relationship between centre and periphery and between political and administrative level is still a strong characteristic of China, the NRCMS is no longer part of the huge bureaucratic and political machine of collectivist China (Appendices A and B). There is no army of Barefoot Doctors and the emphasis has shifted to be more on financial sustainability rather than creating an organization fully integrated with state propaganda. Households and individuals are today subject to higher fluctuations of income and wealth. This has meant, for most, better living conditions but also more uncertainty about their futures. This is why the new scheme is perceived as an insurance against catastrophic healthcare expenses (Yip and Hsiao 2009; Babiarz et al. 2010) in the eyes of both the policy makers and the subscribers. This hope is interesting because it is paradoxically reliant on historical foundations no longer considered relevant for modern China. Although cast differently, several organizational and ideological continuities between the two systems can be discerned. The next sections will describe the theoretical and practical implications of our findings and the needs for further research on this topic.

5. Discussion: history and organization studies

Answering the research questions, we have specifically addressed a gap in the existing literature on the NRCMS, as most medical, political, and economic studies have avoided analysing the heritage of the Maoist version of the scheme when investigating the current one. We consider this to miss a vital part of the story. It is intriguing to look at historical precedents in the light of the dramatically abrupt fall of the past scheme. The subsequent and sudden rehabilitation of the system in 2002, without any apparent mention in the public documents about the past scheme, but clearly embodying a strong ideological similarity to the former incarnation, we argue, needs to be considered. Organization Theory, when combined with historical analysis can offer further insights into the understanding of organizational reality. Institutional Theory has also been drawn upon to provide insights on the way that these organizations emerged, diffused, disappeared, and reappeared under a new institutional context (Powell and DiMaggio 1991; Jepperson 1991).

In the past 30 years there have been increasing calls advocating the wider use of historical research methods of analysis within social science disciplines, particularly those within Management Studies, Organizational Studies and Institutional Theory (Kieser 1994; Gherardi and Strati 1988; Decker 2013; Wadwani and Bucheli 2013; Rowlinson, Hassard, and Decker 2014; Greenwood and Bernardi 2014).

This work responds to these calls, arguing that NRCMS events are both historically contingent and contingent upon modern socio-political dynamics. As it has been argued among historians and organizational studies scholars (Greenwood and Bernardi 2014; Rowlinson, Hassard, and Decker 2014), using historical methods does not mean abandoning discrete disciplinary differences between historically separate fields of enquiry. Indeed, we do not expect any sort of seamless integration between two fields. To this end, we use the example of comparing and contrasting the old and new incarnations of the Chinese Rural Co-operative Medical Scheme using both historical methods and Organization Theory. Our recent visits to rural clinics in China have given us the contemporary perspective, but this is less meaningful if we do not also use history to assess the place from which the new organizational structures and ideological commitments of the scheme have evolved. While history gives us the toolkit to assess change over the passage of time, Organization Studies can additionally give us the means to further critique this analysis by allowing us to examine the structures and power relations that have been present in both schemes.

This study has a few limitations. The language barrier meant we only had access to interviews and Chinese Mandarin documents through the mediation of a translator. Furthermore, the understanding of Chinese politics is a very complex exercise that we make no special claims to have mastered. Finally, the understanding of the Chinese co-operative movement itself presents several challenges, not least because it is so different in many fundamentals to the international model that we assume as a paradigm.

These limitations should be seen as signals for the need for further research. The Chinese co-operative movement deserves more research; it is not clear how much it is in line with the international co-operative movement. Another issue that as well deserves further research is the relationship between contemporary communist leadership and Maoism. Also, the measurement of the effectiveness and efficiency of the NRCMS should be investigated further; 12 years after the establishment, its successes and failures shall be visible.

6. Implications: theory, practice, policy

This research conveys implications for theory (the need of an historical approach in contemporary Chinese Studies), for practice (the need of modernization for the Chinese co-operative movement) and for policy (the effectiveness and efficiency of NRCMS).

With regards to theory, we have learnt that no studies to date have examined the modern system directly comparative to the older one. In particular, most analysis has focused either on the financial or the medical side, without considering the ideological component of the old system and its inheritance to the NRCMS. The later scheme may have differed in emphasis but broadly followed historical patterns in its structure and priority. There were key differences in political context, organizational priorities, and membership terms between the two models, but nevertheless it is arguable that the NRCMS relied on its historical antecedents as part of its modern story of national acceptance. Certainly it seems that the original scheme has left an ambiguous legacy, on one hand its demise was nationally seen with a large amount of regret, certainly if we are to believe the Party line, emanating from the Department of Health which stated that the decline of the RCMS was ultimately to be regretted because the majority of farmers had welcomed this system (Zhang 1982, 32). Yet also by understanding the close associations the earlier scheme had with Maoism and enforced collectivization, we are able to see why there maybe some resistance to co-operatives within modern China. We realize that the health co-operatives that functioned during the 1960s are of a different nature to the NRCMS embraced in 2002. Yet to view modern developments in a vacuum is to ignore an important part of their rationale. Even when contemporary models are significantly different from their forerunners, their divergences from similar past conceptions should be seen as much as a reaction to historical precedents, as it is an adjustment to the social and political factors of the contemporaneous context. Chinese institutions are very ritualistic (Weber 1951) and have a very long memory (Douglas 1987); this makes the understanding of the past very important issue.

With regards to practice, our story of the resurrection of a Maoist co-operative model in post-Maoist China says much about the way co-operatives can adapt, survive, and flourish in different political climates (Scott 2003). Propagandist intent is no longer a central driving force of the new scheme, but nevertheless is present in a subtler and less obvious form. The language has changed from one of collectivism to individualism (all be it with State protection); the spirit of the new scheme is one of voluntary participation and self-responsibility, except for the very poorest sectors of society. The organization seems to have centralized, whilst also simultaneously becoming less authoritarian in its public demands. As explored in Section 4 however organizational differences are perhaps not so bold as the government would have us believe. The 2002 NRCMS policy, together with the 2007 Specialized Farmers Co-operative law, represent the evident resurgence in the interest of contemporary Chinese governments in the co-operative organizational model. The comparison of the old and new Rural Co-operative Medical Scheme confirms that China is indeed involved in a process of convergence (Scott 1995) towards the western notion of co-operation. The reputation of cooperatives was severely damaged by the ideological rule of Mao, but nevertheless, the contemporary Chinese co-operative movement, although different, owes much more than it would like to admit to its troubled past. Further convergence to the international co-operative model will require to deal with that past.

With regards to policy, we have learnt that both schemes have been measurably effective in delivering a broad improvement of health conditions in rural China. Having said this, on the efficiency side, the results are less clear-cut. The measurement of efficiency and effectiveness is beyond the boundaries of this work and would involve broad statistical analysis of the data before and after these schemes were implemented. Leaving the judgement on the efficiency to economics studies, and the judgement on the effectiveness to public medicine studies, we can, however, add to the debate the useful point that (however effective) the organizational form adopted is never neutral, both because of its past heritage and also because of its contemporary influences and objectives. This means that in this case, as in others, the effectiveness and efficiency of Chinese social and economic policies may be affected by the degree of modernization and transparency on politics, ideology, and past Communist leaderships.

7. Conclusions

This paper has described the old and the new Rural Co-operative Medical Scheme. After a detailed narration and historical contextualization, the data analysis made it possible to answer both research questions. We have shown that ideologically and organizationally both schemes are crucially different. However, we argue, these differences are perhaps not that large.

The New Rural Co-operative Medical Scheme is not an ideologically run health care provider, but it nevertheless is far from ideology free. Vitally, under the administration of the national and local authorities, the influence of politics is still visible (as in many other economic sectors) and the CCP are, of course, still conveying some ideological messages, modernized by the new language of individual responsibility and the persuasive appeal of the image of providing a universal entitlement to basic health care. By comparing the ideological commitments of both of the schemes, we can see a distinct reduction in the direct use of political ideology as a cohesive rationale for not only the modern scheme itself, but also for the way it is run and staffed at a micro-level. The NRCMS is still, for sure, part of the policy template put forward by the politicians of modern China, but it is one that now prioritizes long term health affordability and community healthcare management above the need to publicize and justify the central regime.

The old and new RCMS are not similarly organized in the core way in that the NRCMS has aligned itself closer to the western model of mutual insurance. In fact, most of the structure and maintenance of healthcare and public medicine operations are no longer directly managed by the NRCMS. The new incarnation of the scheme is closer now to western models of mutual insurance than it ever has been at any previous point. Political emphasis has shifted and in turn so have consumer expectations. China is now no longer inward looking, but as the second largest economy and a key player in the modern world stage, is attempting to apply broadly western models of insurance to tackle its population challenges.

This work has also argued that using history, as core part of the analytical method, can give deeper insights to organization and management scholars working on contemporary Chinese policies and business practices.

Acknowlegement

The work on original Mandarin Chinese documents was made possible by the support of Ms Xiaojiao WU, Zhejiang Chinese Medical University.

Notes
1. Email: anna.greenwood@nottingham.edu.cn
2. Original Chinese: '至于如何解决广大农民的医疗卫生问题，那时共产党只有一个粗略的思路，既是走合作的道路'.

3. '生产建设与和平生活就无从获得保障', He Cheng, Deputy Minister of Health, quoted in Hu (2007, 51).
4. Original Chinese: '要把过去两年放松了的爱国卫生运动重新发动起来，并且一定要于一九六0年，一九六一年，一九六二年这二年内做出显著的成绩' quoted from Mao Z., *Instructions for Public Health/关于卫生工作的指示*', 18 March 1960.
5. WHO/E/5/418/11 SomnuekUnakul, *Report on Rural Sanitation in China*, February 1975, p. 3.
6. WHO/AFR/MCH/66 3.9.75 V. Agbessi, 'Organisation of Health Services in China'; Report on a Mission, 21 October 1974, p. 2.
7. Original Chinese: '农村合作以来哦是人民公社社员依靠集体力量，在自愿互助的基础上建立起来的一种社会主义性质的医疗制度，是社员群众的集体福利事业' (Article 1).
8. Original Chinese: '尤其应优先挑选具有上述条件的贫下中农子女.'
9. Original Chinese: '合作医疗站是集体福利事业单位，不用办成企业及副业，也不应要求他们上缴利润' (Article 10).
10. See also The Shanghai Porpaganda Poster Mueum and the website database curated by Marien van der Heijden: http://chineseposters.net/.
11. Original Chinese: '举办合作医疗的形式要根据当地的实际情况和条件，经社员群众充分讨论决定' (Article 10).
12. Original Chinese: '赤脚医生的人数，应根据实际需要进行配备' (Article 13).
13. WHO/N52/180/2 CHN (2), File 1, WHO Study Missions to China, 1973–1978, 'Medical Care in Rural Areas', p. 2.

References

Babiarz, K. S., G. Miller, H. Yi, L. Zhang, and S. Rozelle. 2010. "New Evidence on the Impact of China's New Rural Co-operative Medical Scheme and Its Implications for Rural Primary Healthcare: Multivariate Difference-In-Difference Analysis." *British Medical Journal* 341: c5617. doi:10.1136/bmj.

Bloom, G., and X. Y. Gu. 1997a. "Health Sector Reform: Lessons from China." *Social Sciences and Medicine* 45: 351–360.

Bloom, G., and X. Y. Gu. 1997b. "Introduction to Health Sector Reform in China." *IDS Bulletin* 28 (1): 1–11.

Brown, P. H., A. De Brauw, and Y. Du. 2009. "Understanding Variation in the Design of China's New Co-operative Medical System." *The China Quarterly* 198: 304–329.

Brown, P., and C. Theoharides. 2009. "Health-Seeking Behavior and Hospital Choice in China's New Co-operative Medical System." *Health Economics* 18: 47–64.

Bryant, J. H. 1978. "Community Health Workers: The Interface Between Communities and Health Care Systems." *WHO Chronicle* 32: 144–148.

Cai, T. X. 2009. "新中国成立以来我国农村合作医疗的发展历程 [The History of the Development of the Rural Co-operative Medical Care System since the Foundation of PRC]." Literature of Chinese Communist Party No. 3 pp. 20–26.

Central Political Bureau. 1978. "关于湘乡县减轻农民不合理负担的调查报告 [Report on Reducing the Farmer's Unreasonable Financial Burden in Xiangxiang County]." Document No. 37, 23 June 1978. Cited in Wu, S., 2005, p. 4; see also, *People's Daily*, July 5, 1.

Cheng-Chung, L. 1988. "European Co-operativism in Chinese Perspective." *Annals of Public and Co-operative Economics* 59 (3): 369–377.

Cook, I., and J. Clegg. 2012. "Shared Visions of Co-operation at a Time of Crisis: The Gung Ho Story in China's Anti-Japanese Resistance." In *The Hidden Alternative: Co-operative Values, Past, Present and Future*, edited by A. Webster, A. Brown, D. Stewart, J. K. Walton, and L. Shaw, 327–346. Helsinki: United Nations University Press.

CPC Central Committee and State Council. 2002. *中共中央国务院关于进一步加强农村卫生工作的决定* [The CPC Central Committee and the State Council 's Decision on Further Strengthening the Rural Health Work] CPC Central Committee and State Council Document No. 13. Beijing: CPC Central Committee and State Council.

Crozier, M. 1964. *Le phénomène bureaucratique* [The Bureaucratic Phenomenon]. Chicago, IL: University of Chicago Press, 320 pp.

Dahf. 1980. "Department of Agriculture, Health and Finance, Together with State Administration of Medicine 'Code of Conduct of RCMS'."

Decker, S. 2013. "The Silence of the Archives: Business History, Post-Colonialism and Archival Ethnography." *Management and Organizational History* 8: 155–173.

Department of Health. 1965. "关于把卫生工作重点放到农村的报告 [Report Prioritizing Primary Level Medical Services to Rural Areas]." 21 September 1965.

Department of Health. 1976. "Conference Report, 15 June to 23 June 1976." Cited in: Xia, X., 2003, p. 110.

Dong, C., K. T. Kam, Z. Lifeng, and Z. Yuhong. 2013. "Will China's Co-operative Medical System Fail Again? Insight from Farmer Satisfaction Survey." *Health Promotion International*. doi:10. 1093/heapro/dat032.

Douglas, M. 1987. *How Institutions Think*. London: Routledge.

Fairbank, J. K. 1998. *China: A New History*. Cambridge, MA: Belknap Press of Harvard University Press.

Fairbank, J. K., and A. Feuerwerker, eds. 1986. *The Cambridge History of China*. Vol. 13, Part 2. Cambridge: Cambridge University Press.

Gao, S., and F. Chi. 1996. *The Development of China's Non Governmentally and Privately Operated Economy*. Beijing: Languages Press.

Gertler, P., and J. Gruber. 2002. "Insuring Consumption Against Illness." *The American Economic Review* 92 (1): 51–70.

Gherardi, S., and A. Strati. 1988. "The Temporal Dimension in Organizational Studies." *Organization Studies* 9: 149–164.

Greenwood, A., and A. Bernardi. 2014. "Understanding the Rift, the (Still) Uneasy Bedfellows of History and Organization Studies." *Organization*. doi:10.1177/1350508413514286.

Ho, D. Y. F. 1978. "The Concept of Man in Mao-TseTung's Thought." *Psychiatry* 41: 391–402.

Horn, J. S. 1975. "Community Action Pays Off." *World Health Organization*, December: 22–25.

Huang, S. M. 1988. "Transforming China's Collective Health Care System: A Village Study." *Social Science and Medicine* 27: 879–888.

Jamison, D. T., J. R. Evans, T. King, I. Porter, and N. Prescott. 1984. *China: The Health Sector*. Washington, DC: World Bank.

Jepperson, R. L. 1991. "Institutions, Institutional Effects and Institutionalism." In *The New Institutionalism in Organizational Analysis*, edited by Powell, and DiMaggio, 143–163. Chicago, IL: University of Chicago Press.

Kieser, A. 1994. "Why Organization Theory Needs Historical Analyses and How This Should Be Performed." *Organization Science* 5 (4): 608–620.

Klotzbücher, S., P. Lässig, Q. Jiangmei, and S. Weigelin-Schwiedrzik. 2010. "What is New in the 'New Rural Co-operative Medical System'? An Assessment in One Kazak County of the Xinjiang Uyghur Autonomous Region." *The China Quarterly*, , Special Section on Social Insurance in China 201: 38–57.

Kornai, J., and Q. Yingyi, eds. 2009. *Market and Socialism: In the Light of the Experiences of China and Vietnam*. IEA. New York: Palgrave Macmillan.

Lambo, T. A. 1980. "Politics, Ideology, and Health: Reflexions Arising from a Study Tour of the People's Republic of China by Six African Ministers of Health." *World Health Forum* 1 (1): 5–7.

Landsberger, S. R., and M. van der Heijden. 2009. *Chinese Posters*. Munich: Prestel.

Li, Y. A. 1985. "Country Physician." *World Health,* January/February, 4–5.

Liu, Y. 2004. "Development of the Rural Health Insurance System in China." *Health and Policy Planning* 19 (3): 159–165.

Mao, Z. 1956. "高级农业生产合作社示范章程 [Model Guidelines on Agricultural Production Co-operatives]." 30 June 1956.

Mao, Z. 1958. "中共中央关于在农村建立人民公社问题的决议 [Decision on Setting up the People's Commune in Rural China]." 29 August 1958.

Mao, Z. 1960. *关于卫生工作的指示* [Instructions for Public Health]. 18 March 1960.

Mao, Z. 1965. "中央关于卫生工作的指示 [Directive on Public Health]." 26 June 1965 (quoted in Mao 1996, 80).

Mao, Z. 1968. "从"赤脚医生"的成长看医学教育革命的方向:上海市的调查报告 [The Analysis of the Reform of Medical Education from the Perspective of the Growth of the Barefoot Doctor: An Investigation Report in Shanghai]." *Redflag Journal* 3: 1–3.

Mao, Z. 1991. 毛泽东选集 [Selected Works of Mao Tse-Tung]. Vol. 3, 2nd ed. Peking: People's Publishing House.

Merton, R. K. 1936. "The Unanticipated Consequences of Purposive Social Action." *American Sociological Review* 1 (6): 894–904.

Mintzberg, H. 1993. *Structure in Fives: Designing Effective Organizations*. Englewood Cliffs, NJ: Prentice-Hall.

Powell, W. W., and P. J. DiMaggio, eds. 1991. *The New Institutionalism in Organizational Analysis*. Chicago, IL: University of Chicago Press.

PRC. 1978. *Constitution of the People's Republic of China*.

Prescott, N., and D. T. Jamison. 1984. "Health Sector Finance in China." *World Health Statistics Quarterly* 37: 387–397.

Qin, L., S. Pan, C. Wang, and Z. Jiang. 2012. "Adverse Selection in China's New Rural Co-operative Medical Scheme." *China Agricultural Economic Review* 4 (1): 69–83.

Rowlinson, M., J. Hassard, and S. Decker. 2014. "Strategies for Organizational History: A Dialogue Between Historical Theory and Organization Theory." *Academy of Management Review*. doi:10.5465/amr.2012.0203.

Scott, W. R. 1995. *Institutions and Organizations*. Thousand Oaks, CA: Sage.

Scott, W. R. 2003. "Institutional Carriers: Reviewing Modes of Transporting Ideas Over Time and Space and Considering Their Consequences." *Industrial and Corporate Change* 12: 879–894.

Shenkar, O. 1996. "The Firm as a Total Institution: Reflections on the Chinese State Enterprise." *Organisation Studies* 17: 885–907.

Skeet, M. 1984. "Community Health Workers: Promoters or Inhibitors of Primary Health Care?" *World Health Forum* 5: 291–295.

Suchman, M. C. 1995. "Managing Legitimacy: Strategic and Institutional Approaches." *Academy of Management Review* 20: 571–610.

Tsoukas, H. 1994. "Socio-Economic Systems and Organisational Management: An Institutional Perspective on the Socialist Firm." *Organisation Studies* 15: 21–45.

UNDP. 2013. *China Human Development Report. 2013: Sustainable and Liveable Cities: Toward Ecological Urbanisation*. Beijing: Compiled by United Nations Development Program.

United Nations. 2013. *China's Progress Towards the Millennium Development Goals 2013 Report*. Beijing: Ministry of Foreign Affairs of the People's Republic of China.

Wadwani, R. D., and M. Bucheli. 2013. *Organizations in Time: History, Theory, Methods*. New York: Oxford University Press.

Wagstaff, A., and M. Lindelow. 2005. "Can Insurance Increase Financial Risk? The Curious Case of Health Insurance in China." *World Bank Policy Research Working Paper* 3741.

Wagstaff, A., M. Lindelowb, G. Junc, X. Lingc, and Q. Junchengcet. 2009. "Extending Health Insurance to the Rural Population: An Impact Evaluation of China's New Co-operative Medical Scheme." *Journal of Health Economics* 28: 1–19.

Wang, S. 2009. "Adapting by Learning the Evolution of China's Rural Health Care Financing." *Modern China* 35 (4): 370–404.

Wang, H., W. Yip, L. Zhang, L. Wang, and W. Hsiao. 2005. "Community-Based Health Insurance in Poor Rural China: The Distribution of Net Benefits." *Health Policy and Planning* 20 (6): 366–374.

Weber, M. 1951. *The Religion of China: Confucianism and Taoism*. Clencoe, IL: The Free Press.

Whiting, S. H. 2000. *Power and Wealth in Rural China: The Political Economy of Institutional Change*. Cambridge, MA: Cambridge University Press.

WHO. 1973. *Report of WHO Study Mission to People's Republic of China*. Geneva: World Health Organisation.

WHO. 1974. "Round Table Discussion: WHO Visits China." *World Health*, September, 8–15.

WHO. 1978. *Organisation and Functioning of the Health Services in China: Report on Two WHO Study Missions to the People's Republic of China 1973 and 1974*. Geneva: World Health Organisation.

WHO. 1988. "Community Health Workers: Strengthening Community Health Workers for Health for All." *Weekly Epidemiological Health Record* 63 (35): 265–268.

WHO. 1989. "Co-operative Medical System and Barefoot Doctors in Rural China." *Bulletin of the World Health Organisation* 87 (4): 431–441.

Xu, J. 1997. "History of Health Economic Policy." *China Health and Economics* 10: 7–8.

Yip, W., and W. C. Hsiao. 2009. "Non-Evidence-Based Policy: How Effective Is China's New Co-operative Medical Scheme in Reducing Medical Impoverishment?" *Social Science & Medicine* 68 (2): 201–209.

Young, M. E. 1989. "Impact of the Rural Reform on Financing Rural Health Services in China." *Health Policy* 11: 27–42.

Yu, D. 1992. "Changes in Health Care Financing and Health Status: The Case of China in the 1980s." Innocenti Occasional Papers, Economic Policy Series, No. 34.

Zeffane, R. M. 1989. "Centralization or Formalization? Indifference Curves for Strategies of Control." *Organization Studies* 10: 327–352.

Zhang, H. Y. 1982. 公共卫生学 [Public Health]. Taipei: Taiwan Commercial Press.

Zhang, K. N., Y. Q. Wen, and P. Liang, eds. 2002. 从赤脚医生到乡村医生 [From Barefoot Doctors to Village Doctors]. Yunnan City: Yunnan People's Publishers.

Zhu, N., Z. Ling, J. Shen, J. M. Lane, and S. Hu. 1989. "Factors Associated with the Decline of the Co-operative Medical System and Barefoot Doctors in Rural China." *Bulletin of the World Health Organisation* 87 (4): 431–441.

Appendix A. 'Barefoot doctors are all over the mountain villages, cooperation creates a new atmosphere of medical treatment', 1974, IISH / Stefan R. Landsberger Collections

Appendix B. 'Practice birth control for the revolution', 1972, IISH / Stefan R. Landsberger Collections

Appendix C. A clinic in Guanxi, 2012, photo taken by the authors

Appendix D. A picture of Mao Zedong in a clinic in Guanxi, 2012, photo taken by the authors

Appendix E. 'Three barefoot doctors', 1974, from WHO Archive, WHO/N52/180/2 CHN (2), File 2, WHO Study Missions to China

The role and characteristics of social entrepreneurs in contemporary rural cooperative development in China: case studies of rural social entrepreneurship

Hong Lan[a], Ying Zhu[b], David Ness[b], Ke Xing[c] and Kris Schneider[d]

[a]School of Environment and Natural Resources, Renmin University of China, Haidian District, Beijing, China; [b]Australian Centre for Asian Business and Barbara Hardy Institute, The University of South Australia, Adelaide, SA, Australia; [c]School of Advanced Manufacturing & Mechanical Engineering & Barbara Hardy Institute, The University of South Australia, Mawson Lakes Campus, Australia; [d]Faculty of Business, Economics and Statistics, University of Vienna, Vienna, Austria

Rural communities in China have experienced rapid changes in recent years under the government's policy of 'new countryside development'. Remarkably, there has been an increase in social entrepreneurship led by village leaders and capable individuals with an entrepreneurial spirit. This research is based on in-depth interviews with several of these social entrepreneurs in multiple villages in *Yunnan* and *Zhejiang* provinces in China. It aims to explore the key issues related to the role of social entrepreneurship and leadership in developing rural cooperatives. The findings suggest that there are multiple key characteristics of social entrepreneurship in the process of rural cooperative development. The research findings have implications for rural community development in transitional economies in terms of developing social entrepreneurship capabilities.

1. Introduction

Economic reform in China has led to rapid societal changes – rural communities in particular have experienced a rapid transformation (Webber 2012). This transformation has occurred in three stages. During the 1980s, a reform took place based on replacing the 'commune system' with a 'household responsibility system', which allocated land to individual households for agri-production and business. The second stage that began in the early 2000s was a reform based on 'voluntary cooperatives' with the emphasis on new business cooperation among villagers through village enterprises and their connection with markets. The third stage is a more recent reform with the slogan 'new countryside development' (*xin nongcun jianshe*). This concept is based on a comprehensive approach to develop rural community not only for economic growth, but also for the well-being of rural societies in the areas of education, health care, infrastructure and services, and ecological sustainability (Wan 2007). However, there has been limited comprehensive research on rural social entrepreneurship in China either in English or in Chinese. This piece aims to explore the relevant issues and contribute to this research literature.

In recent years, one of the most remarkable elements leading to changes in rural China has been the role of social entrepreneurship among the newly established rural cooperatives managed by village leaders (*nongcun daitouren*) and capable individuals (*nengren*) with the spirit of entrepreneurship and shared core values that send the message of common prosperity for all villagers. These individuals lead rural communities with a clear social mission through the development of villagers' cooperatives as collectively owned enterprises. As the major drivers and leaders of rural cooperative development, rural social entrepreneurs have some extraordinary capabilities as indicated by Huang and Cui (2009), namely self-learning and obtaining knowledge, applying knowledge to practice, and innovation and creativity. In addition, their social networks are an important source for them to obtain information and knowledge related to production, business opportunities and marketing (Li, Schulze and Li 2009).

The unique characteristics of rural social entrepreneurs are summarized by Liu (2004) as being 'the traditional rule/system breakers' and 'new rule/system creators'. In fact, rural social entrepreneurs face many challenges when adopting new approaches; they encounter powerful resistance from time to time. Different stages of market transitions provide different opportunities as well as constraints (Yang and Li 2008). Therefore, these rural social entrepreneurs must be able to overcome difficulties with qualities such as self-determination, proactive thinking and action, self-control and persistence, as well as being able to implement their strategy effectively (Li, Young and Tang 2012). Given the challenging political, social and economic environments in rural China, what role and crucial characteristics are required of rural social entrepreneurs to achieve successful rural cooperative development?

In order to explore the relevant key issues, we have designed this research based on a review of the relevant literature in terms of the social constructivist approach towards the conceptual framework of social entrepreneurship and the leadership role in the process of development. In order to identify similarities and differences between China and other countries, we also provide a historical review of social entrepreneurship in rural communities in China. We selected six leading social entrepreneurs as case studies through semi-structured interviews. The overall contributions include: first, developing a broader definition of social entrepreneurship with a focus on the process of creating value by combining different resources in an innovative way, and particularly in exploring and exploiting opportunities to create common prosperity. Second, scrutinizing conceptualization that relates to a framework comprised of four dimensions as suggested by Sharir and Lerner (2006), namely the individual entrepreneur, the environment, the organization and the process, and these are demonstrated. The most important elements include individual special traits and leadership skills, the strategies and actions at different stages of business, the significance of building social networks and the key challenges in the process of social entrepreneurship under the market economic transformation in China. A framework for the social entrepreneurship process is established and presented in Figure 1 in the discussion section.

2. Literature review

2.1 The underpinning conceptual framework

The concept of entrepreneurship has a long history with a major theme of creation of value through innovation (Drucker 1985). In recent years, the research focus has shifted from pure entrepreneurship towards social entrepreneurship with an emphasis on innovative and exceptional leadership in social enterprises (Dees 1998; Prabhu 1999). However, the concept of social entrepreneurship has been criticized as ill-defined, with more recent literature addressing these concerns (Short, Moss and Lumpkin 2009; Weerawardena and

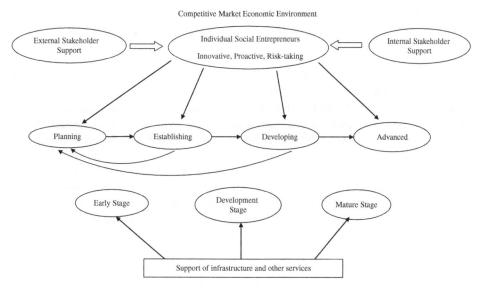

Figure 1. The conceptual framework of the role of social entrepreneurs in the process of cooperative development.

Sullivan Mort 2006). The general direction of conceptualization has two spheres: the first being that social entrepreneurship results in an organization achieving a sustainable competitive advantage, allowing it to achieve its social mission (Weerawardena and Sullivan Mort 2001); the second is that social entrepreneurship should be conceptualized within the broader competitive environment in which it operates (Weerawardena and Sullivan Mort 2006). An increasing consensus is emerging that social entrepreneurship is a bounded multidimensional construct, deeply rooted in an organization's social mission and its drive for sustainability, while being highly influenced and shaped by environmental dynamics.

In recent years, based on consensus building, much broader definitions have been established with the emphasis on social entrepreneurship of individuals or organizations being engaged in entrepreneurial activities with a social goal (Certo and Miller 2008; Van de Ven, Sapienza and Villanueva 2007). As Alvord, Brown and Letts (2004) put it, social entrepreneurship employs entrepreneurial capabilities to solve social problems, such as successful poverty alleviation that leads to sustainable societal transformations. Therefore, social entrepreneurship could be seen as a catalyst for social transformations by producing small changes in the short term through existing systems and eventually leading to large changes in the long term. Based on this logic, some researchers have focused on social entrepreneurship as combining commercial enterprises with social impacts, namely using business skills and knowledge to create enterprises that accomplish social goals as well as being commercially viable (Emerson and Twerksy 1996). On the other hand, others have emphasized social entrepreneurship as an innovative way to achieve social impact by focusing on innovations and social arrangements that have potential to solve social problems, albeit with relatively little attention to economic viability (Dees 1998).

Therefore, a possible expansion of the research target and themes has been discussed and developed. For instance, we have expanded our target of organizations from not-for-profit organizations to others, such as for-profit, that may take some innovative action towards building social capital (Thompson, Alvy and Lees 2000). The leadership characteristics of social entrepreneurs have been considered by including broader criteria such as significant personal credibility, integrity and the ability to generate followers' commitment to the project, with consideration to both economic and social values (Borins 2000). Other aspects, such as developing community organizations and social entrepreneurship, have also been identified as contributing towards the improvement of the living conditions of poor and underprivileged people (Cornwall 1998), and facilitating community development (Wallace 1998). There is now a greater focus on the diversity of social initiatives and economic and social impact on community development (Shaw, Shaw and Wilson 2002). In addition, a social entrepreneur's ability to attract resources (i.e. capital, labour and equipment) in a competitive environment and adopt innovative ways to create social value is a crucial determinant of success (Dees 1998). The factors of innovativeness, proactiveness and risk-taking are central to social entrepreneurship (Weerawardena and Mort 2006). Therefore, a combination of 'business skills' and 'social mission' is fundamental for the social entrepreneur to develop and succeed.

Another area of importance regarding conceptualization is related to the framework and the variables found along four dimensions, namely the individual (or entrepreneur), the environment, the organization and the process (Sharir and Lerner 2006). This conceptual framework links the entrepreneur dimension, such as special traits (Drayton 2002) and special leadership skills (Thompson, Alvy and Lees 2000) with: (1) the organizational dimension (e.g. business activities, structure of organization and capital base); (2) the stage of venture (i.e. start-up, growth and consolidation stages); (3) the environmental dimension (e.g. social network, the existence or absence of support and infrastructure services, the enabling and/or constraining effects thereof); (4) the process dimension (e.g. identifying need and opportunity, planning, network building, creating partnerships, acquiring legitimacy and resources); and (5) the ability to stand the market test (Sharir and Lerner 2006). Therefore, a new venture's success cannot be measured simply in terms of the venture's vision, but it also depends on the ability to plan, manage and market the business as well as build social networks and obtain external support – including support from the government and other relevant stakeholders.

Based on the established research in entrepreneurship and recent studies on social entrepreneurship, Mair and Marti (2006) defined social entrepreneurship broadly as a process involving the innovative use and combination of resources to pursue opportunities to catalyse social change and/or address social needs. In a more detailed discussion, they claimed that, first, social entrepreneurship is a process of creating value by combining resources in new ways; second, these resource combinations are intended primarily to explore and exploit opportunities to create social value by stimulating social change or meeting social needs; and third, social entrepreneurship involves the offering of services and products, while it creates new organizations or develops established organizations. More empirical research has been developed by focusing on the common pattern and trend of social entrepreneurship in recent years. For example, research conducted by Alvord, Brown and Letts (2004) sought to identify common patterns across a small set (seven cases, including Grameen Bank) of successful social entrepreneurship initiatives around the world. They identified three forms in common, namely building local capacity, disseminating a package and building a movement. In a more detailed illustration, they claimed that capacity-building initiatives emphasized scaling up by group organizing and cultural change leverage, and transformational impacts on cultural norms and expectations (Alvord, Brown and Letts 2004, 279). Package dissemination initiatives paid attention to scaling up through packaged services to individuals that enabled the use of economic leverage and had transformational impacts on economic outcomes. Movement-building initiatives emphasized external relations and used indirect scaling-up strategies to have transformational impacts on both political and cultural contexts (Alvord, Brown and Letts 2004, 279). They also suggested some factors that were common across initiatives, regardless of innovation form, including mobilizing and building on the assets of the poor constituencies that the social entrepreneurs served. As a result, they were able to leverage relatively small investments externally to produce sustained changes, and the leadership capacities were a crucial element for the success of social entrepreneurship (Alvord, Brown and Letts 2004, 279). By using the example of Grameen Bank, Yunus, Moingeon and Lehmann-Ortega (2010) also drew a number of lessons, including exercises in challenging conventional thinking, finding complementary partners and undertaking continuous experimentation that were similar to those of conventional business models, as well as recruiting social-profit-oriented shareholders and specifying social-profit objectives from the beginning that were specific to social business models.

Recent research by Short, Moss and Lumpkin (2009) identified several key issues that lack empirical research and need more development. One of them is the examination of leadership in social ventures and the role of social entrepreneurship in developing communities. Freire-Gibb and Nielsen's (2011) empirical research explored the importance of individual creativity and social networks in both urban and rural areas in determining the probability of becoming an entrepreneur and surviving the crucial early years of a business operation, which are referred to as 'the valley of death', namely business failures in its early years.

Therefore, it is our intention for this research to focus on the relevant issues and develop our analysis based on the theoretical basis in the social entrepreneurship constructivist approach that provides a better understanding about the process of creating social ventures and values (Hindle 2010). Jack and Anderson (2002) provided this useful approach to develop a good understanding of the process. They suggested that the process is not merely an economic process but draws from the social context that shapes and forms the outcomes. Elaborating on this key aspect they proposed that social structures affect and encourage entrepreneurial activity, particularly in terms of resource availability or constraint (Jack and Anderson 2002); hence, entrepreneurs utilize their understanding of the context in the creation and operation of their businesses. We find this approach to be very useful in our empirical research and we supplement this approach by drawing on key themes or constructs from already established literature on traditional management and entrepreneurship, for example observing how social entrepreneurs use their experience and knowledge of the context as an important element of their entrepreneurial process to achieve their social objectives and overcome challenges. Following this approach, we are also able to learn the entrepreneurial process and the associated factors contributing to the successes of for-profit social ventures in rural China (Short, Moss and Lumpkin 2009).

The sections that follow will provide some background information on the 'social entrepreneur' in rural community transformation in China.

2.2. The background of the transformation of rural communities and their social entrepreneurship in China

Since economic reform began in the late 1970s and early 1980s, there have been two models of economic development in the rural areas of China, namely a top-down systematic reform led by the governments and a bottom-up innovative change of rural production and business operation initiated by farmers themselves (Liu 2004). The grass-roots-oriented changes have created new systems as well as new production and business opportunities that are led by individuals or groups of individuals referred to as 'rural capable people', who are able to identify opportunities and take risks to lead other villagers to achieve common prosperity.

As we mentioned earlier, the rural social entrepreneurs have faced many challenges when adopting new approaches and have encountered powerful resistance from time to time internally and externally (Yang and Li 2008). For example, due to the negative influence of the collective commune system under the central planning economy during the pre-reform period, villagers became very hesitant in embracing any new attempt to develop cooperatives in their communities. Many villagers also did not have much knowledge about the rule and norm of market economy, and it was very risky for them to put their own assets into a collective entity for developing new business (Liu 2004). Externally, due to the lack of law and regulatory protection for entrepreneurship development, such as land and property protection, and inequality of resource distribution between groups and regions across the country, the phenomena of uneven development of social entrepreneurship and cooperatives in different parts of China were very significant.

Therefore, the reform process in rural areas has been seen as gradual and incremental. Eventually, some capable farmers were able to develop their own agri-production and business. They were driven by a tremendous desire to create greater wealth for their individual households. Their goal then extended through a spillover effect to include other villagers to join them in a new form of cooperative which emphasized equal input (assets) from village members and equal sharing (revenue) among their members at a later stage. The participation of the new form of cooperative was voluntary based and individual farmers could choose a particular cooperative among a number of cooperatives in the village. Village members also formed the cooperative board and decision-making was based on the vote among members (Liu 2004).

Under the leadership of a number of rural capable individuals who were brave enough to take the initial risk, 'test the water' and break the 'old fence' by developing new cooperative enterprises, this grass-roots development has built a foundation of new initiatives of collective agri-business such as township and village industry enterprises, village-based family-run holiday houses for tourism, and multi-family-owned agri-production and trade cooperatives.

So far, four types of rural social entrepreneurs and leaders, known in Chinese as 'nongcun daitouren', have been identified (Wan 2007; Wu, Yu and Huang 2008; Zeng, Li and Yang 2005). The first type is the existing village leaders who were elected by villagers and have held such positions for many years, maintaining a good reputation within the village and networking beyond the village. They lead other villagers to set up new enterprises in the form of village cooperatives for developing agri-business. Most of these leaders have goodwill for achieving common prosperity among the community and their role is to lead their people to achieve their goals. The second type is the new emerging village capable persons who have run their own businesses successfully within the village for many years and have been seen as a good example for other villagers to follow. Most of them are competent entrepreneurs with a wide range of skills and social networks. They normally use their own business as the foundation for forming new cooperatives that include other villagers participating in the business operation and sharing the benefits. The third type is the new generation of migrant workers returning to their home villages with many years of industrial and business experience accumulated through working in cities. On their return, they bring new business opportunities, management skills and their social networks. New cooperatives can be developed through their initiatives. The fourth type is the experts and professional people outside rural communities who work together with these communities and village leaders to develop special products and business with particular know-how and techniques.

As the major drivers and leaders of rural community development, rural social entrepreneurs have some extraordinary capabilities that other villagers may lack. Huang and Cui (2009) summarized three key capabilities, namely self-learning and obtaining knowledge, applying knowledge in practice, and innovation and creativity. These capabilities enable them to accumulate, increase and realize their human capital. As for rural social entrepreneurs, their basic knowledge and skills were obtained from their formal school education, training provided by the local government and other training institutes, and technical development obtained from other professionals. However, the most important factor for their entrepreneurship capability development is their previous experience. The concept of 'learning on the job' is very important for them to accumulate knowledge, skills and know-how to apply these to practice. Their social networks are an important source for them to obtain information and knowledge related to production, business opportunities and marketing (Li, Schulze and Li 2009). These networks include a wide range of people and expertise, such as people conducting the same type of business, sales agents, customers, relevant government officials, technical and professional people, and even competitors. Learning and development for the rural social entrepreneur are a process of continuous revitalization and improvement.

In addition, as we discussed earlier, rural social entrepreneurs have been viewed as 'the traditional rule/system breakers' and 'new rule/system creators'. Generally speaking, different stages of market transitions provide different opportunities as well as constraints (Yang and Li 2008). Therefore, these rural social entrepreneurs must be able to overcome difficulties through self-determination, proactive thinking and action, self-control and persistence, and be able to implement their strategy effectively (Li, Young and Tang 2012). These unique characteristics enable the rural social entrepreneur to survive during the process of reform and transformation.

Based on the literature review on social entrepreneurship and the background of social entrepreneurs in rural communities in China, we can now identify some themes for the current research. First, we adopt the social constructivist approach and a much broader definition of social entrepreneurship developed more recently with the focus on the process of creating value by combining different resources in an innovative way, and particularly in exploring and exploiting opportunities to create social value by stimulating social change and meeting social needs (Mair and Marti 2006). In addition, we scrutinize conceptualization which relates to a framework comprised of four dimensions as suggested by Sharir and Lerner (2006), namely the individual entrepreneur, the environment, the organization and the process. The most important elements include individual special traits and leadership skills, strategies and actions at different stages of business development, the significance of social networks and the key challenges in the process of social entrepreneurship development. By doing so, we can illustrate the characteristics of rural social entrepreneurs in the context of their ability to lead and organize rural cooperative development. Therefore, our four key research questions are developed with these considerations in mind: What are the special traits and leadership skills for achieving the goals of common prosperity and rural cooperative development? What are the strategies and actions adopted by the rural social entrepreneurs at different stages of business development? How significant are these actions for building social networks by the rural social entrepreneurs? What are the key challenges during the process of social entrepreneurship from the planning stage, development, through to the advanced stages of cooperative development?

3. Research design, methods and case selection

This research project is funded by the Australia-China Science and Research Fund as a group mission. A joint research team was formed and the first fieldwork was carried out in several rural communities in *Yunnan* and *Zhejiang* provinces in early 2012. The rationale for selecting these two provinces was based on comparing and contrasting rural villages with less developed and more developed regions, as well as between ethnic minority communities with *Han* (majority) communities. Given that *Yunnan* is located in the south-west and is a less developed region with many remote ethnic minority communities, while *Zhejiang* is located in the developed east coast region with predominately *Han* communities having only one minority (the *She* community); we selected these two provinces as our target rural villages.

This study adopts the methodology of an exploratory qualitative case study analysis, which is considered appropriate for a relatively new research area and tackling research questions rather than testing hypotheses (Yin 2008). The exploratory case study is an inductive study for refining existing theories and making complementary contributions; it is also suitable for research questions related to an unexplored field (Edmondson and McManus 2007).

3.1 Interviewees' profile

Based on the published information pertaining to case studies of rural community development, rural social enterprises and rural social entrepreneurship through the connections of our Chinese research partners at China Renmin University, we selected six social entrepreneurs who are the leaders of the social enterprises in these villages. The size of population in these villages is between 700 and 3000 with household participating these social enterprises between 10 and 520, respectively (see the detailed profiles in Table 1). In early 2012, we conducted face-to-face semi-structured interviews with these six social entrepreneurs and each interview took about 1.5 hours. In order to gain a holistic understanding about the process of the social entrepreneurship in their communities, we also discussed the relevant issues with other village members, professional people assisting with village development, the representatives of local People's Bank branches and local government officials during the fieldwork.

3.2 Interview and analysis

During the interview with these six social entrepreneurs, we asked questions on the following issues: the community governance structure and management decision-making mechanism; the challenges for productivity and quality improvement; the strategies of business development and marketing; the key knowledge, skills and strengths of the community leaders and capable individuals; the main issues and challenges facing the community (i.e. environment and ecosystem, economic conditions, technology and infrastructure, natural disasters, etc.) and the opportunities for improvement; the main sources of income and income level in the community; the major challenges in preparing, developing and running new rural cooperatives; the most important people and institutions as part of business/social networks; assistance given from different stakeholders in the areas of infrastructure, finance, knowledge and know-how, and policy initiatives; special traits and skills required to be a successful rural social entrepreneur; and the needs and challenges for future development in terms of personal development and other areas such as infrastructure, policy, financial and other services.

Table 1. Descriptive profile of six rural social entrepreneurs.

	A	B	C	D	E	F
Role and location	Village chief, *Mangjing* village (*Bulang* minority community), *Lancang* County, *Yunnan* province	Village capable person, leader of village performance team and one village cooperative at *Mangjing* village	Village chief, *Daxi* village (*She* minority community) *Jingning* County, *Zhejiang* province	Village chief, *Baisha* village (*Han* majority community), *Linan* County, *Zhejiang* province	Village capable person, leader of one village cooperative at *Baisha* village	Professional person assisting village development at *Baisha* village; director of Bamboo Research centre
Gender	Male	Female	Male	Male	Male	Male
Age	> 50	> 30	> 40	> 50	> 50	> 70
Business activities and stage	Tea plantation, production and marketing; village-based tourism; developing stage of business	Tea plantation, production and marketing; village-based tourism and *Bulang* cultural products; developing stage of business	Wild rice stem, red rice, bamboo forest and tea production and marketing; village-based tourism; developing stage of business	Village-based tourism, bamboo forest and tea production and marketing; developing stage of business	Village-based tourism and hotels; tea and dry nuts production and marketing; developing stage of business	Bamboo forest protection, eco-diversity development, research and development centre; advanced stage of business
Ownership	Cooperative established in 2006 with 520 households	A new cooperative established in 2009 with 20 households	Cooperative established in 2006 with 130 households	Cooperative established in 2004 with 350 households	Cooperative established in 2009 with 10 households	Research and development centre and village-based bamboo production cooperative with village model households (80% of *Baisha* village households)
Financial sources	Individual household input and mortgage from banks	Individual household input and land deposit mortgage from banks	Individual household input and land and forest deposit mortgage from banks	Individual household input and land and forest deposit mortgage from banks	Individual household input and land and forest deposit mortgage from banks	Individual household cash input and professional know-how and technology input. Bank loans

(*Continued*)

Table 1 – *continued*

	A	B	C	D	E	F
Net per capita annual income among village members	Before 2004, RMB 515 In 2011, RMB 7500	Before 2004, RMB 515 In 2011, RMB 7500	Before 2004, RMB 600 In 2011, RMB 5000	In 1987, RMB 814 In 1997, RMB 3804 In 2000, RMB 7493 In 2011, RMB 30,000	In 1987, RMB 814 In 1997, RMB 3804 In 2000, RMB 7493 In 2011, RMB 30,000	In 1987, RMB 814 In 1997, RMB 3804 In 2000, RMB 7493 In 2011, RMB 30,000
Number of village members belonging to the cooperative	2400	90	600	1500	45	1200
Major customer sources and markets	Domestic customers and markets in China	Domestic customers and markets in China	Domestic customers and markets in China, mainly in *Shanghai* and *Zhejiang* province	Domestic customers and markets in China, mainly in *Shanghai* and *Zhejiang* province; some products for overseas markets	Domestic customers and markets in China, mainly in *Shanghai* and *Zhejiang* province; some products for overseas markets	Domestic markets in China and overseas markets

Interviews were conducted in Chinese at each village and they were tape-recorded. The interview record was transcribed and translated into English, accurately representing the meaning. The analysis of the data involved coding the responses of the social entrepreneurs using the constant comparative method (Silverman 2000) and analytic induction (Glaser and Strauss 1967). The NVivo software programme was used to generate themes that were extracted and clustered across the data set among these cases (Miles and Huberman 1994, 87). The detailed case profiles and analysis are presented in the following section.

4. Results

In Table 1, we identify six leading rural social entrepreneurs. During the interview with them, we observed not only many similarities but also some differences related to their background, gender differences and past experiences. Given that all of these villages are located in mountain regions with a historically poor background, these rural leaders have a strong determination to change these conditions and lead their communities to achieve a better way of life. This is a very common goal among all our samples. However, the way to achieve each goal could be different with many difficulties and even failures. Therefore, in this section, we plan to present these cases by illustrating the process of social entrepreneurship in challenging and difficult environments. By doing so, the key issues defined within our four research questions can be addressed. The ultimate goal is to explore the role of social entrepreneurship in rural community transformation in terms of achieving the social missions of sustainability and common prosperity in a broader competitive environment.

4.1 Social entrepreneurs' special traits and leadership skills

The similarities and differences of the roles and characteristics of the six social entrepreneurs are presented in Table 2. As social entrepreneurs, their special traits and leadership skills are crucial for their business survival and handling routine business challenges. Different historical paths and their personal experiences of dealing with obstacles determine the eventual outcome of the process of rural community transformation.

For example, the transformation of *Mangjing* village, where social entrepreneurs 'A' and 'B' were working and living, has not always been successful, particularly in the early years of rural reform. During these years, thinking and action were driven by short-term plans to generate quick cash income without much consideration to long-term sustainability. For example, the village had many ancient tea trees that were estimated to be more than 1300 years old. These ancient trees produced high-quality tea but in limited quantities. In the 1990s, individual households began cutting down the ancient tea trees and replacing them with young tea plants in order to achieve a higher quantity of tea production. Eventually, the overall tea production in terms of quantity and quality declined due to soil degradation caused by intensive monoculture practices and the amount of chemical products used.

It became obvious to the villagers that this type of tea production was not sustainable and household income could not be maintained for the long term. Village chief 'A' led the change by inviting professional people from Yunnan Agricultural University to advise them on alternative ways of cultivating tea. These changes resulted in a much lower input of chemical products being required and increased the biodiversity of the area by mixing different plants as well as sustaining old and new tea trees. The forest canopies improved

Table 2. Special roles and characteristics of six rural social entrepreneurs.

	A	B	C	D	E	F
Special skills and knowledge	Leadership skills and experience of managing village affairs; effective communications with internal and external stakeholders; strategic thinking and multi-skilling	Knowledge of *Bulang* culture (singing and dancing, costume, arts and crafts production); tea production process; knowledge as a school teacher; experience of leading village women group	Leadership skills and experience of managing village and education system; skills of network building, problem identification and prevention skills; capable ongoing learning and adaptation skills	Leadership skills and experience of managing village affairs; proactive and effective engagement skills with internal and external stakeholders, in particular with professional institutions and experts on agri-business and production	Experiences of working and running small business outside village; entrepreneurship skills of developing new business; network building skills with internal and external stakeholders	Professional knowledge and expertise on bamboo plantation, production, diversification, and marketing; leadership skills of managing institution and facilitating rural community development; entrepreneurship skills of developing new business; network building skills with multiple stakeholders
Key characteristics	Considering collective well-being; leading with good example; risk-taking and sacrifice; flexible and persistent to achieving common goals	Leading with good example, volunteering for village activities; helping other villagers to achieve common prosperity	Efficient decision-making; flexible and adaptable; risk-taking; holistic consideration for decision-making; clear purpose for achieving common goals	Leading by good example; flexible and adaptable; risk-taking, motivating other capable villagers to lead the changes; clear purpose for achieving common goals	Volunteering for village activities as village committee member; leading with good example; knowledge accumulation and sharing; risk-taking; helping other villagers to achieve common prosperity	Leading by good example; motivating other capable villagers to lead the changes; clear purpose for achieving common goals

Major social networks and support	Local government and business networks, infra-structure (road, electricity, water), ICT, and financial services, know-how and professional advice	Local government and business networks, infrastructure and other services, know-how and professional advice	Multi-level government support, business networks, financial support and infrastructure services, professional assistance	Obtaining professional advice from external professional institutions and experts, developing unique business networks, active engagement with government agencies and financial institutions	Accumulating network connections through the work outside village, active engaging customers outside village, bringing expertise and support from professional and financial institutions	National and local government networks; international, national and local research institutes', support of local infrastructure and financial services; support of village leaders and members
Major considerations of social well-being	Improving household income, developing eco-friendly and sustainable agri-business, reserving *Bulang* minority culture for future generations	Reserving traditional culture, developing sustainable business for all villagers, looking after the well-being of women and children	Reserving and developing traditional culture and architecture, eco-development, increasing household income, developing beautiful and livable village	Achieving common prosperity, increasing village household income, maintaining forest and ecosystem	Achieving common prosperity, making village life enjoyable and exciting, helping young people getting good education	Achieving common prosperity, making sustainable ecosystem with a balanced approach of protecting forest and increasing household income
Major challenges for future business	Needs for improved infrastructure and services; competition from large scale commercial production by investors from outside; attracting capable people to manage village-based business from outside; effective brand name and marketing strategies	Getting sufficient loans from financial institutions; difficult to get capable people to manage business from outside; difficult to build brand name	Loosely organized cooperative; barriers for marketing; lack of capable people from outside to manage business; traditional culture and village protection	Building brand name and reputation; sufficient infrastructure and financial services; attracting capable people to manage business from outside; protecting village environment and traditional architecture	Lack of sufficient financial support from formal financial institutions; attracting capable people to manage business from outside	Maximizing carbon credit to benefit villagers, needs more technical support from professional institutions, continuing improvement of eco-diversity and sustainability

(Continued)

Table 2 – *continued*

	A	B	C	D	E	F
Major areas for personal development and improvement	Needs for more knowledge related to production know-how, marketing and tourism management	Needs for more knowledge on marketing and developing brand name	Needs for more knowledge on business management and marketing; eco-development and tourism management	Needs for more knowledge on business management and marketing; eco-development and sustainable architecture and tourism	Needs for more knowledge on business management and marketing; eco-development and sustainable architecture and tourism	Needs for more professional people to support rural community development; needs for more international and national level collaborations

the ecology of the tea gardens and enabled the local people to harness the ecosystem resources of rich biodiversity to support their tea production. Under the leadership of 'A', the village set up the Ancient Tea Gardens Protection Committee in 2005 and *Mangjing* Ancient Tea Cooperative in 2006. Subsequently, the village has developed its own tea brand 'Arbaila', namely 'tea spirit' in the *Bulang* language, and this tea was nominated the official tea of the 2008 Beijing Olympic Games.

As the village chief and leader of the village cooperative, 'A' defined his role very clearly. He said:

> As a leader, you have to lead with a good example and other village members will follow. Given that our village people are very conservative, you have to demonstrate that you can achieve financial success by conducting agri-business in a way that maintains sustainability – and then they will follow. Actually, a leader has to take risks from time to time and not every business deal will make profit.

Social entrepreneur 'B' left her job as a schoolteacher in *Lancang* City and returned to her home village many years ago in order to assist the people achieve better living conditions comparable with those of city people. She volunteered to be a leader, brought together a women's singing and dancing group and helped the village school develop social activities for the children. She felt that preserving the *Bulang* traditional culture was a matter of urgency, so she organized a training class and invited her mother to instruct and teach village women how to make *Bulang* costumes, arts and crafts products. In order to become familiar with tea production, she went to the tea mountains and tea-producing factories to learn the tea production process from experienced people. Then, when a new policy was implemented in 2009 to promote village-based cooperatives, 'B' used her family's tea production capacity as a platform to form a tea production cooperative. She worked with 20 households to establish the cooperative and used the forest use-rights of her family and of other members to mortgage a bank loan for developing the cooperative. She then shared the revenue among the 20 participating households. 'B' established a good example for other village women to follow and she played a nurturing and supportive role to village women and children as she was very keen to preserve the traditional culture for current and future generations.

Another example is social entrepreneur 'F' who was an engineer at Linan Forest Bureau and developed new projects in *Baisha* village by introducing new ideas of sustainable development through effective use of forestry resources at the mountain village. He provided training and helped villagers to change their behaviour from cutting down trees to protecting the forest. He used his own money to set up a community-based cooperative by developing non-wood forest products. Currently, 73% of the villagers' income is derived from non-wood forest products, such as wild baby bamboo, wild tea, pecan and mountain vegetables. 'F' led the villagers to find alternative ways to make a better life without sacrificing the natural environment. 'F' also set up a research centre and used the centre as a training base for people coming from other villages and other provinces. The villagers have also interacted with many international institutions through cooperation and these institutions have provided a new source of export market (such as bamboo seedlings to Africa and the Middle East).

In fact, all six of the social entrepreneurs have identified special traits and leadership skills, with some common elements as well as differences. The major common aspects of these special traits include the consideration of collective well-being and achieving common goals, leading by good example, risk-taking, self-sacrifice and acting with a social mission. The major differences appear between village chief and individual capable person. For the village chiefs, holistic consideration for decision-making and motivating other village members are significant given their role. On the other hand, individual capable persons play a more important role in volunteering to work for the benefit of the village.

In terms of special skills, the village chiefs are normally astute in the areas of leadership; they are experienced in managing village affairs, and are effective communicators when engaged with internal and external stakeholders, as well as being strategic thinkers and generally multi-skilled. As for the individual capable persons, they normally have special skills associated with their previous work experience. Some common elements also exist among them, such as being very capable of network building and vigilant when grasping business opportunities. They are all eager to learn new things and share their knowledge among fellow villagers.

4.2 Strategies and actions at different stages of business

Different villages have experienced different historical paths and stages of transformation. For example, *Jingning* County in general and *Daxi* village in particular have been the poorest regions within *Zhejiang* province largely due to their remote location in the mountains. For many years up until 2004 (see Table 1), the annual per capita income level was below RMB 600. The old agricultural production methods were narrowly focused on rice production; this resulted in the villagers cutting down trees to build 'rice terraces' on the mountains. However, the production output was very low and consequently the villagers' income remained at a very low level. In 2006, the first village cooperative was established by diversifying the agri-business into higher value-added production and ecotourism. The new products included wild rice stem and red rice, which is a more nutritious food that fetches a higher price. In addition, the villagers re-planted bamboo and tea in a move to preserve the forests and produce high price commodities from them. As social entrepreneur 'C' claimed:

> We are in a less developed region, as our business strategies and actions, we need to protect our natural resources, namely our forests and surrounding environments first, then develop our local economy according to our natural advantages so we can achieve sustainability and not make the same old mistakes.

'C' was very clear about capitalizing on the uniqueness of the village and its products. He said:

> *Shanghai* has a lot of high rise buildings, but we have many high mountains. We have *She* culture, clean water, air and a pristine environment which *Shanghai* does not have. We need to protect the natural beauty of our village and our cultural traditions, including preserving the old architecture. We do not need to follow the path of the developed region of fast growth. We can develop in a balanced way, by improving public services and facilities, combining our culture and ethnicity with ecological and economic development in a sustainable way.

Cooperatives were formed based on voluntary participation among villagers with the model of 'large household leading and small household following'. As 'C' claimed:

> Farmers generally do not want to take risks and they are not able to afford any risk. Therefore, leaders and village capable people have to lead and take the risks. When we achieve a better outcome, then other farmers will follow and receive the benefits.

The villagers formed different cooperatives with specialization in a particular commodity, such as wild rice stem, red rice, bamboo and tea cooperatives. Each cooperative elected its leaders and board members. The decision-making was based on members' vote. By adopting these unique strategies, and in combination with the natural advantages and their unique products, the annual per capita income rose from RMB 600 before 2004 to RMB 5000 in 2011, which is more than an eight-fold increase.

In fact, all our sample cases have demonstrated that social entrepreneurship is like any other entrepreneurship that involves risky business, but unique approaches have been developed by combining personal and environmental advantages to overcome risks. In the early years, most social entrepreneurs had to take many risks in terms of obtaining a loan by using personal assets to secure a mortgage, finding a suitable business model and products, developing good networks and markets, dealing with multiple and different suppliers, clients and customers. Given that the rural economy had not been based on a free market for many years, it was very hard for anyone to lead or drive change. However, these social entrepreneurs are very persistent when it comes to achieving their goals and they are quick learners – they learn from negative experiences and look towards positive outcomes.

Therefore, we can see that there is a clear learning curve among these social entrepreneurs integrating both negative and positive experiences along the way to social venture development. In the latter stage of development, the entrepreneurs are more confident about future changes, knowing more about what they should and should not do and becoming more capable of utilizing different resources and social networks.

4.3 Significance of social networks

Generally speaking, the Chinese concept of 'guanxi', namely social networks, is one of the key elements determining business success. Our case studies demonstrate that all six social entrepreneurs were able to obtain support from internal stakeholders in terms of engaging land and forest reform and developing cooperatives within their villages as we discussed earlier. Equally important is to obtain support from external stakeholders, including the initial know-how, financial and policy support, infrastructure, services and marketing networks during the process of development.

For example, social entrepreneur 'A' was actively engaged with external stakeholders such as the Yunnan Social Science Academy and the Provincial Foreign Investment Center and obtained funding support from the Ford Foundation with RMB 200,000 to build a tea processing factory and grow more tea saplings. He worked together with the County Government to develop new roads, and ensure that there were electricity and water supply in the village. He stated: 'Sustainable development needs to rely on government support as well as on the cooperation of village members'.

4.4 Key challenges in the process of social entrepreneurship

The process of social entrepreneurship from planning to developing and advanced rural cooperative transformation is a challenging and difficult process and requires the social entrepreneurs to be trained and developed in order to be more capable in terms of strategic and innovative thinking, to apply consistency and be persistent with their goals and plans, flexible to deal with changes and lead the transformation with competence. Fundamentally, a social mission underpins their commitment to realize these goals and plans. Most of the cases studied indicated that the major consideration was to enhance social well-being, this included increasing villagers' income, developing eco-friendly and sustainable agri-business, preserving ethnic traditional cultures and achieving common prosperity.

On the other hand, they are realistic about the current and future challenges and difficulties. On their journey, they have learnt from the negative experiences of failure. They have become more confident and capable of facing new challenges – but are aware of their limitations.

A good example is *Mangjing* village under the leadership of 'A'. In this village, the per capita annual income increased from RMB 515 before 2004 to the current level of around RMB 7500 with an increase of more than 14 times. Most young people were staying in the village as they did not need to seek jobs in the cities. The *Bulang* culture had been well preserved and a good school was built with donations from external stakeholders, while a training centre – organized by the *Bulang* Prince and funded by UNESCO – was also established for passing on traditional cultures.

However, as 'D' highlighted, these social entrepreneurs were all confronted with the challenges and problems that 'building brand name and maintaining a good reputation are crucial for future success'. Improving infrastructure facilities, such as Information Communication Technology (ICT) for communication, waste treatment and other services such as health care and medical facilities for village people and visitors are important tasks for achieving sustainable development. 'D' stated:

> Given individual households are building their own hotel, different shapes, colors and designs appear in the one village and these give visitors a very bad impression. We have to be cautious about preserving the traditional style of architecture and use local materials. Meanwhile building design must be consistent with the natural environment of the village. We also need to attract capable people from outside to help us to build a professional management team and develop our agri-business and eco-tourism effectively.

In the same village, social entrepreneur 'E' pointed to several key areas as challenges: lack of education infrastructure in the village (the closest school is 15-km away); a need to build more waste treatment facilities for maintaining eco-sustainability; preservation of traditional architecture by using local materials and consistent design practices that harmonize with the mountain environment; developing and maintaining a good brand name and improving the quality of services offered.

5. Discussion

This study is based on in-depth interviews with several rural social entrepreneurs in multiple villages in *Yunnan* and *Zhejiang* provinces in China. It aimed to explore the key issues related to the leadership role and unique characteristics of social entrepreneurship in rural cooperative development. Based on studying six cases of rural social entrepreneurs, the findings identify that there are multiple key characteristics of their leadership role in the process of establishing and developing rural cooperatives that could lead and unite rural community members to achieve common prosperity. In this discussion section, we identify the key implications for the conceptual framework in terms of developing social entrepreneurship among rural cooperatives and communities.

5.1 Implications for theory

There are a number of meaningful implications for the development of a new conceptual framework. Based on the literature we reviewed earlier and our research findings, we summarize our new conceptual framework in Figure 1 with the identification of the following key aspects (see Figure 1). First, our findings provide the broader concept and definition of social entrepreneurship based on the social constructivist approach. This approach of aligning the process and the organization of the social venture to the local historical and cultural context is not just desirable, it is important for the acceptance and survival of the organization (Jack and Anderson 2002; Tapsell and Woods 2010).

Our evidence shows that social entrepreneurship emphasizes innovative and exceptional leadership in social enterprises (i.e. village cooperatives), with the goal of achieving sustainable development and a social mission (Weerawardena and Sullivan Mort 2001) of common prosperity. Our sample village cooperatives and their leaders are good examples of profit-driven business working for community development and operating in a competitive economic market environment.

Second, we have obtained sufficient evidence to demonstrate social entrepreneurs' ability to attract and utilize different resources in a competitive environment and adopt innovative ways to create social value; this is consistent with the claim made by Dees (1998). Three key factors for successful social entrepreneurship, namely innovativeness, proactiveness and risk-taking, identified by Weerawardena and Sullivan Mort (2006), could be found in our case studies. In fact, our case studies show that a combination of 'business skills' and 'social mission' is fundamental for a social entrepreneur to obtain and develop during the entire business development process (Sharir and Lerner 2006). In addition, based on the conceptual framework of four dimensions, namely the individual, the environment, the organization and the process (Mair and Marti 2006), our case studies provide a meaningful outcome and enable us to have a better understanding of the leadership role of social entrepreneurs in relation to the competitive environment, the support of external and internal stakeholders, as well as the way of managing the process of social enterprise development. In Figure 1, we highlight the leadership role of social entrepreneurs and their key relationships in the process of social enterprise development. Besides these important relationships and support in a competitive environment, the different stages of social enterprise development also require particular attention, especially in the early stage and developing stage. Sometimes business failures can lead to a reverse process of returning business to the beginning stage of planning and starting the business process once again.

Our research outcomes are consistent with the general common patterns suggested by Alvord, Brown and Letts (2004) regarding the successful social entrepreneurship initiatives, namely local capacity building, package dissemination and movement building. Our samples show that their efforts to help village groups through their leadership and example influence the transformation of mindset, cultural norms and expectations among villagers who could be hesitant to participate in new cooperatives given the negative history of the commune system in the past. In addition, through the hard work of social entrepreneurs with packaged services and economic leverage, the eventual economic outcome in these villages was remarkable. Furthermore, these social entrepreneurs can be seen as 'old rule breakers' and 'new rule creators' during the economic transformation in China. Their active external engagement with local governments and other institutions enabled them to influence policy formation and a better business environment gradually developed in favour of their entrepreneurship activities.

However, some differences exist between these Chinese social entrepreneurs and those in other developing countries due to some key contextual factors, in particular related to historical path, economic development stage and personal experiences. The historical transformation from communist planning system (commune system in rural areas) during the pre-reform period to market-oriented economic system (individual household economy and later recollectivism with new forms of cooperatives in rural areas) creates certain unique characteristics among Chinese rural social entrepreneurs. Combining the historical factor with the level of economic development and social entrepreneurs' personal experiences, we observed that the social entrepreneurship model has shifted from traditional social-work orientation (i.e. emphasis on charity and social outcome and less on economic viability; Dees 1998) to the current model, which balances economic success and social goals. This presents a phenomenon in which social entrepreneurship can no longer be either social work-oriented or commercial entrepreneurship-oriented; it has to combine both elements with multi-characteristics. Our evidence shows that the combined contextual factors influence the process of social entrepreneurship and indicates different characteristics compared with other countries (e.g. India).

5.2 Implications for practice

The practical implications are equally important. These social entrepreneurs could be vulnerable to market competition and sometimes the risk-taking could lead to personal sacrifice. They need both institutional and community support during the process of social entrepreneurship development in terms of policy initiatives, resources, financial and even emotional support from other stakeholders. We also observed that the family support given to these social entrepreneurs during difficult times was crucial to their survival. In addition, providing continuous learning opportunities for these social entrepreneurs could build their ability to face challenges, in particular related to knowledge of new products, technology and markets. More voluntary support from professional bodies and individuals in these areas would enhance social entrepreneurs' capability and confidence. In addition, we need to think about an integrated approach to connect all the necessary elements together in order to make the development of social enterprises and social entrepreneurship sustainable. For example, strong mentality of self-determination by the community, controlling its own destiny and setting its own goals could be crucial element for developing leadership in the rural community. In addition, strong champions and leaders who draw together individual social entrepreneurs and enterprises under cooperative mechanisms, with a common village brand and identity, could lead all villagers to participate effectively. Recognition of village context, such as demographical, cultural, natural environments, skills, ideas and capacities, and associated challenges and opportunities could help designing more appropriate policy and strategy for rural development. Shared utilization and integration of village capabilities and resources, including facilities and infrastructures, unique natural assets and ecosystems, and ideas and human talents could enable these villages to build long-term capability for sustainable development. It is also important to point that partnership of the community with external public and private institutions, corporations, scholars and NGOs is very important element in order to gain capital and investment, capability building, education and training, and technical, business and financial advice and support. The last but not least, government policy support through fostering cultural identities of ethnic minorities (e.g. the *Bulang* and *She* people), and promoting conservation of traditional architecture and crafts would be very significant for future generations to keep their cultural identities in the process of development.

6. Conclusion

Our research has demonstrated the leadership role and special characteristics of social entrepreneurship in rural China. Certain similarities and differences between these Chinese rural social entrepreneurs and those in other countries have been identified through our case study analysis. The outcome of this research could have some meaningful implications for other countries, in particular developing countries in the transitional stage with mixed economic and ownership systems, limited financial and other resources, and potential market opportunities. Such environments require a more innovative and proactive approach towards the development of social enterprises. In this sense, social entrepreneurship plays a vital role in the process of community development as well as making a significant contribution to nation-building and common prosperity. This is an alternative business model from the mainstream of business operations under market capitalism that focuses on individual self-wealth building and expansion. Based on this research, it is hoped that, through our case studies based on the rural social entrepreneurship models, this could lead to more meaningful research projects with a focus on equitable and mutually beneficial development models that would foster stronger cooperation among citizens to achieve common goals for the entire society.

References

Alvord, S. H., L. D. Brown, and C. W. Letts. 2004. "Social Entrepreneurship and Societal Transformation: An Exploratory Study." *The Journal of Applied Behavioral Science* 40: 260–282.

Borins, S. 2000. "Loose Cannons and Rule Breakers, or Enterprising Leaders? Some Evidence about Innovative Public Management." *Public Administrative Review* 60: 498–507.

Certo, S. T., and T. Miller. 2008. "Social Entrepreneurship: Key Issues and Concepts." *Business Horizons* 51 (4): 267–271.

Cornwall, J. 1998. "The Entrepreneur as Building Block for Community." *Journal of Developmental Entrepreneurship* 3 (2): 141–148.

Dees, J. G. 1998. "Enterprising Nonprofits." *Harvard Business Review* 76: 55–67.

Drayton, W. 2002. "The Citizen Sector: Becoming as Entrepreneurial and Competitive as Business." *California Management Review* 44 (3): 120–132.

Drucker, P. F. 1985. *Innovation and Entrepreneurship Practice and Principles*. New York: Harper & Row.

Edmondson, A. C., and S. E. McManus. 2007. "Methodological Fit in Management Field Research." *Academy of Management Review* 32 (4): 1155–1179.

Emerson, J., and F. Twerksy, eds. 1996. *New Social Entrepreneurs: The Success, Challenge and Lessons of Non-profit Enterprise Creation*. San Francisco, NC: Roberts Foundation, Homeless Economic Development Fund.

Freire-Gibb, L. C., and K. Nielsen. 2011. "Entrepreneurship within Urban and Rural Areas Individual Creativity and Social Network." Danish Research Unit for Industrial Dynamics, Working Paper No. 11-01. Accessed July 2 2012. http://www3.druid.dk/wp/20110001.pdf

Glaser, B., and A. Strauss. 1967. *The Discovery of Grounded Theory*. Chicago, IL.: Aldine.

Hindle, K. 2010. "How Community Context Affects Entrepreneurial Process: A Diagnostic Framework." *Entrepreneurship & Regional Development* 22 (7–8): 599–647.

Huang, Z. J., and P. Cui. 2009. "Nongcun zhifu daitouren nengli jiegou ji xingcheng jizhi yanjiu." [The research of rural leaders' capability structure and formation mechanism] *Hunan Agricultural Sciences* 8: 176–178.

Jack, S. L., and A. R. Anderson. 2002. "The Effect of Embeddedness on the Entrepreneurial Process." *Journal of Business Venturing* 17: 467–487.

Li, S., W. Schulze, and Z. Li. 2009. "Plunging into the Sea, Again? A Study of Serial Entrepreneurship in China." *Asia Pacific Journal of Management* 26: 667–680.

Li, J., M. N. Young, and G. Tang. 2012. "The Development of Entrepreneurship in Chinese Communities: An Organizational Symbiosis Perspective." *Asia Pacific Journal of Management* 29: 367–385.

Liu, B. 2004. "Nongcun jingji fazhan yu nongcun zhifu daitouren." [Rural economic development and rural leadership] *Commercial Research* 292: 180–181.

Mair, J., and I. Marti. 2006. "Social Entrepreneurship Research: A Source of Explanation, Prediction, and Delight." *Journal of World Business* 41: 36–44.

Miles, M. B., and A. M. Huberman. 1994. *An Expanded Sourcebook: Qualitative Data Analysis*. 2nd ed. London: Sage.

Prabhu, G. N. 1999. "Social Entrepreneurial Management. Career Development International." *MCB Internet Conference Special Issue on Leadership* 4 (3): 140–145.

Sharir, M., and M. Lerner. 2006. "Gauging the Success of Social Ventures Initiated by Individual Social Entrepreneurs." *Journal of World Business* 41: 6–20.

Shaw, E., J. Shaw, and M. Wilson. 2002. *Unsung Entrepreneurs: Entrepreneurship for Social Gain*. Durham: University of Durham Business School – The Barclays Centre for Entrepreneurship.

Short, J. C., T. W. Moss, and G. T. Lumpkin. 2009. "Research in Social Entrepreneurship: Past Contributions and Future Opportunities." *Strategic Entrepreneurship Journal* 3: 161–194.

Silverman, D. 2000. *Ding Qualitative Research*. London: Sage.

Tapsell, P., and C. Woods. 2010. "Social Entrepreneurship and Innovation: Self-Organization in an Indigenous Context." *Entrepreneurship & Regional Development* 22 (6): 553–556.

Thompson, J. L., G. Alvy, and A. Lees. 2000. "Social Entrepreneurship: A New Look at the People and the Potential." *Management Decision* 38: 328–338.

Van de Ven, A. H., H. J. Sapienza, and J. Villanueva. 2007. "Entrepreneurial Pursuits of Self- and Collective Interests." *Strategic Entrepreneurship Journal* 1 (3–4): 353–370.

Wallace, S. L. 1998. "Social Entrepreneurship: The Role of Social Purpose Enterprises in Facilitating Community Economic Development." *Journal of Developmental Entrepreneurship* 4: 153–174.

Wan, B. R. 2007. "Yao zhongshi xinnongcun jianshe de liangzhi shenglijun." [The importance of two forces for new countryside construction] *Agricultural Economic Issues* 11: 4–7.

Webber, M. 2012. *Making Capitalism in Rural China*. Cheltenham: Edward Elgar.

Weerawardena, J., and G. Sullivan Mort. 2001. "Learning, Innovation and Competitive Advantage in Not-For-Profit Aged Care Marketing: A Conceptual Model and Research Propositions." *Journal of Nonprofit & Public Sector Marketing* 9 (3): 53–73.

Weerawardena, J., and G. Sullivan Mort. 2006. "Investigating Social Entrepreneurship: A Multidimensional Model." *Journal of World Business* 41: 21–35.

Wu, J. H., H. L. Yu, and Z. J. Huang. 2008. "Nongcun zhifu daitouren chengzhang de shihui ziben fengxi." [The social capital analysis about the growth of the rural wealth-leader] *Rural Economy* 24 (1): 95–97.

Yang, J. Y., and J. Li. 2008. "The Development of Entrepreneurship in China." *Asia Pacific Journal of Management* 25: 335–359.

Yin, R. 2008. *Case Study Research: Design and Methods*. 4th ed. Beverly Hills, CA: Sage.

Yunus, M., B. Moingeon, and L. Lehmann-Ortega. 2010. "Building Social Business Models: Lessons from the Grameen Experience." *Long Range Planning* 43: 308–325.

Zeng, P. S., D. X. Li, and X. N. Yang. 2005. "Guanyu qianfada diqu nongcun zhifu daitouren peiyu de sikao." [The consideration of the training of rural leadership in less developed countryside] *Chengren Jiaoyu [Adult Education]* 225: 71–72.

Governmental influences on the evolution of agricultural cooperatives in Vietnam: an institutional perspective with case studies

Anne Cox[a] and Viet Le[b1]

[a]Faculty of Business, School of Management and Marketing, University of Wollongong, Wollongong, Australia; [b]Leadership and Management Group, Faculty of Business and Enterprise, Swinburne University of Technology, Melbourne, Australia

Using an institutionalist approach as the main framework, this research examines the evolution of Vietnamese agricultural cooperatives over the last six decades through four distinct phases – the voluntary collectivization period of 1954–1975, the compulsory collectivization period of 1975–1981, the de-collectivization period of 1981–1997 and the neo-collectivization period since 1997. Based on two case studies, this research examines the role of the Vietnamese government in the development of Vietnamese agricultural cooperatives. It argues that a stable legal environment and appropriate government support are extremely important for the successful development of cooperatives. In terms of theoretical contribution, the study calls for an integration of the notion of institutional dynamics into the current 'static' institutionalism and emphasizes the need to analyse institutions' influences at central, local and organizational levels to understand the formation and development of organizations. It also offers some policy implications that are relevant to the development of cooperatives in other economies.

1. Introduction

Agriculture has long been an important sector in the Vietnamese economy. In 2011, earnings from the agriculture sector, which includes farming, forestry and fishery, accounted for 22.02% of Vietnam's gross domestic product (GDP) (GSO 2012). The agriculture sector's share of economic output has declined in recent years, falling as a share of GDP from 40.49% in 1991 to 25.77% in 1997 and to around 20% since 2005, as growth in other sectors of the economy has gained pace. However, Vietnam can be still called an agricultural country, as this sector remains the major source of employment (Wolz and Pham 2010). About 50% of the Vietnamese labour force work in the agricultural sector (Nguyen 2012). In 2012, 68% of the total population live in rural areas (GSO 2013a, 2013b, 63).

Agricultural cooperatives were an essential tool in combatting poverty in the 1950s and today play a crucial role in promoting effective allocation of resources and efficiency in production in Vietnam. However, ever since the birth of the cooperative movement in the agriculture sector, the development and evolution of this form of economic organization have not been an easy process. The present day concept of agricultural cooperatives in Vietnam is the outcome of a long drawn out process of development. In retrospect, the development of Vietnamese agricultural cooperatives can be classified into four distinct phases: (1) the voluntary collectivization period of 1954–1975; (2) the compulsory collectivization period of 1975–1981; (3) the de-collectivization period of 1981–1997 and (4) the neo-collectivization period since 1997.

Despite the fact that agricultural collectivization is a significant issue in contemporary Vietnamese political and economic history, there has been a limited amount of research on Vietnamese agricultural cooperatives. Existing research in this area has focused predominantly on the impact of agriculture sector on the Vietnamese economy (Truong 1987; Pingali and Vo 1992; Asian Development Bank 2002), land reform and distribution (Moise 1983; Ravallion and van de Walle 2003a, 2003b ; Kerkvliet 2006), agricultural techniques and innovation (Kaiser 1997; Foerster and Nguyen 1999; Nguyen 2000, 2007), agricultural productivity (Bui 2003; Ho 2012), economic reforms and their impact on agriculture (Tran 1998a), and government policies on agricultural development (Cohen 2001). Nevertheles, agricultural cooperatives have been understudied. In particular, there is a dearth of empirical studies on the evolution of agricultural cooperatives after Vietnam's new Cooperative Law of 1997 was launched and the role of the government and its agencies in this process. While there are a few notable studies, such as Truong (1987), Kerkvliet (1994, 1998, 2005, 2006), Tran (1998a, 1998b) and Wolz and Pham (2010), which provided excellent analyses of agricultural cooperatives in different periods and of the impact of economic reforms on agricultural cooperatives, surprisingly there has not been a review of the performance of Vietnamese agricultural cooperatives that covers their development from their establishment in the 1950s until today.

The purpose of this study is, therefore, twofold. First, it aims to fill the gap in the literature by presenting a comprehensive review on Vietnam's agricultural cooperatives in the past six decades, with an emphasis on the period after the issue of the new 1997 Cooperatives Law. Second, it examines the development of contemporary agricultural cooperatives and the role that government agencies have played in this process. It explores some interrelated research questions, namely: (1) How have Vietnamese agricultural cooperatives developed in the last six decades? (2) How do government agencies support the operations of agricultural cooperatives? and (3) How will the agricultural cooperatives evolve in the future?

2. Literature review

This section highlights the relevance of the institutional framework for the analysis of economic structures and their behaviours. The institutionalist approach provides a valuable method for understanding the evolution and perpetuation of firms' behaviours. It then discusses the formation and evolution of Vietnamese agricultural cooperative models over the last six decades.

2.1 *The institutionalist approach and its application in understanding the evolution of firms*

Recent decades have witnessed the strong development of institutionalism. Comparative institutionalism analysis shows how different forms of economic organization have been established, reproduced and changed in different market economies. It focuses on macro-level societal institutions, in particular those that govern 'access to critical resources, especially labour and capital' (Whitley 1999, 47).

A systematic analysis of main national institutions and the interactions between these institutional arrangements and the activities of business organizations has been conceptualized in terms of 'societal logic' (Maurice, Sellier, and Silvestre 1986), 'social systems of production' (Hollingsworth and Boyer 1997), 'industrial orders' (Herrigel 1996), 'national industrial order' (Lane 1992) or ' national business systems' (Whitley 1999). Lane's framework (1992), for example, consists of the state, the financial system, the system of education and training, and to a lesser extent, the network of business associations and the system of industrial relations. Institutionalism explains how national institutions impose structural limitations on social actors and mediate or modify international pressures.

The effects of variations in businesses' institutional contexts on firms' behaviour are prominent, as a 'firm will gravitate towards the mode of coordination for which there is institutional support' (Hall and Soskice 2001, 9). It is now widely accepted that the influence of such social institutions is so strong that they can almost be regarded as additional factors of production which become the basis of competitive advantage or disadvantage (Maurice, Sellier, and Silvestre 1980; Lane 1992; Porter 1990). The role of the government for instance in economic planning and controlling in different countries affects a firm's organizational structure, its willingness to undertake long-term investments and its dependence on state agencies in making decisions. In this case, what is 'rational' strategic behaviour is determined according to the role of the state.

The main contribution of the institutionalist approach is the establishment of a conceptual framework allowing study of firms' behaviours. However, the institutional perspective is criticized, first, as being insensitive to the 'soft' part in business organizations. Firm behaviour is over-determined by national stereotypes and the potential for human agency neglected within this framework (Gamble 2001). Second, it might be problematic when applying an institutionalist approach to understand a business system in its transitional period, where 'previously latent institutions may suddenly become salient, old institutions may be put in the service of different ends or actors goals or strategies may shift within existing institutions' (Thelen and Steinmo 1992, 16).

2.2 The formation and evolution of Vietnamese agricultural cooperative models

The International Cooperative Alliance defined a cooperative as 'an autonomous association of persons united voluntarily to meet their common economic, social, and cultural needs and aspirations through a jointly-owned and democratically-controlled enterprise' (ICA 2013). Neoclassical economists suggested that economic agents will coordinate their actions and engage in industry development activities whenever the benefits from doing so outweigh the costs. Chloupková (2002) argued that one of the characteristics of the cooperatives under the communist regime was forced membership, and as a result these cooperatives did not obey the principles set by ICA, even though they were touted by the government as collective farms aimed at 'joining resources and sharing benefits'. Parnell (1992) aptly pointed out that in communist countries, cooperatives were considered as a stepping stone to less centralized economies and in capitalist countries as a counterbalance to the strongly capitalist market-based system.

3. Agricultural cooperatives in the voluntary collectivization period of 1954–1975

During the French colonial period, there was a high concentration of land in the hands of a small elite group of French and Vietnamese. According to Wolf (1999, 166), in the Northern region of Vietnam, 500 large landowners, both French and Vietnamese, owned

20% of the land; another 17,000 held a further 20%. The remaining small holders, about 1 million, owned the rest of the agricultural land. This situation caused great class conflicts between landowners, small land owners and tenant farmers, which contributed directly to periodic rural unrest in the 1920s–1930s and the revolutionary war for independence (1945–1954) (Kerkvliet 2006).

In 1954, after the defeat of the French at the battle of Dien Bien Phu, the Vietnamese communists took control of North Vietnam. The Geneva Accords effectively resulted in a fragmented Vietnam with two sovereign states – the Democratic Republic of Vietnam in the North, led by the Vietnamese Communist Party, and the Republic of Vietnam, supported by America, in the South. The North and the South developed along two very different paths in terms of politics and economics. The North's economy developed all the characteristics of a Soviet-style socialist centralized economic system, while the South's economy was decentralized and heavily dependent on America.

In the South, the Vietnamese-American government emphasized private property and was in favour of large land owners at the expenses of the peasants (Callison 1983; Kerkvliet 2006). This policy continued until 1970, when the government began a redistribution of land and implemented the 'land to the tiller' programme. The result was that approximately 1.3 million hectares of agricultural land was redistributed to over 1 million farmers by the end of 1974 (Pingali and Vo 1992).

In the North, large landowners and rich peasants were publicly denounced as landlords, and their land redistributed to poor and middle class peasants, particularly to those with ties to the Communist Party. By 1956, this programme of redistribution had transferred ownership of substantially all the available land to farmers in a largely equitable manner which benefitted approximately 73% of the North's rural population (Truong 1987, 35). The North also entered a stage of agricultural collectivization.

The initial steps were to establish work-exchange teams (*to doi cong*), a simple form of agricultural collectivization, which included the majority of the farmers. This collective economic form was organized on the principle of voluntary participation. Farmers retained ownership of land and equipment and were in control of production on their land but were encouraged to assist each other during periods of peak labour demand by joining seasonal or permanent working teams. The work-exchange teams helped to improve agricultural production during the post-war period. As a result, food output increased 57% with average food per capita of 303 kg per year. This not only ensured food for domestic consumption but also yielded a surplus for export in 1956 and 1957 (Tran 1998a, 32).

Encouraged by the positive results of this 'golden period' (Tran 1998a, 32), the government decided to accelerate the agriculture collectivization programme throughout North Vietnam. Work-exchange teams were transformed into agricultural cooperatives, starting out at a low level (1958–1960) and advancing to the high level of cooperatives (1960–1972). The low level of cooperatives worked on the principle that farmers also kept their own land, traction animals and equipment but farmed according to the general plan of the cooperative, while in the high level of cooperatives, all land and farm instruments were put under cooperative properties and farmers worked under a unified management (Pingali and Vo 1992).

Initially, the collectivization movement achieved some success. The stage of low level agricultural cooperatives, between 1959 and 1960, witnessed a sharp increase in the number of cooperatives established. By the end of 1960, 40,422 cooperatives were set up throughout North Vietnam, encompassing over 2.4 million peasant households, accounting for 86% of the total households (Tran 1998a, 32). However, this early success was short-lived. Between 1962 and 1975, the average growth in the yield of rice, the most important crop of the country, was only 1.1% per year with negative growth in 7 out of 14 years (FAO 2000 as quoted in Nguyen 2000, 25). The reasons that the system did not function as expected are many. Agricultural cooperatives constrained individual choice and eliminated the economic incentives required for efficient agricultural production and markets. The mandatory collectivization policies resulted in the removal of private farm ownership, and reduced the economic incentives for farmers to produce and market their crops. These factors ultimately dampened farmers' enthusiasm for work and resulted in both low agricultural efficiency and productivity (Tran 1998b).

4. Agricultural cooperatives in the compulsory collectivization period of 1975–1981

After the country was reunited in 1975, the Communist Party quickly sought to establish a socialist production in the hitherto capitalist-oriented South and thus bring this part of the country in line with the North. The Communist Party outlawed tenancy and enforced agricultural cooperatives in the South. In these cooperatives, the cultivation of crops, the division of labour and the distribution of the harvest were bureaucratically managed and the state retained the ownership of land. Farmers were subjected to a food obligation policy that was implemented in 1978 and 1979, which required them to sell a quota of grain to the state at fixed prices in exchange for fertilizer, gasoline, bricks and consumer goods at subsidized prices. Free market prices for grain were eight times higher than state prices while state-supplied goods were usually inferior in quality, insufficient in quantity and delivered late, which interrupted planting and thereby hurt production (Raymond 2008).

The policy faced with stiff resistance from farmers from the very early stage. The level of success of collectivization and the forced cooperatives programme varied significantly in different regions. According to Tran (1998a, 33), in central of Vietnam in 1978, over 67,000 peasant households participated in cooperatives. By the end of 1980, there were 673,500 households in cooperatives, accounting for 83.8% of the number of agricultural households. In the eastern region of South Vietnam, only 1.6% of the total peasant households had joined cooperatives by the end of 1978. In the western region, the Mekong delta, the situation was even worse with only 0.2% of all peasant households joining cooperatives. Despite all efforts, the government's attempt to use a collective mode of production to increase productivity and achieve a large surplus was mostly unsuccessful. By the late 1970s, after two decades of collectivization, only 10–15% of all farming collectives in the North fulfilled the Communist Party government's standards. About 15% were 'relatively good'. The rest, 70–75%, failed to reach the government's expectations of cooperatives (Nhu 1979, 42 as quoted in Kerkvliet 2006, 293). During the post war period of 1976–1981, the national rice yield grew by a rate as low as 1% per year. Vietnam was a major food importer during this period (Nguyen 2000, 25).

5. Agricultural cooperatives in the de-collectivization period of 1981–1997

This period was marked by signicant reform in the Vietnamese economy in general and agricultural cooperatives in particular. After the unification, under the socialist economic system, the state and collective sectors, which were highly subsidized by the state budget, were the foundation of the economy. Large-scale private economic organizations were forced or encouraged to join the state or collective sectors. This process effectively eliminated the market mechanism except in small-scale (household) activities. Therefore, it became clear as early as 1976 that the economic strategy was not working, with the economy witnessing steady declines in production and productivity in vital industries, including agriculture (Le and McCarty 1995). In 1980, Vietnam's GDP growth rate was − 1.6% (Statistical Yearbook 1995). In the same year, food production reached only 69% of its target (Vu 1995, 19). By the mid-1980s, Vietnamese economy was barely sustained, thanks to significant assistance from the Eastern bloc (now a burdensome debt for Vietnam). The lowest point was reached in 1985, when a miscalculated currency reform plan was introduced, effectively revaluing the Dong, in a bid to reduce the amount of money circulating and encourage the import-reliant economy but in fact resulted in an escalating inflation rate.

At the Sixth National Congress of the Communist Party in 1986, the Vietnamese government introduced a comprehensive reform programme, known as *Doi Moi*, with the objective of liberalizing and deregulating the economy. The agricultural reform in Vietnam actually started before the *Doi Moi*. On the 13 January 1981, Vietnam introduced the Directive No. 100 CT/TW on 'improvement of contractual activities and extension of product contracts to labour groups and individuals in the agricultural production cooperatives' ('Contract 100' for short) into the agricultural production sector. For the first time since the establishment of agricultural cooperatives, the government recognized market forces in the operation of cooperatives. Under the 'contractual' mechanism, cooperatives entrusted land to a member household on a contract. Farmers were responsible for sowing, seedling transplanting, tending and harvesting of the crop (known as the three production links). Subsequent phases in processing and marketing were still the responsibility of the cooperatives. All land and production means were still placed under the management and disposition of the cooperatives. The household had to deliver a quota of food to the state as stipulated in the contract but could use a small part of their land privately and sell the surplus product in the market. The new system enabled individual farm households to cultivate more independently and to be responsible for providing the contracted amount of output to the state (Pingali and Vo 1992; Nguyen 2000).

The initial reform had positive effects on agricultural production. National rice production increased from 226 kg per person in 1981 to 256 in 1982 and annual harvests of food crops rose from 15.0 million tons in 1981 to 17.8 million tons in 1984 (Raymond 2008, 52). However, the growth occurred mainly in the first year after 'Contract 100' was implemented. After 1982, the country again experienced a continual decrease in the rice yield growth rate from year to year, which became negative in 1987. Pingali and Vo (1992) argued that the main reasons for this failure was the cumbersome, top down planning approach in production, the frequent failure of the state to buy all the contracted products from farmers due to limited funds and the lack of security in land tenure resulting in insufficient investments at the farm level. Fundamentally, the cooperative model was still based on collective ownership, centrally run management and the uniform distribution of products based on workdays. Collective farmers were paid 'work points', which were converted into amounts of agricultural products such as rice and other food and occasionally money through an elaborate assessment method that assured everyone a basic share of each collective's net income but provided little reward for productivity and innovation (Kerkvliet 2006).

In response to the problem of critically low agricultural production in the second half of the 1980s, the Vietnamese government promulgated Resolution No. 10 NQ/TW in 1988 (All Around Renovation of Economic Management in Agriculture), which created fundamental changes to the agricultural sector and to rural development. The significance of Resolution No.10 was the full recognition of the market mechanism in the operations of cooperatives. The Resolution recognized farming households as the main units of agricultural production and further empowered farmers to manage all stages of production. The only obligation of the peasants and of the cooperatives to the state was to pay agricultural taxes (Pingali and Vo 1992). Resolution No. 10 was strongly supported by the Land Law 1993 and its revisions in 1998 and 2000, which provided security in land use rights for farmers. The main feature of the land reform policies was the privatization of land-use rights with farmers granted 25 years of land use right for rice and other annual crops and 50 years of land use right for perennial crops (ownership right to the land, however, remained with the State) (Pham and Nguyen 2005).

6. Agricultural cooperatives in the neo-collectivization period since 1997

Although cooperatives continued to exist, their major traditional tasks in agricultural production were no longer needed (Wolz and Pham 2010). Many of them failed to provide the necessary services to the newly established family farmers, especially input supply (Sultan and Wolz 2012). In this context, the Cooperative Law was introduced in 1997. According to Sultan and Wolz (2012), the Cooperative Law was developed based on the basic principles of the international cooperative movement and reflected user-centred policies and voluntary membership. Compared with the old model, the new model focuses more on providing services and marketing activities to its members (Table 1).

There were three options for previously existing agricultural cooperatives under the new law (Wolz and Pham 2010). They included: (i) the conversion of the old style agricultural cooperatives into viable agricultural service cooperatives that had to be newly registered; (ii) the dissolution of old style agricultural cooperatives and (iii) the formation and registration of new agricultural service cooperatives. There was an initial lack of interest from cooperatives in the conversion process and it took much longer than anticipated to finalize (Sultan and Wolz 2012).

Since the new Cooperative Law became effective in 1997, it has been revised twice in 2003 and 2012. The legal environment has been improving gradually to encourage the formulation and development of the new model of cooperatives. The second revision of the Cooperative Law in 2012 for example simplified the administrative procedures for cooperatives including the registration, setting up of branches and closure of cooperatives. The time it takes to register a cooperative was cut from 15 to 5 days. This aimed to facilitate the registration of new cooperatives, and expansion and even closure of current ones.

The development of the cooperatives has been further supported in recent years with the establishment of the National Cooperative Assistance Fund in 2006. These funds were established to provide credit to cooperatives in their respective provinces and to help them

Table 1. Basic information on agricultural service cooperative development in Vietnam.

Development periods after de-collectivization	Main characteristics
1986–1996: collective farms still operated as service providers	• Basic services to farmers: extension, input supply, irrigation, electricity; no marketing • Government promotion, but almost no financial support
Since 1997: Cooperative Law became effective: recognized as registered legal entities under the law; transformation of still operational cooperatives ('old style' into 'new style'), set up of new ones from scratch	• Better services: extension, input supply, irrigation, electricity, basic marketing activities • Limited support from government

Source: Adapted from Son (2009) and Wolz and Pham (2010).

expand business activities. Furthermore, since 2002, the concept of contract farming has been strongly supported by the Vietnamese government. There has been an increase in the number of agricultural cooperatives participating in contract farming since the promulgation of Decision 80 in 2002 which aimed to promote agricultural transformation from subsistence farming to a commercialized and export-oriented agricultural sector. This decision, often known as 'four-party' contract, promotes cooperation between the state, farmers, research institutions and enterprises (Asian Development Bank 2005). It aims to improve procurement of agricultural cooperatives' products, and to promote technology innovation in the rural economy. Neverthelesss, the model has not been very sucessful due to lack of trust, lack of professionalism, mismanagement of contract and lack of cooperation among parties. There is a need for clearly defined roles of the four parties, good governance of the contract and an effective value chain.

6.1   Performance of the new agricultural cooperatives

As of 31 December 2010, there were 6302 agricultural cooperatives (GSO 2012, 58). This represented a decline of 12.9% during a 5-year period from 2006 when the number of agricultural cooperatives was 7237. The fall in number of agricultural cooperatives could be due to the closure and exit of inefficient cooperatives during the period when the Vietnamese economy experienced a downturn with GDP growth dropping from 8.23% in 2006 to 5.89% in 2011. In addition, the global financial crisis contributed to a fall in demand of Vietnamese agricultural products in international markets and as a result cooperatives also suffered. In terms of economic performance, the capital–employee ratio in agricultural cooperatives reached 59.8 million Vietnamese dong (VND) in 2010 (equivalent to about 3000 USD in 2010), which was an increase of 13.9% compared to 2005. However, the average income for agricultural cooperative members is still very low, standing at only 201,000 VND (about 11 USD) a month in 2010.

Figures from the 2011 Rural, Agricultural and Fishery Census revealed that agricultural cooperatives employed 136,100 permanent workers in 2010, achieving a growth rate of 7.8% compared to 2006 (GSO 2012, 59). Of the permanent workers, about 128,000 are members of the cooperatives. As such, cooperative members made up 94.1% of the total employment in the sector. The remaining 5.9% of the workers are employed outside the cooperatives. The average size of a cooperative is about 22 workers of which 20 are members (GSO 2012, 59). Hence, their size is relatively small and it is difficult to achieve economies of scale. Nevertheless, the average size of a cooperative has risen by 24% compared to the average size in 2006. Most of the workers employed in the agricultural cooperatives were between the ages of 35 and 55 accounting for almost 70% of the employment in 2012. The second largest age group in the agricultural cooperatives is the 15–34 age group with a share of about 18% (GSO 2012, 59). The expanding size of cooperatives and the relatively young ages of cooperatives' members appear as encouraging signs that potentially show the popularity of this economic organization form with the new generation.

In sum, as suggested by the insitutionalist theory, the government has played an extremely important role in the formation and development of Vietnamese agricultural cooperatives. This form of economic organization has undergone significant transformation since 1954. The statistics show a picture with some encouraging sights for the whole sector. Questions remain, however, on what happens at the micro-level (cooperative level). These questions include: How have the changes in the government's policies impacted on the daily operations of agricultural cooperatives? How do government agencies support the operations of agricultural cooperatives? How will the agricultural cooperatives evolve in the future?

7. Research methodology

A case study approach is used in this study because of its suitability for exploratory and descriptive research, and studies where the phenomenon under investigation is very much socially and contextually situated (Yin 1994; Marshall and Rossman 1995). Case studies enable researchers to observe phenomena as they occur in their settings, a feature that allows surrounding social and structural intricacies to be exposed and unravelled (Yin 1994). This essentially provides a more accurate conception of events and behaviours, and a more comprehensive understanding of the associations that influence the phenomenon in question (Eisenhardt 1989).

Two agricultural cooperatives were chosen to study, coded in this research as AG1 and AG2 (Table 2). Some criteria govern the choice of cooperatives: (1) the size of the cooperatives – priority is given to cooperatives that have a larger number of members; (2) age of the cooperatives. AG1 represents old cooperatives that have a long history dating back to pre-*Doi Moi* period. It has survived many waves of changes in government policies and thrived in the new context. Meanwhile, AG2 represents the newcomers that have only been established in the last decade; and (3) accessibility to the cooperatives.

Interviews were the primary source of research data and the focal point of the empirical research element of this work. There were two groups of interviewees: those inside the cooperatives and outside the cooperatives. The first group included the Chairman and/or Vice Chairman and members of the cooperatives (at least two at each cooperative). It was considered necessary to conduct interviews at two levels to cross check the information as well as to examine whether the policies stated and described by the board of management were indeed implemented at lower levels of the organizations. There was also a need to corroborate the information provided, and thereby reduce hidden bias and aid reliability.

The second group included government officials from the Cooperative Department at the Ministry of Planning and Investment and the provincial Departments of Agriculture and Rural Development (DARD). These departments have played a very active role in implementing Decision 80, by supporting the establishment of cooperatives and facilitating the signing of contract farming between cooperatives and agricultural product purchasing companies. Interviewing personnel outside the enterprise context was considered vital, given that one of the aims of the research is to understand the role of the government and its agencies in the development of agricultural cooperatives.

Table 2. Case study profiles.

	AG1	AG2
Year of establishment	1978	2004
Location	Tien Giang province	Vinh Long province
Product	Rice (main product), poultry farming, handicraft production, construction services, ice factories, mixing of animal feeds (other products)	Clean vegetables (green vegetable, fennel, roots and fruits)
Area of cultivation	500 ha	85 ha
Number of members	3000	34

Table 3.   Interviewee distribution and characteristics.

	AG1	AG2	Government official
Management staff	Two (Chairman and Deputy chairman)	Three (Chairman, Vice Chairman and Chief Accountant)	Three (one from the Cooperative Department at the Ministry of Planning and Investment, and two from the provincial DARD)
Cooperative member	Four (two females and two males)	Five (two females and three males)	N/A

Interview questions were organized into six themes: history of the cooperatives, profiles of the households, their agricultural production, the households' current use of cooperative services, the respondents' assessments on the services provided by cooperatives and any factors that hinder or facilitate the operations of cooperatives. Semi-structured interviews were conducted on site in 2004 and over the phone in 2013 to update data. The length of the interviews ranged from 30 to 80 minutes. In total, 17 interviews were carried out. The distribution and characteristics of the interviewee are depicted in Table 3.

Ethical considerations were taken into account in this research. Throughout the research process, steps were taken to ensure key interviewees were protected particularly in terms of their privacy and confidentiality. All participants were assured that the information they provided would only be used to fulfil the aims of research, and were informed of their right to withdraw from the study at any time for any reason.

8.   Empirical study

8.1   AG1

AG1 was established during the period of central planning in 1978. During the compulsory collectivization period, the whole production process from the cultivation stage to the distribution of the harvest was bureaucratically managed. The management of labour extended even to working hours which were announced by the village bell. Regardless of their productivity, farmers were required to sell a quota of grain to the state at fixed prices. In the de-collectivization period, following Contract 100 issued in 1981, land was distributed to the households according to family size. Land that was brought in to the cooperative by households during the collectivization phase was also returned to them. In this period, the role of agricultural cooperatives was reduced and households were recognized as the primary units of production.

The Cooperative Law 1997 established the foundation for the old style agricultural cooperatives to convert into membership-oriented service providers. AG1 was revived and has successfully diversified services to its members, including input supply (fertilizers, pesticides and seeds), irrigation services, land preparation services, field protection services, marketing and selling of output and development of extra income-generating activities (such as poultry farming, handicraft production, construction services, ice factories, mixing of animal feeds). Irrigation services, in particular the maintenance of the distribution canals and the pumping of water, was considered one of the most important services offered by AG1 as it required a level of cooperation between farmers. The fees and contributions for irrigation services was 450 kg paddy/ha per year. To operationalize this service, AG1 bought water from the irrigation companies and then provided water to internal channels leading to the rice fields. It collected a fee from farmers for this service.

AG1 was also involved in the signing of contract farming with purchasing companies. Based on farmers' production abilities of a specific agricultural product, the cooperative looked for markets for these products and represented farmers in contract negotiations and agreements with the purchasers. After signing the contracts with the companies, the cooperative established subsequent contracts for agricultural product procurement with its members and as such the cooperative played the intermediary role in this process.

The interview with the commune authorities revealed that there was an emergence of linkages between cooperatives. AG1 formed linkages with other cooperatives in nearby localities and has maintained a regular exchange of information on market conditions, prices of materials and commodities, and sub-contracting prices in consumption contracts. This has helped to enhance the competitiveness of the cooperatives.

According to its Chairman, AG1 is now a strong and viable organization. It comprises over 600 households with more than 3000 family members, and controls over 500 ha of agricultural land. However, total capital of the cooperative is still very low, about 2175 million VND (87,000 USD). The operating capital for running service activities is even lower, accounting for only 25% of total capital or just 21,750 USD. The rest is the value of fixed assets. The Chairman of AG1 noted that the low level of operating capital has impeded the implementation of service provision to members of the cooperative.

8.2   AG2

Compared to AG1, AG2 is a 'newcomer' having been established in 2003. Interviewed farmers noted that before joining the cooperative, they operated as individual households. Every morning, farmers brought their vegetables to a local market to sell. If the vegetables were accepted by vegetable stall owners, farmers would sell all their products at a wholesale price; otherwise, they would sell them to consumers in the market. If they could not sell all their vegetables, they would bring them back to the village and sell them to other households as poultry food. Farmers did not maintain a long-term plan for crop selection, rather they planted based on the current price in the market. If a particular vegetable price was low, its cultivation would be stopped and a different vegetable crop would be sown. Therefore, their income from vegetables was very low and highly dependent on the fluctuations in market prices. This led to most farmers lacking surplus capital and prevented them from purchasing pesticides and fertilizers. Farmers did not pay attention to cultivation techniques to improve output because they were either unaware of or lacked information about market demand.

By 2002, purchasing companies, such as supermarkets and food catering companies came to the province to propose a plan to purchase clean vegetables on a large scale. This triggered authorities into considering the establishment of a cooperative to meet the projected demand. AG2 had a very modest start with 20 members, each of whom contributed a total amount of 200,000 VND (roughly 8 USD), mostly to build a cooperative office (on the borrowed land of the commune committee) and for other administrative costs. The management board of the cooperative initially had three people who worked without salary.

From the outset, AG2 was actively supported by the provincial DARD. For example, the DARD distributed a budget of nearly 100 million VND (4000 USD) to support the cultivation of clean vegetables by providing training on cultivation techniques to all members of the cooperative. Most importantly, DARD facilitated the signing of contract farming between the cooperative and agricultural product purchasers. Previously, the cooperative focused on production, and passively waited for purchasers to come to them.

Based on their wide networks, DARD was in touch with a large number of potential purchasers and acted as a link between these companies and AG2. At present, there are 36 companies including both small retail stores and large purchasing companies that have signed contracts with AG2 for the supply of vegetables.

The terms and conditions in these contracts specify that the cooperative is responsible for vegetable origins and their quality, and that government food safety standards will be strictly adhered to. The board members of the cooperative thus monitor closely the cultivation process at each household member to ensure that the quality is met. Also, AG2 is responsible for delivering the products in accordance with the terms of the contract relating to quantity, time and place of delivery. Selling prices are set at the market level. However, the cooperative offers purchasers preferential conditions such as deferred payment after the delivery of the products. If the price set in the contract is higher than the market price due to price fluctuations, the purchasers have the right to deduct the difference during the next trading round.

Interviewed farmers believed that they now have much better knowledge of cultivating, harvesting, packaging, categorizing and transporting their products as well as better access to market information. Therefore, their incomes from clean vegetable have significantly improved. Members are committed to the cooperative and always give priority to the cooperative when it comes to selling their products. They appreciate that their products are bought at a fair market price and that they are shielded from fluctuations in market demand, which was a big concern for farmers prior to the cooperative. The Chairman shared that cooperative membership has increased from 20 persons in 2003 to 34 persons currently. According to him, on average, the cooperative members earn around 50–70 million VND per ha (2000–2800 USD), compared to 20–50 million VND per ha (800–2000 USD) when they operated individually prior to 2003.

9. Discussions

Smallbone and Welter (2001) observed that the dominant feature influencing the nature and pace of entrepreneurship development in transition economies is the external environment, which, in some cases, appears hostile in social, economic and political terms. In addition, the social context inherited from the former socialist period appears to affect both the attitudes and behaviour of entrepreneurs and the attitudes of society at large towards entrepreneurship. Like the private sector, agricultural cooperatives in Vietnam have encountered numerous problems from the lack of enterprise culture during the socialist period. In addition, the support infrastructure has not always been sufficient to help them to overcome such problems. The Vietnamese economy has market institutions and infrastructures that are largely undeveloped (Le, Venkatesh, and Nguyen 2006). They face higher transaction costs and have limited access to credit and other inputs.

Transition economies have experienced a combination of privatization, entry of new private firms and fundamental changes in the legal, institutional and regulatory systems. Vietnam has experienced similar changes which improve the overall business environment including the legal framework for agricultural cooperatives. The development of the new model of cooperatives in Vietnam since the Law on Cooperatives was adopted in 1997 has been supported by different agencies in Vietnam. They include the Cooperative Department at the Ministry of Planning and Investment, which is responsible for formulating strategies and policies for the development of cooperatives in Vietnam; the Vietnam Cooperative Alliance, which aims to support, promote and represent cooperatives at different policy levels; and the Department of Cooperatives and

Rural Development at the Ministry of Agriculture and Rural Development, which solely focuses on agricultural cooperatives. The activities of these key agencies aim at promoting the establishment of new cooperatives, training to existing cooperative staff, trade promotion, and upgrading facilities, equipment and technology to expand production. Government policy documents indicate that the government intends to support cooperatives by providing (i) incentives for the establishment of cooperatives; (ii) training for management staff; (iii) access to land and premises; (iv) access to credit; (v) tax cuts; (vi) trade promotion; (vii) technology and extension services; (viii) facilities and equipment and (ix) establishment of the cooperative development fund (Government of Vietnam 2005). The government allocates a portion of the budget to different agencies to carry out activities in the above areas according to a yearly plan (MPI 2012).

The case studies indicate that appropriate support from the government can greatly enhance the performance of agricultural cooperatives. Government policy has had a strong influence on farmer cooperative establishment and development. This finding is similar to studies of farmer cooperatives development in China, a country that shares many similarities to Vietnam in terms of historical traditions, domestic economies, which are predominantly agrarian and rice cultivating, and the transition from formerly central-planned into increasingly market-oriented economies (see e.g. Garnevska, Liu, and Shadbolt 2011). However, it is contrary to van Bekkum's (2001) research findings that show that government policy has a limited impact on cooperative development in liberalized economies.

Although an extensive range of support policies is available to cooperatives, there is still a problem with their implementation. The policies have not been consistently implemented across agencies or at different administrative levels. Therefore, the support seems to be dependent on the efforts of government officials or cooperative leaders. For example, it is always difficult to get access to credit for cooperatives to invest and expand their production, but a personal relationship between the cooperative manager and local government officials can make it easier. Another issue is the lack of targeted support measures for sectors and sub-sectors. The high level support programmes have not been effective in meeting the needs of specific sectors. For example, training courses are provided in the area of product marketing but not at the level of marketing of agricultural produce.

Agricultural cooperatives account for more than half of the existing cooperatives in Vietnam. They have contributed significantly to creating employment and income for their own members and additional workers. Despite the decline in the number of agricultural cooperatives in the last 10 years, they still provide a large number of employment. However, the share of the collective sector in general and agricultural cooperatives in particular in GDP is still limited. The collective sector contributed only 5.2% to GDP in 2011 making it the smallest sector in the economy of Vietnam (GSO 2012). Furthermore, the size of agricultural cooperatives in Vietnam is relatively small with 20 members on average for each cooperative (GSO 2012, 59). Thus, they could increase their size to reach a more efficient scale.

Future development of cooperatives in Vietnam need to focus on supporting cooperatives to expand, become more diversified in their activities, and improve management staff capacity and worker skills. In the agriculture sector, provinces are asked by the Ministry of Agriculture and Rural Development to identify models that work in different sub-sectors and in different types of products and services so that they can be replicated in similar contexts (Nguyen 2012). Efforts are being focused on innovating, developing and improving the efficiency of current agricultural cooperatives. In addition, the development of agricultural cooperatives with operations in production, business and general services as well as specialized agricultural cooperatives are being encouraged by the government. Increasingly, agriculture cooperatives attempt to offer quality produce with better value to not only the local market but also export markets.

10. Implications

10.1 Theoretical implications

As discussed in the literature review, an institutionalist approach is a very useful tool to analyse firms' behaviours. It highlights the causal relation between institutional arrangements and firms' structure and characteristics. This study acknowledges the contributions of the institutionalist approach. However, it is argued that the institutionalist analysis comes short in investigating transitional economies and the form of economic organizations which exist within them as it fails to convey a sense of 'changefulness' of a business system (Martin and Beaumont 2001). Taking into account profound changes and volatility within the Vietnamese business system in the last three decades and in the external environments (the process of regionalization and globalization), this research sees the need to integrate the notion of institutional dynamics into the current 'static' institutionalism (Thelen and Steimo 1992).

Furthermore, it is clear that in the context of Vietnam, despite the availability of extensive institutions set out to govern and and support agricultural cooperatives, their successful development is not guarranteed. Formal institutions could not make agricultural cooperatives work in the earlier periods. Many initiatives failed or encountered strong resistance because without the basic principles of voluntary participation, there was a lack of participation from cooperative members. In addition, formal institutions alone do not automatically lead to the implementation of supporting policies at the local level to benefit agricultural cooperatives. Thus, an institutionalist approach which solely relies on a rational assumption of a direct link between institutional arrangements and the development of business organizations (Maurice, Sellier, and Silvestre 1986; Hollings-worth and Boyer 1997; Lane 1992; Whitley 1999) will fail to fully explain the success or failure of cooperatives as demonstrated in this study. An integrative approach that highlights the roles all the stakeholders, their bargaining powers and the interaction amongst them is needed in any analysis of firms' behaviours. Furthermore, it is not only institutional arrangement at the national level that needs to account for the development of organizations, their agencies at provincial and local levels are also extremely important in this process.

10.2 Practical implications

Vietnam's experience with the transformation of the cooperative sector could offer several useful lessons for other economies attemping to develop agricultural cooperatives. First, the formation of cooperatives should be based on voluntary participation. The coercive nature of agricultural cooperatives in earlier periods in Vietnam resulted in the limited success of the cooperatives as it did not provide incentives for members to perform and deliver. Second, new policy and regulation to support cooperatives do not automatically lead to growth in the number of cooperatives. In fact, the number of cooperatives established should not be seen as a success factor of government policy. Administrators shoud also focus on quality and efficiency of the newly formed cooperatives and not only on growing the number per se. Third, policy implementation has to be monitored closely as it is the key to delivering intended outcomes and this is particularly important at the local level. It is important to make timely adjustments that are relevant to sectoral and local conditions to support the growth and development of cooperatives. Fourth, the transition towards a market economy requires cooperative managers to upgrade their business management knowledge and skills which had been poorly developed during the central planning period and are not suitable in the current situation. Fifth, diversifying products, upgrading technology, introducing innovation have the potential to increase efficiency and this will help cooperatives to add value, become more competitive and move up the value chain. Finally, policymakers and cooperative managers will need to set priorities for each period in the development of cooperatives so that their limited and valuable resources can be maximized to achieve their respective goals for each period.

11. Limitations

This research has been conducted within a definite time scale and is subject to some limitations in research methodology and scope. First, adopting a qualitative method, it does not rely on a large sample as with a survey approach. The rationale of choosing the qualitative method is provided in Section 3, and the approach has been proven to be a sharp tool to solve the research questions posed by this research; nevertheless, broad generalization to a large number of cooperatives can be problematic. Second, the study concentrates only on one industry. If the research had encompassed other industries, the outcomes would have consisted of a more complete picture of cooperatives across industries. Lastly, the focus of this study is on two successful cooperatives, thus unsuccessful cooperatives are excluded from this study. An analysis of unsuccessful firms could have provided valuable lessons on the management of cooperatives, especially in the context of transforming economies.

12. Conclusion

Vietnamese agricultural cooperatives have witnessed great changes and transformation in the last six decades and are still in a transformation phase, whereby there is a slow conversion of the old-type cooperative to the new cooperative type guided by the Cooperative Law. The successful cases of agricultural cooperatives outlined in this study suggest that the new model of agricultural cooperatives could work well in the context of a transitioning economy. Most agricultural cooperatives have been able to provide valuable services to their members, especially input supply, marketing and selling of agricultural outputs. Some cooperatives have diversified their services by mobilizing investment capital, developing production planning, building market share, creating jobs and achieving high returns (Phung 2008).

Using an institutionalist approach, this research argues that the legal environment and appropriate government policy and support are extremely important for the successful development of cooperatives. The Cooperative Law 1997 and its revisions in 2003 and 2012 have set up the legal framework to encourage the formulation and development of commercialized agricultural cooperatives at the national level. However, the two case studies presented here have demonstrated that not only national institutions' influences but also those of the 'human agencies' at local and organizational level are equally important.

Note

1. Email: clle@swin.edu.au

References

Asian Development Bank. 2002. *Program Performance Audit Report on the Agricultural Sector Program (Loan 1340-VJE[SF]) in the Socialist Republic of Vietnam.* Report PPA: VIE 25325. Manila: ADB.

Asian Development Bank. 2005. *30 Cases of Contract Farming: An Analytical Overview. Making Markets Work Better for the Poor.* Hanoi: ADB, Vietnam Resident Mission.

Bui, D. T. N. 2003. "Vietnam." In *Agrarian Reforms and Agricultural Productivity*, Report of the APO Study Meeting on Agrarian Reforms and Agricultural Productivity, edited by M. G. Chaudhry, 199–208. Tokyo: The Asian Productivity Organization.

Callison, C. S. 1983. *Land to the Tiller in the Mekong Delta.* Berkeley: Center for South and Southeast Asia Studies, University of California.

Chloupková, J. 2002. *European Cooperative Movement. Background and Common Denominators*, Working Paper 24204 from the Royal Veterinary and Agricultural University, Department of Economics and Natural Resources, Copenhagen.

Cohen, M. 2001. "Vietnam – Reluctant Cooperation. The Government's New-Style Agricultural Cooperatives Meet Resistance from Many Farmers and Jack the Preconditions Vital for Success." *Far Eastern Economic Review*, Hong Kong, November, 22, 28–29.

Eisenhardt, K. M. 1989. "Building Theories from Case Study Research." *Academy of Management Review* 14 (4): 532–550.

Foerster, E., and T. H. Nguyen. 1999. "Technical Agriculture and Agroforestry Options for Sustainable Development Promoted by SFDP in the Song Da Watershed." Working Paper Number 5, Social Forestry Development Project Song Da, Hanoi.

Garnevska, E., G. Liu, and N. M. Shadbolt. 2011. "Factors for Successful Development of Farmer Cooperatives in Northwest China." *International Food and Agribusiness Management Review* 14 (4): 69–84.

Gamble, J. 2001. "Transferring Business Practices from the United Kingdom to China: The Limits and Potential for Convergence." Paper Presented to 'Multinational Companies and Human Resource Management: Between Globalisation and National Business Systems' Conference, De Montfort University Graduate School of Business, Leicester.

Government of Vietnam. 2005. "Decree No 88/2005/ND-CP on Policy to Support and Promote Cooperatives." Issued on July 11.

GSO (General Statistics Office). 2012. *Results of the 2011 Rural, Agricultural and Fishery Census.* Hanoi: Statistical Publishing House.

GSO (General Statistics Office). 2013a. *Statistical Yearbook of Vietnam.* Hanoi: Statistical Publishing House.

GSO (General Statistics Office). 2013b. *Report on Initial Results of the 2012 Establishment Census.* Hanoi: Statistical Publishing House.

Hall, P., and D. Soskice. 2001. "An Introduction to Varieties of Capitalism." In *Varieties of Capitalism: The Institutional Foundations of Comparative Advantage*, edited by P. Hall and D. Soskice, 1–68. Oxford: Oxford University Press.

Herrigel, G. 1996. *Industrial Constructions: The Sources of German Industrial Power.* New York: Cambridge University Press.

Ho, B. D. 2012. "Total Factor Productivity in Vietnamese Agriculture and Its Determinants." PhD thesis, University of Canberra, Faculty of Business, Government & Law.

Hollingsworth, R. J., and R. Boyer. 1997. "Coordination of Economic Actors and Social Systems of Production." In *Contemporary Capitalism the Embeddedness of Institutions*, edited by R. J. Hollingsworth and R. Boyer, 1–48. Cambridge: Cambridge University Press.

ICA (International Co-Opeative Alliance). 2013. "Cooperative Identity, Values & Principles." Accessed November 10. http://www.ica.coop/en/what-co-op/co-operative-identity-values-principles

Kaiser, K. 1997. *Proposals to Increase the Efficiency and Effectiveness of Extension Services Supported by SFDP Song Da in the Districts of Yen Chau and Tua Chua.* Consultancy Report Number 07, Social Forestry Development Project Song Da, Hanoi, March.

Kerkvliet, B. J. T. 1994. "Village State Relations in Vietnam: The Effect of Everyday Politics on Decollectivisation." *Journal of Asian Studies* 54: 396–418.

Kerkvliet, B. J. T. 1998. "Wobbly Foundations: Building Cooperatives in Rural Vietnam." *South East Asia Research* 6: 193–251.

Kerkvliet, B. J. T. 2005. *The Power of Everyday Politics: How Vietnamese Peasants Transformed National Policy.* Ithaca: Cornell University Press.

Kerkvliet, B. J. T. 2006. "Agricultural Land in Vietnam: Markets Tempered by Family, Community and Socialist Practices." *Journal of Agrarian Change* 6 (3): 285–305.

Lane, C. 1992. "European Business Systems: Britain and Germany Compared." In *European Business Systems Firms and Markets in Their National Contexts*, edited by R. Whitley, 64–97. London: Sage.

Le, D. D., and A. McCarty. 1995. "Economic Reform in Vietnam: Achievements and Prospects." In *Asian Transitional Economies*, edited by S. F. Naya and J. L. H. Tan, 99–153. Singapore: Institute of Southeast Asian Studies.

Le, N. T. B., S. Venkatesh, and T. V. Nguyen. 2006. "Getting Bank Financing: A Study of Vietnamese Private Firms." *Asia Pacific Journal of Management* 23 (2): 209–227.

Marshall, C., and G. Rossman. 1995. *Designing Qualitative Research.* 2nd ed. London: Sage.

Martin, G., and P. Beaumont. 2001. "Transforming Multinational Enterprises: Towards a Process Model of Strategic Human Resource Management Change." *International Journal of Human Resource Management* 12 (8): 1234–1250.

Maurice, M., F. Sellier, and J. J. Silvestre. 1980. "Societal Differences in Organizing Manufacturing Units: A Comparison of France, West Germany and Great Britain." *Organization Studies* 1: 59–86.

Maurice, M., F. Sellier, and J. J. Silvestre. 1986. *The Social Foundations of Industrial Power.* Cambridge, MA: MIT Press.

Moise, E. 1983. *Land Reform in China and North Vietnam.* Chapel Hill: University of North Carolina Press.

MPI (Ministry of Planning and Investment). 2012. *Report on the Situation Regarding Collective Economic Sector in 2011 and Plan for 2012.* Hanoi: Ministry of Planning and Investment (MPI).

Nguyen, T. Q. 2000. "Farmers' Training and the Adoption of Upland Agricultural Technologies in the Black River Watershed, Northwest of Vietnam." Master thesis, Department of Agricultural and Resource Economics, The University of Arizona.

Nguyen, V. T. 2007. "Agricultural Cooperatives in Vietnam: Innovations and Opportunities." Paper presented at the international conference on Agricultural Cooperatives in Asia: Innovations and Opportunities for the 21st Century, Seoul, National Agricultural Cooperative Federation (NACF), September 11–15.

Nguyen, D. K. 2012. "Some Development Solutions for Agricultural Co-Operatives in Vietnam." Speech by Deputy Minister of Agriculture and Rural Development of Vietnam at the Ninth Asia – Pacific Co-Operative Minister Conference, Bangkok, February 27–March 1.

Parnell, E. 1992. "A New Look at Cooperatives and Their Role in Developing Countries." *Small Enterprise Development* 13 (1): 103–105.

Pham, D. H., and C. H. Nguyen. 2005. "Reforming Vietnam's Legal Institution." Chap. 7 In *The Vietnamese Economy and Its Transformation to an Open Market System*, edited by W. T. Alpert, 128–142. Armonk, NY: M.E. Sharpe.

Phung, Q. C. 2008. "Roles and Functions of Cooperative and Rural Producer Organisations in Vietnam." Presentation at Rural Institutions and Sustainable Livelihoods Workshop, Addis Ababa, April 10–11.

Pingali, P. L., and X. T. Vo. 1992. "Vietnam: Decollectivisation and Rice Productivity Growth." *Economic Development and Cultural Change* 40 (4): 697–718.

Porter, M. 1990. *The Competitive Advantage of Nations*. London/Basingstoke: MacMillan.

Ravallion, M., and D. van de Walle. 2003a. *Land Allocation in Vietnam's Agrarian Transition*. Policy Research Working Paper 2951, The World Bank.

Ravallion, M., and D. van de Walle. 2003b. *Land Allocation in Vietnam's Agrarian Transition: Part I, Breaking Up the Collective Farms*. World Bank Policy Research Working Paper, January.

Raymond, C. 2008. "No Responsibility and No Rice: The Rise and Fall of Agricultural Collectivisation in Vietnam." Faculty and Staff – Articles & Papers. Paper 21. Accessed July 23, 2013. http://www.digitalcommons.salve.edu/fac_staff_pub/21

Smallbone, D., and F. Welter. 2001. "The Distinctiveness of Entrepreneurship in Transition Economies." *Small Business Economics* 16 (4): 249–262.

Son, D. K. 2009. *Agriculture, Farmers and Rural Development in Vietnam: Present and Future*. Hanoi: Gioi Publishers.

Statistical Office of Ho Chi Minh City. 1995. *Statistical Yearbook*. Hanoi: Hanoi Publishing House.

Sultan, T., and A. Wolz. 2012. "Agricultural Cooperative Development in China and Vietnam Since Decollectivisation: A Multi-Stakeholder Approach." *Journal of Rural Cooperation* 40 (2): 239–257.

Thelen, K., and S. Steinmo. 1992. "Historical Institutionalism in Comparative Politics." In *Structuring Politics: Historical Institutionalism in Comparative Analysis*, 1–32, edited by S. Steinmo, K. Thelen, and F. Longstreth. New York: Cambridge University Press.

Tran, T. Q. 1998a. "Economic Reforms and Their Impact on Agricultural Development in Vietnam." *ASEAN Economic Bulletin* 15 (1): 30–46.

Tran, T. Q. 1998b. *Vietnam's Agriculture: The Challenges and Achievements*. Singapore: Institute of Southeast Asian Studies.

Truong, Q. 1987. *Agricultural Collectivisation and Rural Development in Vietnam: A North/South Study, 1955–1985*. Amsterdam: Vrije Universiteit te Amsterdam.

van Bekkum, O.-F. 2001. *Cooperative Models and Farm Policy Reform: Exploring Patterns in Structure-Strategy Matches of Dairy Cooperatives in Regulated Vs. Liberalized Markets*. Assen: Van Gorcum.

Vu, T. A. 1995. "Economic Policy Reform: An Introductory Overview." In *Vietnam in a Changing World*, edited by I. Nørlund, C. L. Gates, and C. D. Vu, 17–30. Surrey: Curzon Press.

Whitley, R. 1999. "How and Why are International Firms Different? The Consequences of Cross-Border Managerial Coordination for Firm Characteristics and Behaviour." Presented to Sub Theme 3 "Business System in Their International Context" of the 15th EGOS Colloquium, University of Warwick, July 4–6.

Wolf, E. R. 1999. *Peasant Wars of the Twentieth Century*. Norman, OK: The University of Oklahoma Press.

Wolz, A., and B. D. Pham. 2010. "The Transformation of Agricultural Producer Cooperatives: The Case of Vietnam." *Journal of Rural Cooperation* 38 (2): 117–133.

Yin, R. K. 1994. *Case Study Research: Design and Method*. 2nd ed. London: Sage.

Development and challenges of cocoa cooperatives in Papua New Guinea: case of Manus province

Elena Garnevska[a], Harold Joseph[a] and Tanira Kingi[b]

[a]Massey University, Institute of Agriculture and Environment, Palmerston North 4442, New Zealand; [b]AgResearch, Palmerston North 4442, New Zealand

In Papua New Guinea (PNG), cooperatives have a long and dynamic history, and since 2000 they have been promoted by the government as a vehicle for economic and social development. There have been few studies on cooperatives in PNG and no prior research into cocoa cooperatives. This study explores the development and challenges of cocoa cooperatives in PNG. Cooperatives were mainly formed as a response to governmental initiatives as well as to provide access to processing facilities, overcome market difficulties, reduce unemployment and improve living conditions. Cooperatives and collectives among farmers and growers are important mechanisms in fostering social and economic development in PNG. Problems associated with land tenure insecurity, small land holdings, lack of access to capital, poor rural infrastructure, among others, have been reduced with farmer collectives and cooperatives across the Pacific countries. This paper outlines the role that cooperatives, and cocoa cooperatives in particular, have had in rural development in the Manus province of PNG.

1. Introduction

Cooperatives having a long history and stories of their success in terms of contribution to economic and social development can be found in every country around the world. The cooperative movement in Papua New Guinea (PNG) has a dynamic history and has significantly contributed to the country's development in the last few decades. Despite some cooperative failures, the government of PNG in 2000 tried to revitalize cooperatives and implemented a reformed cooperative policy for economic recovery and growth, empowerment of the people, poverty alleviation and infrastructure development (CSU 2008). The PNG government, through the Ministry of Trade and Industry (MTI), promoted agricultural-based cooperatives in order to: (1) increase farm production and income, (2) create employment opportunities, (3) promote self-reliance and (4) contribute to the community and national development (CSU 2008; Duncan 2008).

PNG is a constitutional parliamentary democracy and a Commonwealth country. It is the largest nation in the South Pacific with a land area of 462,840 km^2 and population of about 7 million in 2011. Estimated land area of PNG is 452,860 km^2 and 80% of this is under natural vegetation (primary or replanted forest) and less than 7% of the land area is in food production. Concentrations of intensive plantation, cash crops and smallholder tree crops estimated at around 3000 km^2 can be found in New Britain, New Ireland, Morobe and Madang provinces. Intensive food crops of approximately 8000 km^2 are predominantly located in the Highlands of PNG. Agriculture provides about 27% of the country's GDP and subsistence livelihood for 85% of the people who produce food and cash crops for home consumption, or for sale (Gwaiseuk 2000; FAO 2014; UN Data 2014).

The cocoa industry is PNG's third most important sector in terms of export earnings after palm oil and coffee (Allan, Bourke, and McGregor 2009). The cocoa industry in Manus province has been decreasing in the last few years and the local government tried to revitalize the cocoa industry by promoting cocoa cooperative development. There has been only a small number of studies undertaken relating to cocoa cooperatives in PNG, and no study on cooperatives in the Manus province. The purpose of this research is to analyse the historical and socio-political factors that have influenced the cooperative development of the cocoa cooperatives in PNG and in the Manus province in particular. The role of cooperatives among farmers in developing countries has been shown to be a critical mechanism to overcome constraints in the ability of small holder farmers under traditional land tenure systems to move beyond subsistence farming and to function effectively in commercial agricultural markets. This study is structured into eight sections. The following section reviews the literature on cooperative development theory and the development of cooperatives in PNG. Sections 3 and 4 outline the research questions and the methods employed in this study. Section 5 summarizes the results of this research, while the discussion is provided in Section 6. Sections 7 and 8 include implications and conclusions.

2. Literature review

2.1 Cooperative development

The evolution of cooperatives has shown that the cooperative movement has been influenced by various social and economic conditions. The diversity of cooperatives worldwide has been influenced by their emergence within different time periods, classes, communities, economic sectors and regions (Fairbairn 2004). Sargent (1982) categorizes the factors for cooperative development into social, political, economic, business, administration and management. Members' attitudes towards cooperation, relationships and participation, and cooperative governance and management have been important factors in the development of cooperatives (Banaszak 2008). Political factors such as the legal environment and government policies have also strongly influenced their development. Although almost all nations have now enacted cooperative laws to promote and foster cooperative development in their countries, their effectiveness has been different, due to the implementation of such laws – and whether some of these laws have done more harm than good was debatable according to FAO (2004). Close links with the interests of political leaders at regional, state and national levels have also been influential (Baviskar and Attwood 1984). Economic and business factors such as sound finance, increase in profit, better marketing capacities, reduced risk and business planning, and management have also been important indicators for cooperative development (Fulton 2000; Ortmann and King 2007). Administration and management in terms of leaders' strength and the relationship between the Board of Directors (BODs), management and members of the cooperative have certainly been an important part of the successful cooperative development (Sargent 1982; Adrian and Green 2001; Banaszak 2008).

Cooperatives play a significant role in agriculture, in both developed and developing countries. ICA (2013) reports that cooperatives have around 1 billion members worldwide and 40% of the African households belong to a cooperative. Clegg (2006) suggests that in general cooperatives have evolved because they have provided a mechanism for small farmers to work together, share risk and solve common problems. In the Pacific, a major constraint that cooperatives help overcome is the large number of small farm landholdings that are owned under traditional land ownership systems. Cooperatives assist these farmers to increase their bargaining influence with processors and market agents. It is estimated that over 50% of global agricultural output has been marketed through cooperatives (UN Report 2009). In several African countries, it was found that cooperatives have the potential to create employment and to open up rural market opportunities, generating revenue and enabling access to social services and education (Chambo, Mwangi, and Oloo 2007).

With specific reference to agricultural cooperatives, cocoa cooperatives have also contributed significantly to the development of economies and the livelihood of farmers and governments in many developing tropical countries in Africa, South America and the Asia Pacific regions. In Ghana, the Kuapa Kokoo Cooperative contributed to improving the social and economic well-being of almost 35,000 farmers and their families. In the Dominica Republic, the Conacado Cooperative improved the livelihood of almost 9000 members (Global Exchange 2007). Furthermore, large agribusiness organizations (such as Fair Trade) also have an impact on cocoa cooperative development by providing technical support/training and processing facilities as well as establishing social services (schools and medical centres) (Global Exchange 2007). In Vanuatu, the Vanuatu Cocoa Growers Association and Vanuatu Organic Cocoa Growers Association have been very effective in the collection, marketing and exporting of cocoa produced from almost 19 cooperatives. A key lesson from Vanuatu is that these cooperatives were successful because of management competence (McGregor, Watas, and Tora 2009). They also pointed out that a cooperative can be an effective organizational structure for solving the problems that small-scale farmers face in developing countries in the Pacific region.

The evolution of cooperatives as an international institution has faced different challenges due to their rapid development, changing environment and increasing members' demands. Due to the unique user-driven features of cooperatives, Cook (1995) outlines five general problems in their development: horizon problem, free rider problem, portfolio problem, control problem and influence on cost problems. Borgen (2004) summarizes the first three as 'investment-related problems' and the last two as 'decision-related problems'. Baldwin (2001) explains that the problems with cooperatives have been linked with members' multiple objectives, decision-making processes, control of power, limited pool of director skills and knowledge, under- and over-investment, weak incentives to perform, unbalanced portfolios and member moral hazards (Baldwin 2001). Apart from the common cooperative problems, every cooperative has its own specific problems.

Cooperatives, owned and controlled by small-scale farmers, have enormous potential for delivering economic and social growth in developing countries (Clegg 2006). However, it has been recognized that lack of capital and business management capability had been a key element for the disappointing cooperative history in many developing countries (Birchall 2004).

2.2 Cooperative development in PNG

Cooperatives were first introduced in PNG by the Australian Colonial Administration in 1947 and they worked successfully until 1970 (Singh 1974) (see Appendix 1 for key milestones of PNG cooperative development). The overall objective of the cooperative movement at that time was to mobilize land owners and enable them to undertake cooperative farming activities to increase family incomes and improve their livelihoods (Singh 1974). By the end of 1968, it was estimated that there were approximately 316 multipurpose cooperatives, with membership between 109 and 175 (Singh 1974). Towards the end of the 1960s, signs of failure began to emerge due to mismanagement and incompetency of the cooperative managers and directors, corruption and conflicts of interest, mismanagement by colonial administrators and competition from investor-owned firms (IOFs) (Singh 1974; Mugambwa 2005; Murray-Prior, Sengere, and Batt 2009).

In the 1980s, several politicians attempted to promote the cooperative movement in PNG; however, their initiative was not supported by the government and their attempt failed. As a result of this in 1985, the Cooperative Societies Act was amended and remained on the statutory books for the next 23 years (Mugambwa 2005).

In 2000, another attempt was made by PNG politicians to revitalize cooperative development for two main reasons. First, the government promoted the cooperative concept aiming to encourage and empower people (who were experiencing economic and social hardship) to mobilize themselves and to participate in economic activities. Second, the government viewed cooperatives as a mechanism to effectively deliver goods and services to the majority of the people in the rural areas (CSU 2008). In 2008, the Cooperative Society Act, 1985, was replaced with a new Cooperative Society Act, 2008, which provided the legal basis for the establishment of the newly registered cooperatives as independent and viable business entities responsible for their own operations and activities (CSU 2008). This initiative resulted in the development of the 2008 Cooperative Society Development Policy (CSDP) aiming to regulate and promote cooperative development in PNG within the context of a changed socio-economic environment. The government also provided financial and technical assistance together with training support to the newly registered cooperatives. Financial support was available in two ways: (1) support grants – distributed in the form of grants to help establish cooperatives and (2) revolving funds – available in the form of loans, for registered cooperative only. The standard loan was between PGK 5000 (1 PGK = 0.386 USD or 1 PGK = 0.285 EUR in October 2013) and PGK 10,000. Training support was available via the Cooperative Society Unit (CSU) (part of MTI), which developed training modules and programmes for cooperative members and managers. Technical training was provided by the governmental agricultural extension agents (CSU 2008).

Cooperatives in PNG conform to a four-tier system that includes primary (local), secondary (provincial), tertiary (comprising primary and secondary) cooperatives and the National Federation of Cooperatives at the highest level (CSU 2008). Almost all of the cooperatives in PNG are still primary cooperatives. The four-tier cooperative structure in PNG is similar to cooperative structures in some parts of Africa, such as Zambia, Ghana, Kenya and South Africa (Lolojih 2009; Ortmann and King 2007; Wanyama, Develtere, and Pollet 2009). The advantage of the four-tier structure is that it encourages vertical and horizontal integration, which enables cooperatives to extend their services to members of other cooperatives, which a single cooperative may not be able to provide (Lolojih 2009).

Previous studies on PNG cooperatives found that the copra and coffee cooperatives faced challenges in their development such as incompetency in management, misappropriation of funds, abuse of processes and competition with IOFs (Singh 1974; Duncan 2008; Mugambwa 2005; Murray-Prior, Sengere, and Batt 2009). Murray-Prior, Sengere, and Batt (2009) pointed out that one of the major challenges identified in PNG is poor institutional structure and governance.

3. Research questions

Agriculture is an important economic sub-sector and a source of livelihood for the people of PNG (Gwaiseuk 2000; Allan, Bourke, and McGregor 2009). The cocoa industry in PNG is the third most important cash crop after palm oil and coffee in terms of agricultural exports value (Figure 1), with exports to the USA, Singapore, Malaysia and others. The cocoa industry produces an average of 40,000–50,000 tonnes of cocoa per year – 80% of which comes from small holders, some of them organized in cooperatives (Allan, Bourke, and McGregor 2009).

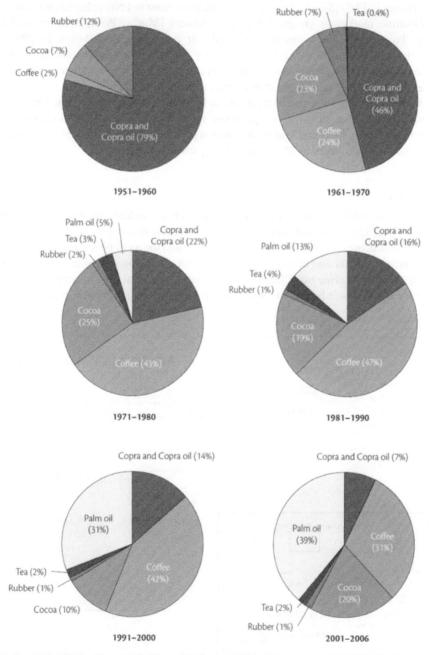

Figure 1. Contribution by value of the main cash crops to agricultural exports, by decade, 1951–2006. *Source*: Bank of PNG and various industry sources.

Cooperative development has been influenced by different factors (political, economic, social, business, managerial, etc.) (Sargent 1982; Fulton 2000; Adrian and Green 2001; Ortmann and King 2007; Banaszak 2008; McGregor, Watas, and Tora 2009) and depends on region/country, community, economic sector, industry structure and other specific issues (Fairbairn 2004; Clegg 2006; UN Report 2009). There have been a small number of studies undertaken relating to cooperatives in PNG, including a history of cooperatives in PNG (Singh 1974), cooperative movement in PNG (Mugambwa 2005) and collaborative marketing groups for coffee growers (Murray-Prior, Sengere, and Batt 2009). To date no study has been carried out on cocoa cooperatives in PNG and cooperative development in the Manus province. The purpose of this study is to analyse the key factors that underpin cooperative development and the challenges of the cocoa cooperatives in PNG and in the Manus province in particular. In order to achieve the overall aim, the following research questions need to be answered: (1) What are the key factors that influence effective cooperatives internationally? (2) Why do cooperatives succeeded/failed in PNG and Manus province in particular and (3) What are the challenges of the cocoa cooperatives in PNG and Manus province in particular?

4. Methods

This research used a multiple-case study approach as outlined in Yin (2003). Manus province (see Figure 2) was chosen as the location for this study because there was no prior research conducted on cooperatives in the province and the local government had a history of encouraging social and economic cooperation in the region (e.g. promoted cash crops such as cocoa and coffee using financial incentives). The local government identified that collective actions have helped to reduce the problems of tenure insecurity, lack of access

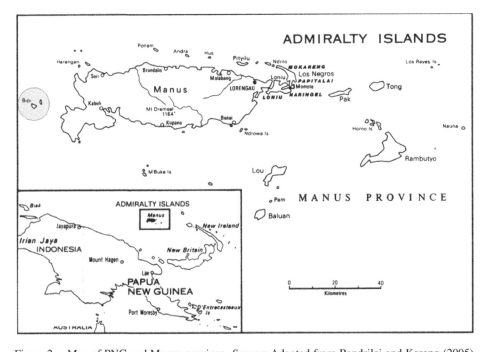

Figure 2.   Map of PNG and Manus province. *Source*: Adapted from Pondrilei and Kareng (2005).

to capital and poor rural infrastructure. The researcher was fluent in the local language, had local knowledge of the area and the province was safe for data collection.

The selected cases represented an opportunity to observe a mixture of registered cooperatives (some not working) and other cooperative groups working collaboratively. According to the MTI in 2010 there were about 3062 registered cooperatives under various industries in PNG comprising 149,130 individual memberships in 2010. Among these registered cooperatives, 12 were in Manus province: 5 were registered as cocoa cooperatives, 6 as fishing cooperatives and 1 as a poultry cooperative. Out of the five cocoa cooperatives, only two were producing, processing and selling cocoa. The other three cocoa cooperatives were registered officially but not producing, processing and selling cocoa because they lacked capital for buying, transporting and planting cocoa seeds even though they received the initial governmental financial support. It was also found by the Provincial Agriculture and Livestock (PAL) office (part of the Ministry of Agriculture and Livestock (MAL)) that there were a few cocoa cooperative groups in Manus province which were working cooperatively for producing, processing and selling cocoa but were not registered officially as cooperatives according to the new Cooperative Society Act from 2008. Therefore, four cooperatives/cooperative groups were studied in this research: only two registered and working cocoa cooperatives, Akale and Musio Paiai, and two unregistered and working cooperative groups: Mohe and Manus cocoa.

Secondary data were collected from published and unpublished reports and documents from different governmental organizations in the Manus province, and the CSU in Port Moresby. Statistical information was collected from the office of the registrar of cooperatives in Port Moresby and provincial offices.

Primary data were collected in June–August 2010 through face-to-face semi-structured interviews. Semi-structured interviews were used because it provided an opportunity for deeper understanding of the issues from the respondents' perspectives. Furthermore, it allows respondents the freedom to express their views in their own terms (Ritchie and Lewis 2003).

For this research, 22 respondents were interviewed using questionnaires:

- Four government officers – an assistant registrar for New Guinea islands region based in Port Moresby, a regional cooperative coordinator based in ENB province, a cooperative development officer for Commerce and Industry based in Manus province and an officer from the PAL representing the stakeholders involved in the promotion of cooperative development at the provincial level. The interview locations were urban, the language used was English and the duration of the interview was about 1 hour and sometimes longer. All of these respondents were in the age group between 30 and 50 years old and well educated.
- Two leaders (out of the cooperative management committee) from each cooperative and cooperative group – most of the interview locations were rural (where the cooperatives were placed), local Pidgin language was used and the duration of the interview was about 1 hour. The interviewees were between 40 and 60 years old with some education.
- Three members from the two registered cooperatives using snowball sampling – interview locations were rural (where the cooperatives were placed), local Pidgin language was used and the duration was less than an hour. The respondents were under 50 years old and with limited education.
- Two members were from the two cooperative groups using snowball sampling – interview location was rural (where the cooperatives were placed), local Pidgin

language was used and the duration was less than an hour. Three of the respondents were young under 40 years old and one over 40 years old, all with limited education.

A qualitative data analysis technique developed by Dey (1993) was used to analyse the data. This is a three-step iterative process comprising description, classification and connection. During the description process, the data (primary and secondary) were summarized to provide a comprehensive account of the phenomenon of interest and the context in which it occurred. Once the description had been written, the data were categorized (Dey 1993). The final step in the analysis process was connection, where relationships between categories were identified and defined. Such connections were identified through linking words or conjunctions (Dey 1993) such as 'and then', 'because', 'therefore', 'as a result', 'and after that', 'as a consequence' and so on. Having undertaken an iteration of Dey's (1993) process, it was then repeated and the outputs from the individual steps were refined and finally combined into a more general description of the phenomena of interest. The results were then compared with the literature to identify areas of similarity and difference between this study and other relevant studies (Yin 2003). The issues of triangulation, validity and reliability were very important in social science studies (Robson 2002). Ensuring triangulation, validity and reliability in this research was a difficult task because the researcher dealt with people's attitudes and behaviour and the quality of the data depended on their individual responses. Furthermore, the quality of the secondary data was limited and the cocoa industry and cooperative situation in PNG were very dynamic and unpredictable. However, these threats were partly overcome by using face-to-face interviews, which reduced the misunderstanding of the questions and ensured that the necessary data were collected. Governmental officers were also interviewed to assess the reliability of the secondary data collected. Ethical issues were a high concern in this research, particularly relating to the participants' privacy and confidentiality.

4.1 Manus province

Manus province is one of the island provinces (comprising a chain of 18 smaller islands) situated on the north-eastern part of the mainland of PNG with a population around 43,387 and provincial capital being Lorengau. The majority of the province's population (80%) live in rural areas. Manus has a tropical climate and rich volcanic soils and the main food crops grown are sago, betel nut, sweet potato, cassava, banana, taro, fruits and leafy vegetables. Traditionally the food harvested is consumed by the families and the surplus is sold at local markets for cash income. Export cash crops including cocoa, coconut, rubber and recently vanilla are also grown in Manus. Cocoa is a very important crop in Manus province and is produced by smallholder farms between 0.01 and 0.1 hectares (Pondrilei and Kareng 2005). The farmers harvest the cocoa using knives and transport the wet cocoa beans to the fermentary, most often by foot. Cocoa processing (fermentation and drying) is a labour-intensive process. Dried cocoa beans are put in bags for further storage and then transported to Lorengau for sale. The marketing of cocoa has been monopolized by the PAL for the last 5 years.

Cocoa production in Manus province had decreased prior to 2007 due to lower market price, poor transport infrastructure, poor rehabilitation and crop husbandry practices, and a lack of effective extension services (Toreu 2005). In 2008, PAL introduced a Manus Agriculture and Livestock Development Plan (MALDP) promoting a cocoa rehabilitation programme. They provided both initial funding for buying cocoa seeds from the Cocoa Coconut Institute (CCI) and fermentaries. Since 2008 and the introduction of the cocoa cooperatives, there has been an increase in volume of cocoa production and exports.

5. Descriptive analysis

5.1 Akale cooperative description

Akale cooperative is located on Lou Island and it is approximately 40 km from Lorengau. The smallholder farmers on the island experienced market difficulties in selling their cocoa produce, and in 2003, some of them decided to organize themselves into a farmers' association which was officially registered in 2007, named Lou Island Producer Association (LIPA) with a total membership of 400. The aim of this association was to assist the cocoa farmers with start-up capital, seek markets, provide new income-generating opportunities and improve standards of living for the members. All members paid a registration fee of PGK 5.00. The reasons for the delay in registration were due to complex bureaucratic procedures, lack of start-up capital and delay in payments of the member registration fees. In 2009, LIPA was officially registered as an Akale cooperative by the CSU under the new Cooperative Act 2008. The primary motivation for their official registration was the potential access of financial and training governmental support. Between 2009 and 2010, two cocoa fermentaries were purchased using grants acquired under the scheme. In 2010, the membership increased to 460 due to good cooperative performance and access to cocoa seeds. The cooperative is involved in the production, collection, processing and selling of cocoa to the market in Lorengau (see Appendix 2 for key details).

5.2 Musio Paiai cooperative description

Musio Paiai cooperative is located in Lawes village approximately 20 km from Lorengau. Over the last two decades, the people of Lawes experienced many economic difficulties and a high rate of unemployment. These challenges motivated 30 smallholder cocoa farmers to form a farmer's association in 2005 named Musio Paiai Cocoa Producers Association. The aim of the association was to improve the standard of living of the members by pursuing opportunities in the cocoa business. The registration fee was PGK 10.00 per member. In 2008, Musio Paiai cooperative was officially registered as cooperative by the CSU. The cooperative assets included a large fermentary. In 2010, the PAL delivered a small size fermentary and the total membership increased to 54 (see Appendix 2 for key details). The fermentary distribution was part of the PAL cocoa rehabilitation programme which was funded by the MALDP which targeted the rehabilitation of cocoa industry in Manus to seek better markets with higher prices.

5.3 Mohe cooperative group description

Mohe cooperative group is located in Patu village on the south coast of Lorengau, which is approximately 60 km from Lorengau. The major economic and social problem of the village in the last 20 years has been the lack of employment of young people and non-involvement in any income-generating activities. This situation motivated 10 farmers to form a cooperative group in 2006 named Mohe, taken from the name of a major clan in Patu village. The membership increased to 30 in 2010 (see Appendix 2 for key details). The Mohe cooperative group is involved in cocoa production, collection and processing in the field and the selling of cocoa (on behalf of its members) to the market in Lorengau. In early 2010, they have initiated the process of formal cooperative registration but at the time of the research they were still not officially registered as a cooperative.

5.4 Manus cocoa cooperative group description

The Manus cocoa cooperative group is located in Lorengau. This cooperative group was established with 20 cocoa farmers in 2008 who received significant extensive assistance by the PAL. The name of the group implies that the membership of this cooperative group is open to all cocoa farmers of Manus but no new members had joined the group by 2010. Manus cocoa cooperative group is not officially registered as a cooperative. The group has 10 small cocoa fermentaries purchased with the PAL cocoa rehabilitation programme. These were distributed per village depending on the members of the group (see Appendix 2 for key details).

Akale, Musio Paiai and Mohe are based in rural areas, while Manus cocoa is based in Lorengau. The rapid development of cooperatives in rural areas was because many people who live in the rural areas were with limited level of education, high unemployment and limited income streams. The cooperative structure of Musio Paiai, Mohe and Manus cocoa included a four-people management committee (chairman, deputy chairman, treasurer and secretary), while only Akale had a management committee and a BODs (including three people working for different governmental organizations). Akale was more advanced in its cooperative structure than Musio Paiai cooperative due to the important governance role of the BODs and the existence of a written constitution. The BODs provided support to Akale through the complex registration process, applying for financial support and controlled the work of the management committee. In comparison, the Musio Paiai cooperative experienced internal conflicts between members and management committees over financial issues. In addition, the cooperative did not have a constitution and BOD to control the management committee. Musio Paiai cooperative obtained financial and technical assistance from the PAL and politicians to start up its business. The cooperative also received financial support from the MTI (via CSU) because they are a legally registered cooperative. The progress of Mohe cooperative group has been slower than that of the registered cooperatives because it was not legally registered and its location was far away from the main city Lorengau. The Manus cocoa cooperative group has been performing poorly since its establishment initiated by the PAL because of complexity of coordinating and managing their members who come from different cocoa growing areas. In addition, the Manus cooperative group did not have an effective management structure, constitution and regular meetings.

The findings also revealed that cocoa was harvested by the members and supplied to the cooperatives/cooperative group for processing, transportation and sale. The use of family members as farm labour promotes an opportunity for small-scale farmers to be actively involved in the cooperative farming business. In addition, the cooperative members also grew some food crops (taro, cassava, sweet potato and other), which acted as an 'income safety net', especially during the cocoa off-season. All the cooperatives were selling their semi-processed produce at the Department of Agriculture and Livestock market, which was a subsidiary of the government.

6. Data analysis and discussion

6.1 Why farmers form cooperatives

This study suggested that the most important reasons for establishing cooperatives and cooperative groups were achieving economies of scale by pooling resources (mainly land) and sharing costs of production, responding to government policy and seeking government support (financial and training), overcoming market constraints due to high cost of transport (mainly fuel), increasing efficiency in cocoa processing due to availability of cooperative processing facilities, increasing employment opportunities and raising household incomes. These findings were similar to the results of studies conducted in other developing countries (including Pacific and African countries) and in terms of responding and seeking assistance from the government (Pathak and Kumar 2008; Lolojih 2009; Nganwa, Lyne, and Ferrer 2010) or reducing poverty by creating employment opportunities and improving living standards (Lolojih 2009; Wanyama, Develtere, and Pollet 2009; Nganwa, Lyne, and Ferrer 2010). There were no distinctive differences between cooperatives and cooperative groups due to the nature of the cocoa production and processing in PNG and in Manus province. Manus cocoa cooperative group was mainly formed as a direct response to the policy programme for the rehabilitation of cocoa industry in Manus province. Mohe cooperative group was looking to reduce unemployment among the tribes' young people. The two registered cooperatives have been involved in the cocoa sector for a number of years and took the opportunity that the new cooperative policy presented.

6.2   Factors for cooperative development

A range of social, political, governance/management and economic factors influenced the cooperative development of the cocoa cooperatives and cooperative groups in the Manus province of PNG.

6.2.1   Social factors

This study suggested that the *standard of living* of the members of the registered cooperatives has improved since they have joined the cooperatives as well as for the members of the Mohe cooperative group. The members were able to use the income from the cocoa sales for repairing their houses, paying school fees for their children and purchasing essential store items in the village. This was similar to other studies relating to the social importance of cooperatives in developing countries (UN Report 2009; Nganwa, Lyne, and Ferrer 2010; Garnevska, Liu, and Shadbolt 2011; ICA 2013).

The *member participation* in cooperative meetings and training had a positive impact on the development of both cooperatives and cooperative groups studied. Only registered cooperatives were allowed to participate in training courses organized by the CSU. The results revealed that the technical training received by Akale and Musio Paiai increased the member's knowledge and skills on cocoa technology, which resulted in higher production, better quality and consequently higher incomes. This also promoted a high cooperation spirit among the members. This research further suggested that active participation of the members during the cooperative meetings promoted better working relationship between the members and the management committee of both cooperative and cooperative groups. For example, the Manus cocoa cooperative group experienced low member participation to the annual meetings which reflected negatively on their development. This is consistent with Fulton (1999) who said that the success of a cooperative development was determined by members' knowledge of the cooperative, technical skills, active participation, commitment and the relationship between the members and cooperative managers. Another very important social factor for the Mohe cooperative group was job creation for the young people of the tribe.

6.2.2 Political factors

Government policy was another factor that significantly influenced the development of cooperatives in PNG and in Manus province in particular. It was found that Akale and Musio Paiai cooperatives were once farmer associations which were later transformed into registered cooperatives, resulting from the new governmental policy on revitalizing cooperatives in 2008. This is consistent with the study by Garnevska, Liu, and Shadbolt (2011) who found that a stable political environment with well-developed cooperative policy, with clear laws and rules, contributed to the success of the farmer cooperatives in north-west China. Both registered cooperatives (Akale and Musio Paiai) included in this study required guidance from governmental officers during the complicated registration process and financial support applications. They were assisted by external people with experience in the PNG governmental institutions through the formal registration process. The UN Report (2009) highlights that effective cooperative development depended on a government working together with its people. This was consistent with the result of a study conducted in north-west China, which concluded that effective communication between the cooperative and government officials must be maintained, to ensure the efficient flow of vital information (Garnevska, Liu, and Shadbolt 2011). The results also showed that the cooperative groups were disadvantaged by governmental policy. They were not eligible for significant support (financial and training) due to the fact that they were not officially registered even though they were working collectively. The managers of the Mohe cooperative group identified that the promotion of the new cooperative policy was not well advertised in the rural areas of PNG and in the Manus province, and the formal process of registration seemed too long, complicated and expensive for the small-scale rural farmers.

This study demonstrated that the *governmental financial support* was vital for the establishment and development of the cooperatives. This is consistent with Lolojih (2009) who suggested that the provision of government support was important for the development and viability of a cooperative. The funding available for the cocoa cooperatives studied was provided by two PNG Ministries. The MTI (via CSU) targeted cooperative development for registered cooperatives only. In contrast, MAL (via PAL) funding was aiming at development of the cocoa sector available for both registered cooperatives and cooperative groups. MAL funding was the only available governmental financial support for the cooperative groups and it was limited. Each cooperative and cooperative group studied received initial capital that they used for buying cocoa seeds, transporting them to Manus and planting them in their orchards. Both registered cooperatives and the Mohe cooperative group also received support (mainly financial) from politicians. It was found that Akale was a recipient of a grant from the provincial governor in 2008. This grant (PGK 80,000) aimed to help the formal registration process. Musio Paiai cooperative also received financial assistance from politicians. According to their manager, financial assistance (PGK 2,000) was gained from the provincial governor in 2005. The money was used to subsidize the cost of freight for the cocoa seeds from the Tavilo research station to Manus. The managers of the Mohe cooperative group also obtained financial assistance from a politician who grew up in their village. The grant was PGK 2000 and was used to buy cocoa seeds for planting. These findings were supported by Attwood and Baviskar (1987) who found that cooperatives which have closer relationships with political leaders have a better chance of getting support.

Governmental training support was another very important factor for the development and viability of cooperatives (Sargent 1982; Pollet and Develtere 2004; Ravensburg 2009). In this study, it was found that cooperative management and technical training were only provided for registered cooperatives. Only one of the managers of Musio Paiai cooperatives participated in cooperative management training. Formal technical training was received by Akale and Musio Paiai cooperatives which helped the members to acquire necessary skills, which helped them to improve their cocoa farming practices. Musio Paiai received a second technical training after most of their production was rejected by the buyer in 2010. On the other hand, the cocoa cooperative groups received partial assistance from extension officers and learned from each other. The analysis also suggested that the government stakeholders (e.g. CCI) provided technical support only to Akale and Musio Paiai, such as facilitating the ordering process of cocoa seeds, which was beyond the cooperative capacity. This is consistent with the literature (Pollet and Develtere 2004; Ravensburg 2009; Garnevska, Liu, and Shadbolt 2011), who suggested that training is vital for the successful development of the rural cooperatives in many developing countries.

6.2.3   Governance and management

In this study it was found that only Akale cooperative had efficient *governance structure*, including a BOD. The other cooperative and cooperative groups (Musio Paiai, Mohe and Manus cocoa) had only management committees, which was a result of poor cooperative skills and lack of cooperative constitution. As a result of this, many members distrusted their leaders and several conflicts (including physical) between members and management arose with the worst experienced in Musio Paiai. According to Staatz (1989), a well-structured cooperative organization provided better delivery of services to its members (owners). A study conducted by Garnevska, Liu, and Shadbolt (2011) finds that a well-established governance structure and a good leader were very important factors for the success of the farmer cooperatives in China. A well-informed governance structure enhances the relationship between the members and their BOD and managers (Chaddad and Cook 2004).

According to this study, the Akale cooperative used government employees in their governance structure as BODs, which promoted a wider experience and helped them through the complex process of formal registration. In this study the cooperative managers were elected due to their leadership skills and previous experience in managing a farmers' association (Akale and Musio Paiai). This was supported by Adrian and Green (2001) and Sargent (1982) that good leadership, commitment honesty and open communication are important for the development of a cooperative. Manus cocoa cooperative group experienced poor leadership which resulted in stagnation of their development.

This research identified that the *management* team of the Akale cooperative comprised a mixture of semi-subsistence farmers and government workers, which was an advantage, since it provides a wide spectrum of experience that was essential for their development. The experience of the management team, based on their previous involvement in farmers' associations, was also an advantage towards better management of the cooperative. The management team provided written reports from their meetings to the BODs. This arrangement promoted transparency and a better working relationship between the members and the management team. Musio Paiai management team provided better management and leadership skills due to their previous experiences as a farmers' association, which helped them to become a registered cooperative. They were also successful in applying/requesting multiple funding from different sources. The members of the management team of Mohe cooperatives comprised solely of semi-subsistence farmers with limited education and experience as well as knowledge of the external environments, such as working with the government sector. Their management committees were extensively seeking external technical advice and support from government officials from the PAL. In case of the Manus cocoa cooperative, the management team comprised members with farming backgrounds and an extension officer helped to establish the cooperative group. Despite the different backgrounds and experience of the members, they were not committed to working together and they lacked clear vision for their future development.

The members of both cooperatives and cooperative groups studied were individual farmers. The membership was open to any farmer interested to join them, except for the Mohe cooperative group where the membership was restricted to clan members. The members' democratic process says 'one member–one vote' in both cooperatives and cooperative groups built up their reputation and sense of responsibility to the development of their organization.

6.2.4   Economic factors

In this study, it was found that individual farmers were disadvantaged when selling their cocoa to the market because they had very little market power due to low production volume. Farmers coming together and forming cooperatives have more economic power associated with economy of scale in processing, storage and transportation as well as lowering input costs (Fulton 2000; Ortmann and King 2007). Analysis suggested that the members of all four cases studied brought their cocoa produce to their cooperative or cooperative group which was then processed, stored, transported and sold as bulk dry cocoa at reduced transaction costs.

This study suggested that the Akale cooperative doubled their production and revenue from 2009 to 2010. The Musio Paiai cooperative provided inconsistent data for production and revenue due to the fact that they changed the buyer in 2010 and over 60% of their production was rejected by the new buyer. The two cooperative groups studied started to record their data in 2010 and generated some income (see Appendix 2 for key details).

6.3   Challenges

This study identified that some of the members of both cooperatives and cooperative groups were not actively participating in some cooperative activities such as processing of cocoa. The increase of the membership of three of the organizations studied could lead to a free-rider problem in future. Cook (1995) explained that the new cooperative members have access to assets and equities that have been built up by long time members. It was also found that the Akale and Musio Paiai cooperatives began to get bigger in terms of assets and production, therefore, their members could demand some distribution of payments, similar to the horizon problem explained in detail by Cook (1995). This was very evident in the Musio Paiai cooperative and the physical conflict they had in resolving financial issues. Having members from different and distant villages (as in case of the Manus cocoa cooperative group) led to poor coordination, communication and control. The Musio Paiai cooperative, the Mohe and Manus cocoa cooperative groups did not have a BOD in their organization structure which may have led to a lack of clear vision and strategy for their future development. According to Cook (1995), internal problems, such as poor control of the members and poor decision-making by the management, were the likely problems that may arise in a cooperative that does not have a BOD in its governance. In this study, it was found that the Musio Paiai and the two cooperative groups, which were managed and controlled by management committees only, created confusion and conflict due to their dual roles and responsibilities. Finally, this study also found that a lack of cooperative management skills and knowledge had a negative impact on the performance of both cooperatives and cooperative groups. Studies conducted in Africa found that poor cooperative management was the main reason for cooperative failures (Mugambwa 2005; Ortmann and King 2007; Wanyama, Develtere, and Pollet 2009). The empirical results of a study conducted in Fiji also found that a major problem with cooperatives was a lack of management skills (Pathak and Kumar 2008).

This study found that the slow progress and development of the two cooperative groups studied was a result of poor awareness and also a lack of efficient promotional programmes, organized by cooperative government agencies such as CSU. The Mohe cooperative group wished to register officially as a cooperative but they lacked skills, information and knowledge for the registration process and they expressed their difficulty to find good advice due to their distance from Lorengau. It was also demonstrated that the majority of the members of the registered cooperatives lacked basic cooperative skills and were not aware of the cooperative concept. They perceived their cooperative membership as a way for seeking governmental financial assistance. This was consistent with the empirical results of a study conducted in Fiji (Pathak and Kumar 2008). Second, insufficient technical training resulted in significant crop losses experienced by both cooperatives and cooperative groups, due to poor nursery management practice and poor orchard farm management practices and the rejection of cocoa produce at the market due to poor export quality (e.g. Musio Paiai cooperative). Insufficient training provided to cooperatives was a result of insufficient funding by the national government. Third, both the cooperatives and cooperative groups in this study (except Musio Paiai) have encountered many economic difficulties in obtaining cooperative assets (cocoa seeds, fermentaries and storage shed) as a result of a lack of or limited start-up capital. Members of both cooperatives and cooperative groups were small-scale farmers with limited financial resources who needed time to pay their membership fees. However, the membership fees were too low and were only used to maintain the office administration. Therefore, the cooperative organizations in PNG, irrespective of whether they were registered cooperatives or not, relied heavily on support and incentives from the government, politicians, private sector or donors, to get them 'off the ground'. Birgegaard and Genberg (1994) stated that a poor capital base is a contributing factor towards the slow progress (and even some failures) of cooperatives, in most parts of Africa.

7. Implications

Cooperatives are important organizational structures in agriculture that could successfully help to overcome institutional (cultural and legislative) and market constraints. Problems associated with land tenure insecurity, small land holdings, subsistence farming, poor rural infrastructure, lack of access to capital, among other socio-economic problems, have been reduced with farmer cooperatives and collectives across various developing countries, including some Pacific countries such as Vanuatu and PNG.

The development of cooperatives in Manus was advocated by the PNG government in 2000 and it gained momentum among the rural population. Enthusiasm was relatively high and most of the rural population took a 'trial and error' attitude towards the cooperative development in their area. A number of groups were established and worked collectively in order to be able to improve their economic and social conditions; however, they were not registered as cooperatives.

The lessons learnt from this study identified several important factors and challenges faced by the cooperatives in the Manus province that could help to improve the policy decision-making in PNG at the national, regional and local levels. Cooperative policy has to outline clearly the structure of the cooperative (BODs, management committee and shareholders) prior to their official registration. The national government should also consider establishing a Cooperative Training Institution (1) to cater for the training needs of cooperative members and management so that they become sufficiently competent to manage the office and development of their cooperative and (2) to cater for the cooperative groups in assisting them through the official cooperative registration process.

Improved standard monitoring and evaluation tools were necessary because there were an unknown number of registered cooperatives that were registered but inactive. A better promotion of the benefit of cooperatives among the farmers in rural areas was also required together with an effective extension/support service.

More frequent technical training using educational tools suitable for poorly educated member-farmers was also essential for the successful development of the cooperatives in the Manus province and in PNG.

8. Conclusion

Cooperatives are unique organizations and have been successful in many countries worldwide. Cooperatives in PNG which began to appear in the 1940s were influenced by the Australian colonial government. Their development was strongly influenced and reinforced by political forces over that last few decades. In early 2000, the PNG government decided to revitalize cooperatives as means of economic and rural development, and a new cooperative law was enacted in 2008. Influenced by the cooperative spirit, cooperative groups emerged, which followed the cooperative principles, but not all were registered as cooperatives.

Cooperatives in the Manus province were in their initial stage of development and the key reasons for their establishment were to seek governmental support, manage market problems, share processing and achieve better standards of living. The key reasons for the establishment of the cooperative groups were to access processing facilities, reduce unemployment, improve standard of living and respond to MAL governmental initiative to revitalize the cocoa sector. Cocoa is one of the three main cash crops in PNG and is an important cash crop in PNG, in terms of exports revenues (Allan, Bourke, and McGregor 2009).

This study demonstrated that registered cooperatives have a great advantage in securing financial and training support (cooperative and technical) from the government and politicians, which resulted in obtaining more cooperative assets than the non-registered Mohe and Manus cocoa cooperative groups. The limited technical training received only by the registered cooperatives increased the member's knowledge and skills on cocoa technology and promoted a high cooperation spirit among their members.

Key social, political, governance/management and economic factors contributed to the development of both cooperatives and cooperative groups in PNG. The most common problems experienced by both cooperatives and cooperative groups were lack of member participation, poor control over organizational management, lack of operational management skills, a lack of understanding about cooperative policies and principles, and poor cooperative awareness and promotion by the governmental offices. The importance and potential of the cooperative movement in many developing countries has been identified (Clegg 2006) and this study suggests that cooperatives in PNG could also play a significant role in fostering social and economic development in the country.

This study had several limitations including the unavailability of potential respondents, because of financial constraints and the inaccessibility of cooperatives/ cooperative groups – they were only accessible by sea dinghy. Other difficulties emerged in accessing reports and documents on cooperatives in PNG and Manus province in particular, which had influenced our selection of interviewees. The choice of sampling and the limited sample size was also a limitation due to time and logistical constrains.

Future research with more reliable governmental information and with a greater number of cocoa cooperatives in PNG could provide more reliable and valid results. Cooperatives in different regions of PNG should be studied further due to their different levels of cooperative development. Cooperatives producing/marketing other cash crops could also provide useful insights into the development of the PNG cooperatives. Cooperative member perceptions study could also provide some useful information relating to the success of cooperative development in PNG.

References

Adrian, J. L., and T. W. Green. 2001. "Agricultural Cooperative Managers and the Business Environment." *Journal of Agribusiness* 19 (1): 17–34.

Allan, M., R. M. Bourke, and A. McGregor. 2009. "Cash Income from Agriculture." In *Food and Agriculture in PNG*, edited by R. M. Bourke, and T. Harwood, 283–420. Canberra: ANU E Press.

Attwood, D., and B. Baviskar. 1987. "Why do Some Co-Operatives Work but Not Others? A Comparative Analysis of Sugar Co-Operatives in India." *Economic and Political Weekly* 22 (26): 38–56.

Baldwin, M. 2001. "Working Together, Learning Together: Cooperative Inquiry in the Development of Complex Practice by Teams of Social Workers." In *Handbook of Action Research: Participative Inquiry and Practice*, edited by P. Reason and H. Bradbury, 287–293. London: Sage.

Banaszak, I. 2008. "Determinants of Successful Cooperation in Agricultural Markets: Evidence from Producer Groups in Poland." *Strategy and Governance of Networks* 27–46.

Baviskar, B. S., and D. W. Attwood. 1984. "Rural Co-Operatives in India: A Comparative Analysis of Their Economic Survival and Social Impact." *Contributions to Indian Sociology* 18 (1): 85–107.

Birchall, J. 2004. *Cooperatives and the Millennium Development Goals.* Geneva: International Labour Organization.

Birgegaard, L. E., and B. Genberg. 1994. *Co-Operative Adjustment in a Changing Environment in Sub-Saharan Africa* ICA Document, Geneve, Switzerland.

Borgen, S. O. 2004. "Rethinking Incentive Problems in Cooperative Organisations." *Journal of Socio-Economics.* 33: 383–393.

Chaddad, F. R., and M. L. Cook. 2004. "Understanding New Cooperative Models: An Ownership-Control Rights Typology." *Applied Economic Perspectives and Policy* 26 (3): 348–360.

Chambo, S. A., M. Mwangi, and O. Oloo. 2007. *An Analysis of the Socio-Economic Impact of Cooperatives in Africa and Their Institutional Context.* Nairobi: ICA Regional Office for Africa.

Clegg, J. 2006. "Rural Vooperatives in China: Policy and Practice." *Journal and Small Business and Enterprise Development* 13 (2): 219–234.

Cook, M. L. 1995. "The Future of US Agricultural Cooperatives: A Neo-Institutional Approach." *American Journal of Agricultural Economics* 77 (5): 1153–1159.

CSU (Cooperative Society Unit). 2008. *Co-Operatives Societies Development Policy.* Waigani, Port Moresby: Cooperative Society Unit.

Dey, I. 1993. *Qualitative Data Analysis: A User-Friendly Guide for Social Scientist.* London: Routledge.

Duncan, L. 2008. "Potential of Co-Operatives." *Post Courier* p. 12.

Fairbairn, B. 2004. "History of Cooporatives." In *Cooporatives and Local Development, Theory and Application for the 21st Century*, edited by C. D. Merrett and N. Walzer, 23–51. New York: M.E. Sharpe.

FAO. 2004. "Cooperatives and Their Environments, New Strategies for Mobilizing Capital in Agricultural Cooperatives." Accessed March 24 2010. http://www.fao.org/docrep/007/y5469e/y5469e04.htm

FAO. 2014. "Country Profile: PNG." Accessed May 10. from http://www.fao.org/countryprofiles/index/en/?iso3=PNG

Fulton, M. 1999. "Co-Operative and Member Commitment." Paper presented at the the role of cooperative entrepreunership in the Modern Market Enviroment, Findland. http://www.scholar.google.co.nz/scholar?hl=en&q=Cooperatives+and+member+commitment&btnG=Search&as_sdt=2000&as_ylo=&as_vis=0

Fulton, M. 2000. "Traditional Versus New Generation Cooperatives. A Cooperative Approach to Local Economic Development." Accessed January 25 2013. http://www.scholar.google.co.nz/scholar?cluster=14360156035777991881&hl=en&as_sdt=2000

Garnevska, E., G. Liu, and N. Shadbolt. 2011. "Factors for Successful Development of Farmer Cooperatives in Northwest China." *International Food and Agribusiness Management Review.* 14 (4): 69–84.

Global Exchange. 2007. "Cocoa." Accessed January 25 2013. http://www.globalexchange.org/fairtrade/campaigns/cocoa

Gwaiseuk, W. 2000. "The Role of Agriculture in PNG Economy." ACIAR Proceedings, No. 99. Accessed January 25 2013. http://ageconsearch.umn.edu/bitstream/135368/2/PR099.pdf

ICA (International Cooperative Alliance). 2013. *Blueprint for a Cooperative Decade.* Oxford: International Cooperative Alliance.

Lolojih, P. K. 2009. *Bearing the Brunt of a Liberalized Economy: A Performance Review of the Cooperative Movement in Zambia.* International Labour Organisation.

McGregor, A., P. C. Watas, and L. Tora. 2009. *The Vanuatu Organic Cocoa Growers Association (VOCGA): A Case Study of Agriculture for Growth in the Pacific.* FAO. http://www.fao.org/docrep/013/am013e/am013e00.pdf

Mugambwa, J. 2005. "The Saga of the Cooperative Movement in Papua New Guinea." *Journal of South Pacific Law* 9: 1–12.

Murray-Prior, R., R. Sengere, and P. J. Batt. 2009. "Overcoming Constraints to the Establishment of Collaborative Marketing Groups for Coffee Growers in the Highlands of PNG." In XVIth International Symposium on Horticultural Economics and Management, June 28. Chiang Mai, Thailand: International Society of Horticultural Science.

Nganwa, P., M. Lyne, and S. Ferrer. 2010. "What Will South Africa's New Cooperatives Act do for Small Producers? An Analysis of Three Case Studies in KwaZulu-Natal." *Agrekon* 49 (1): 39–55.

Ortmann, G. F., and R. P. King. 2007. "Agricultural Cooperatives I: History, Theory and Problems." *Agrekon* 46 (1): 18–46.

Pathak, R. D., and N. Kumar. 2008. "The Key Factors Contributing to Successful Performance of Cooperatives in Fiji for Building a Harmonious Society." *International Journal of Public Administration* 31 (6): 690–706.

Pollet, I., and P. Develtere. 2004. *Development Co-Operation: How Co-Operatives Cope.* Leuven: HIVA-CERA-BRS.

Pondrilei, S., and Z. Kareng. 2005. *Manus Provincial Agriculture Development Plan.* Lorengau: MAL.

Ravensburg, N. G. 2009. *Enterprise Future Lies in Cooperation: Entrepreneur Cooperatives in Africa.* International Labour Office. Accessed January 25 2013. http://www.ilo.org/public/english/employment/ent/coop/africa/download/wp2_enterprisefuture.pdf

Ritchie, J., and J. Lewis. 2003. *Qualitative Research Practice: A Guide for Social Science Students and Researchers.* London: Sage.

Robson, C. 2002. *Real World Research.* 2nd ed. Oxford: Blackwell.

Sargent, M. 1982. *Agricultural Cooperation.* Hampshier: Gower.

Singh, S. 1974. *Co-Operatives in Papua New Guinea.* Canberra: New Guinea Research Unit, Australian National University.

Staatz, J. 1989. *Farmer Cooperative Theory: Recent Developments.* Washington, DC: U.S. Department of Agriculture.

Toreu, B. 2005. *Cocoa Development on Manus Island*. Kokopo: Cocoa Board of PNG.

UN Data. 2014. "PNG Country Profile." Accessed May 10. http://www.data.un.org/CountryProfile. aspx?crName=Papua+New+Guinea#Summary

UN Report. 2009. "Cooperatives in Social Development." Accessed January 26 2013. http://www. undesadspd.org/Cooperatives/UNDocumentsonCooperatives.aspx

Wanyama, F., P. Develtere, and I. Pollet. 2009. "Reinventing the Wheel? African Cooperatives in a Liberalized Economic Environment." *Annals of Public and Cooperative Economics* 80 (3): 361–392.

Yin, R. K. 2003. *Case Study Research: Designs and Methods*. Vol. 5, 3rd ed. Thousand Oaks, CA: Sage.

Appendix 1. Historical development of cooperatives in PNG

Period (year)	Events in the cooperative movement
1947	Cooperative society movement was introduced in PNG by the Australian Colonial Government under legislation called the 'Native Societies Ordinance'.
1960	More administrative officials were assigned to assist cooperative societies in managing their affairs, preparing budgets and accounts and general policy formulation. A cooperative education centre was established, to provide training for cooperative management.
1965	The legislation changed from 'Native Societies Ordinance' and became 'Cooperative Societies Ordinance' in 1965. The objective of the cooperative society was to transform the indigenous people from a subsistence economy to a cash economy and it was also an instrument for delivering goods and services to the majority of members living in the rural areas, to basically improve their livelihoods.
1970	The Cooperative College was established in Laloki, with assistance from the United Nation Development Program. The Cooperative College expanded cooperative education and training for members. The office of the Registry of Cooperatives was upgraded to a Division of Cooperative Extension within the Department of Trade and Industry. The House of Assembly established a committee of inquiry to examine the achievements and problems of the cooperative movement in the territory. These findings confirmed that cooperatives were facing serious problems and they were collapsing.
1975	PNG gained its independence. The Cooperative Societies Ordinance 1965 was repealed and replaced by the Companies Act 1975, under which the majority of cooperatives were transformed into companies under the Company Act, or under the Business Group Act.
1982	The Governor General (the late Sir John Guise) introduced a private members bill to the House of Assembly, to re-introduce cooperative societies, which also led to the enactment of the Cooperative Society Act.
1985	The Cooperative Society Act was amended to its present-day form: The Cooperative Society (Amended) Act 1985.
1995	The Department of Trade and Industry made an attempt to revive the cooperative concept. The rationale behind this attempt was that cooperatives would be effective in driving the government's small and medium enterprises Policy, by mobilizing people in rural areas to participate in economic activities.
2000	The government accepted the cooperative movement initiated by the Ministry of Commerce and Industry.
2003	The Department of Trade and industry (now called the Department of Commerce and Industry) established the CSU) and it was allocated NZ$202, 020.00 (PNGK 400,000.00) to start operations.
2008	The CSU developed the first CSDP and amended the Cooperative Society Act (2008).
2008 and 2009	The CSU established Regional Cooperative Centres in the four regions, which are headed by regional cooperative coordinators.

Source: Cooperative Society Unit (2008), Mugambwa (2005) and Singh (1974).

Appendix 2. Summary of key characteristics of the four cooperatives/cooperative groups

Items	Akale cooperative	Musio Paiai cooperative	Mohe cooperative group	Manus cocoa cooperative group
Interviewed – plus two officers in Port Moresby, and two regional officers in Manus province	Two leaders Three members	Two leaders Three members	Two leaders Two members	Two leaders Two members
Location (LLG)	Balopa – rural	Penabu – rural	Pobuma – rural	Lorengau – urban
Establishment	Started in 2003 as farmer association, transferred to cooperative in 2008	Started in 2005 as farmers association, transferred to cooperative in 2008	Started in 2006	Started in 2008
Founding members	400	30	10	20
Members – 2010	460	54	30	20
Travelling distance to Lorengau (km)	40	20	60	0
Mode of transport to market	Sea dinghy	Sea dinghy	Sea dinghy	Road
Total land area (ha)	76	16.6	6	20
Cooperative constitution	Yes	No	No	No
Training: (1) Managerial	None	One for managers	None	None
(2) Technical	One for members	Two for members	None	None
No of cocoa trees	47,000	9000	3500	12,000
Assets	Two fermentaries (one big and one small), storage Shed	Two fermentaries (one big and one small), storage Shed	One small fermentary	Ten small fermentaries
Financial sources	Membership Politicians PAL	Membership CDS PAL CSU	Membership PAL	Membership (not paid yet) PAL
Production sold (kg) – 2009	515	1500	Nil	Nil
Production sold (kg) – 2010	1161	1060	305	750
Sale revenue – 2009	PGK 1957[a]	PGK 5700	Nil	Nil
Sale revenue – 2010	PGK 4413	PGK 4028	PGK 1159	PGK 2850

Notes: PAL, Provincial Agriculture and Livestock; CDS, Community Development Scheme in 2005; CSU, Cooperative Society Unit.
[a] PGK = 0.386 USD or 1 PGK = 0.285 EUR in October 2013.

Growth pattern of an employee-owned business: a narrative inquiry concerning the new venture creation experience of Wowprime in Taiwan

Li-Chung Chang[a], Chao-Tung Wen[b], Yeg-Ming Chang[c] and Pei-How Huang[d]

[a]Department of Management, Guangzhou Vocational College of Science and Technology, Guangzhou, China; Management School, University of Electronic Science and Technology of China, Zhongshan Institute, Zhongshan, China; [b]Graduate Institute of Technology, Innovation and Intellectual Property Management, National Changchi University, Taipei, Taiwan; [c]Department of Business Administration, National Chengchi University, Taipei, Taiwan; [d]Department of Business Administration, National Sun Yat-Sen University, Kaohsiung, Taiwan

The current private- and shareholder-ownership pattern has found its limits. The aim of this research is to explore a growth pattern of employee-owned business adopting the narrative inquiry approach. The findings show that there are four growth stages: the 'family-owned', the 'family- and manager-owned', the 'family-, manager-, and staff-owned' and the 'family-, manager-, staff- and franchisee-owned' stages. This study explains why the pattern is becoming an important part of the business environment around the world and why mutual ownership can better grasp opportunities and turn environmental threats into new opportunities. This study contributes to advancing the understanding of the ownership pattern from private (family), to shareholder (manager) to employee.

Introduction

The 'standard' business model or pattern that is generally regarded to be private ownership, either owned directly by an individual or family, or by external shareholders, has found its limits.

The earliest and most popular business pattern in the world is family- or private-owned business with centralized ownership and control (Neubauer and Lank 1998; Sharma 2004). It is a family (capital)-, relationship- or collective interest-driven growth pattern. In the running of such a business, capital is the key for sustained growth. The patriarch rules through the family to maintain capital inside the business for expansion without the need for external capital (Wu 1993). Talent is the other key for sustained growth (Bewayo 2009; Dyer 1989). The patriarch will also educate family members to equip them for top management positions, so as to prevent untrusted non-family members from controlling the business. This growth pattern can be seen as 'a growth pattern based on internal resources'.

The advantages of a centralized structure of ownership and control such as in family (private)-owned businesses are obvious: (1) pre-existing business involvement, which results in lower agency costs; (2) competitive advantage ensues when the horizons of decision-makers are broadened due to commitment to long-term support of the family; and (3) firm value is enhanced due to the access to family resources, especially when access to other capital is limited (James and Kaye 1999). The disadvantages that limit its growth are also obvious: (1) nepotism, (2) autocracy, (3) difficulties of delegation, (4) paternalism, (5) confusion regarding cash flows, (6) manipulation by family members and (7) lack of definition of organizational structure (Ginebra 1999).

In contrast, the current mainstream shareholder-owned businesses with separated ownership and control operate on the idea that family ownership is only suitable for small firms and modern enterprises should be operated by professional managers to pursue efficiency and economies of scope and scale. That is the reason why western economies are prosperous (Chandler 1977).

It is a personal (capital)-, performance (effectiveness and efficiency)- and individual interest-driven growth pattern. Firms expanding in scale or hiring professional managers will gain more capital to release entrepreneurial equity (Romano, Tanewski, and Smyrnios 2000). Ownership will then gradually transfer from insider to outside shareholders. These shareholders (owners) with dispersed and a tiny number of shares will find it hard to gain control over the election and operation of the board of directors, because only the owner who holds the majority of shares (more than 50%) can control the board and force management decisions. Therefore, shareholders (owners) will need to empower managers by giving them a greater number of shares, allowing them more control and operative power over the firm. That is the agency mechanism (Wang and Jiang 2010). Such growth patterns of moving resources from inside entrepreneurs to outside shareholders are 'a growth pattern based on external resource'.

The disadvantages that limit the growth of such businesses come from managers who pursue their own maximum personal interest under the assumption of self-interest, so the agency mechanism becomes the agency problem because of the conflict of interest between shareholders (owners) and managers (management controllers). The 2007–2008 credit crunch has therefore called into question the appropriateness of the shareholder-owned pattern. An improved mechanism design of the ownership-driven growth pattern is needed.

A new pattern called employee-owned business (EOB) has rapidly grown (Pierce and Furo 1990) and is becoming an important aspect of the business environment around the world (Poutsma, Nijs, and Poole 2003). It is a blend of capitalism and communitarianism (Sauser 2009) and a combination of individual and collective interest (Ridley-Duff 2009).

This study adopts the definition of EOB as a business or organization majorly owned (more than 50% of the shares) and controlled by employees (Mygind 2012). That is, employees have ownership, return and control rights (Ben-Ner and Jones 1995). Pierce and Furo (1990) further define EOBs as taking four forms: social ownership, worker (producer) cooperatives, employee stock-ownership plan and direct ownership. Ben-Ner and Jones (1995, 534) define it further as 16 cells based on an involved degree of ownership and control.

Current research on EOBs mainly emphasizes the content (of cause and effects). Some studies have pointed out its advantages which are mainly rooted in participation, involvement (Cacioppe and Kenny 1987) and control that motivate employees (Cohen and Quarrey 1986). Through participation, employees as owners (Chiu, Hui, and Lai 2007) will make their company advance further to become better than other firms via improvement (innovation) (Chiu, To, and Iun 2006), providing revolutionary concepts to bring about societal transformation (Logue et al. 1998, 79). Leadbeater (1997, 25) even concluded that 'employee ownership is the most powerful way to give employees a direct, tangible stake in their company' (46) and 'we want companies which are dynamic and entrepreneurial, and yet socially responsible and inclusive'. Hence, EOBs can be seen as adopting an 'entrepreneurship-' or a 'new venture-driven growth pattern'. The following provides a review of the literature on new venture growth patterns (models) to elaborate on the EOB growth pattern in order to answer the key research question of this special issue: 'What frameworks, models and theories might be useful in analysing mutual and their development?'

Literature review

Definition of a new venture

The development of the definition of a new venture (creation) basically has three stages. An early definition was that it meant creating a new organization in order to integrate ongoing interdependent actions and then to achieve positive results (Gartner 1985). Later, the definition followed the industrial organization paradigm that emphasizes the opportunity of recognition influenced by industry structure and environment (McDougall, Robinson, and DeNisi 1992). The resource-based view has been adopted recently, addressing the importance of valuable resources and capabilities that an entrepreneur possesses and exploits in an effective manner (Arthurs and Busenitz 2006). Therefore, entrepreneurship can be viewed as a process by which entrepreneurs or entrepreneurial teams identify, acquire and accumulate resources to pursue perceived opportunities (Ireland et al. 2001; Jarillo 1989).

In brief, the definitions have different emphases at different stages, and this research defines new venture creation as the process of opportunity recognition, resource development and team (organizational) development in order to constitute a pattern.

Growth pattern of new venture creation

There are 'static' and 'dynamic' growth patterns (Park and Bae 2004). The 'static developmental pattern' features the entrepreneurial process as consequent stages (Block and MacMillan 1985; Kazanjian 1988; Kazanjian and Drazin 1990), while the 'dynamic developmental pattern' emphasizes the co-evolving process between environments and the organization (Bruyat and Julien 2001; Timmons 1999; Timmons and Spinelli 2006).

In the static development pattern school, Block and MacMillan (1985) analyse the steps of commercialization and conclude that there is a 10-step pattern. Holt (1992) then demonstrated the growth cycles of new venture creation. Later, a new pattern combining life cycle and commercialization was formulated by Kazanjian (1988) and Kazanjian and Drazin (1990).

In addition, the dynamic developmental pattern school places more emphasis on the balance and fit between environment and organization (Maidique 1980; Timmons and Spinelli 2006; Vesper 1990). For example, Gartner (1985) points out that new venture creation needs to include entrepreneurs, entrepreneurial process, organization and environments. Bruyat and Julien (2001) adopted the concept of the open system to emphasize the focus of a new venture, which is the co-evolution between individual and new value creation. Timmons and Spinelli (2006, 56–57) concluded that the new venture process is a dynamic process of balancing between opportunities, resources and teams, the dynamic circles among these three elements during its growth. The new venture plan starts from the process of recognizing opportunities, acquiring resources and then building up a team.

Theoretical framework

The EOB pattern is a dynamic venture process strongly influenced by the environment. Therefore, this research adopted Timmon's pattern (a pattern belonging to the above-mentioned dynamic school) as a theoretical framework of dynamic circles starting from opportunities, moving on to resources and then to team to extrapolate the EOB growth pattern. The pattern of circles depends on the fit and balance among the three (Timmons and Spinelli 2006, 56). The role of the lead entrepreneur and the team is to juggle these key elements in a changing environment. Its dynamic nature is like a juggler bouncing up and down on a trampoline that is moving on a conveyor belt at unpredictable speeds and in unpredictable directions. Another role of the lead entrepreneur is to manage and redefine the risk-reward equation to make a new balance (from imbalance) and improve the fit of the ambiguity and risk (Timmons and Spinelli 2006, 57) (Figure 1). Following are the three elements.

First, opportunity is defined as selling valuable products and services at a higher price than the total cost. Timmons and Spinelli (2006, 58) depict the characteristics of good opportunities as the greater the growth, size, durability and robustness of the gross and net margins and free cash, the greater the opportunity. In addition, opportunity can be recognized from the process.

Second, resources mainly include talent and capital (Chang and Chen 2010). Chang and Chen (2010) summarized factors related to the resources for a new venture. For example, talent with diversified background has a positive impact on a team's performance, bringing high efficiency. Capital is the other important resource, especially for new venture performance and technology adjustment. Capital for a new venture is usually from private (network) sources. Once a new venture can raise capital from an external network, such as banks or venture capital companies, it means new venture growth begins. It is especially important for the new venture's survival, because it has no reputation to acquire such resources (Brush, Greene, and Hart 2001).

Finally, teams invariably are formed and led by a very capable entrepreneurial leader who is a pacemaker and culture creator. The lead entrepreneur is central to the team as both a player and a coach (Timmons and Spinelli 2006, 58). Members of a new team are usually built up from friends, colleagues or relatives (Kamm et al. 1990). Timmons (1999) points out that teams can generate more creativity than a single person, and past evidence shows that interaction among team members can achieve better solutions. Past evidence also indicates that a new venture built up by an entrepreneurial team has a wider social and business network, more technology and a wider capability base (Lechler 2001).

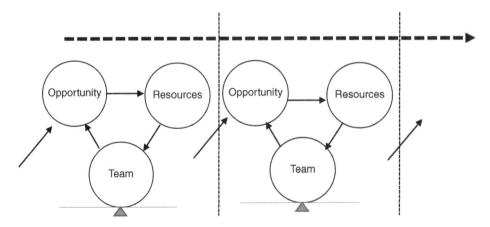

Figure 1. Theoretical framework: growth pattern of new ventures among opportunity–resources–team. *Source*: Timmons and Spinelli (2006), pp. 60–61.

The external environment also impacts new venture creation. Chang and Chen (2010) claim that the entrepreneur needs to adjust himself/herself dynamically at different stages. It is best to adopt transformational leadership in a fast-moving environment. Once a new venture is well developed, connection with an external network is important to supplement resources so as to establish a derivative firm (Larson 1992), to enter into a new market (Prashantham 2008) or to implement a diversification strategy (Steier 2001).

Methodology

A narrative inquiry is a qualitative (Bansal and Corley 2011) interpretive approach (Cope 2005). It is the study of the stories that people tell to register and systematize the stored nature (Dawson and Hjorth 2012) of EOB life. It traces the order of events to know how episodes are related to each other and the binding of organizational life (Czarniawska 1997). Through narrative inquiry, a theory is developed, neither through absolute generalization nor by statistical generalization, but through the analytical induction (Williams 2000) of meaningful patterns and a conceptual bridge (Greenblatt 1990).

Narrative methods concerning 'how' questions (Tsoukas and Chia 2002) can indeed help us to step into that 'time machine' (Dawson and Hjorth 2012). The process of narrative inquiry is the process of search and research (Clandinin and Connell 2000, 181) in order to explore the meaning of sequential actions. Therefore, it is a suitable approach to answering the research questions and can help to focus on the pattern of growth and to understand the nature of the advantages of EOBs.

This research selected 'Wowprime' as a 'critical case' of extending a well-formulated theory and to examine propositions (Yin 2009). This 'critical case' was selected from numerous cases, which adopted the EOB model, as it can be used to analyse its 'critical factors'. The data sources included primary and secondary data in Chinese. We collected secondary data from the websites of Wowprime and the United Daily Network database in order to have a complete understanding of the historical development of the founding and operation of the chain restaurant EOB.

Then, primary data were collected via interviews of key decision-makers (for details of who was interviewed, please refer to Appendix) who know the growth process very well during 2011–2012. We interviewed them mainly at the Taichung headquarter, restaurants and hotels. They were selected because they knew how and what decisions were made regarding the growth of the company. Such selection was by 'theoretical sampling' rather than by 'random sampling', because the study was focused on useful persons for the theory of the growth pattern to fill the theoretical gap. Therefore, the theoretical sampling involved continually collecting and selecting useful persons, which were able to be used to make theoretical replication and to extend the theory. Such a process will continue until theoretical saturation, which means that no new information seems to emerge. That is, data collection and selection of interviewees will stop when no new properties, dimensions, conditions, actions, interactions or consequences are seen in the data (Eisenhardt 1989).

Questions were designed from general to specific in semi-structured and open-ended format as presented to the interviewees (Yin 2009). Then, we carried out and recorded the interviews based on the theoretical framework to guide us in exploring how the company grew and where the advantages came from. This led to tracing the development process and to building a complete story of the EOB. Data collection ceased upon saturation (Eisenhardt 1989; Yin 2009). Triangulation was applied to verify the interview and secondary data (Yin 2009). Concurrently, an evidence chain was built up to verify the reliability of the data (Xiao 2006; Yin 2009).

The processes of narrative analysis included four levels to find the 'themes' (such as 'family-owned stage') from the data: word-by-word script, storytelling, dialectical induction and reorganization, to add to Timmons' theoretical framework. Through such writing processes, the researchers created the fourth section of thick description and the fifth section of findings. The process was conducted as follows: first, the case data were analysed chronologically (see Table 2) in order to have a fundamental understanding of how it grew and what made it grow. After the interviews, the content of the field text and research text was typed up as 'word by word script'. These texts needed to be completed within one week of discussion with the co-authors. Second, based on the time, the 'word by word script' was transferred into a meaningful 'story'. The story was written based on the persons, work, time, places and objects.

Third, 'dialogical induction' was processed further. During the discussion with the co-authors, the researchers discussed the growth pattern with the interviewees. Through thoughts and reconnection with the story, meaningful statements were made. Then, the researchers re-examined the pattern that was built and the source of the advantages that were found (Klein and Myers 1999). The study transfers from objective to subjective and new constructs gradually emerged such as 'family-owned stage', 'family-manager-owned stage', etc. Fourth, reorganization and proper dialogue with the framework made unclear constructs gradually clearer. Then, the framework was added to the dialogue of the story. This study seeks to find the growth pattern and source of advantages for the EOB to explain why the pattern is increasingly important. In the practice of narrative analysis, the third and fourth steps are actions of continuity and iteration that are not so clearly divided.

Finally, the themes were developed and tested through four quality criteria (Riessman 1993). First, the themes developed were cross-examined by the co-authors and interviewees in order to achieve persuasiveness or plausibility. Second, all interview texts were checked by the interviewees to ensure correspondence between authors and interviewees. Third, replicated and extended themes were developed based on the growth source from the EOB to ensure coherence among themes. Finally, all analysis processes based on the development of the advantages of the EOB with text and explanation were described in detail to have pragmatic usage. However, this method suffers from the disadvantage that its reliability cannot be evaluated (Riessman 1993).

Inquiry into the EOB of Wowprime

Wowprime is a company currently up to 90% owned by employees. Established in 1993 in Taichung, Taiwan, it had become the biggest domestic chain restaurant in Taiwan by 2008, and one of the leading chain restaurants in mainland China.

Currently, Wowprime has 10 brands and 189 stores in Asia (see Table 1). A time- and key events-ordered table (see Table 2) provided a fundamental understanding of its growth path for the subsequent interviews. Figure 2 also exhibits its performance since it was established. In revenue, Wowprime grew from US$50,000 in 1993 to US$340 million in 2012, and the recent five-year average growth rate was 63% with a margin of more than 20% (see Figure 2).

Episodes and stages

The analysis of the data focuses on selected episodes as growth stages (themes) according to the temporal dimension of four turning points of new venture creation of the Wowprime EOB.

Table 1. Brands, price, stores and appeals of Wowprime.

	Brand symbol	Found	Product	Price (US$)	Customer	Store #	Main appeals
Wang steak		1993	Steak	High 40	25–50	14	Dignity and enjoyable meal
Tasty		July 2001	Steak	Middle 14–16	25–45 DINK	37	Low price with high quality
Taoban		May 2002	Japanese Food	Middle 16	25–45	31	Mix of Japanese and Western food
Yuanshao		2003	Barbecue	Middle 16	30–45	20	Smoke free, elegant dining
Gather		2004	Chafing dish	MidHigh 18–26	20–45 Masses	28	Time spent together
IKKI		July 2005	Kaiseki	High 27–40	30–45	11	New East style
Chamonix		October 2005	Teppanyaki	High 33	25–45	13	French romantic, elegant style
Pintian		April 2007	Pork chop	Low 6–10	All	22	Happiness-taste
12 Sabu		2009	Chafing dish	Low 7	All	30	Mix of stone chafing dish and BBQ
Sufood		2011	Milan vegetable foods	Low 14	All	13	Feeling the beauty of food with the heart
Famonn		2012	Coffee cake	Low 1–3	All	7	Savouring world coffee culture

Sources: This research

Table 2.   Main events of Wowprime.

Years	Important events
1993	Established first restaurant of Wang Steak with professional manager partners in Taichung City with revenue of US$50,000 in 1993
1994	From autocracy to group decision mode as Central Standing Committee (CSC) and to monthly share bonus
1995	Established Mongolia Mutton Dinner Restaurant
1996	Established Guinness World Records Museum in Taichung
1997	Executing McDonalds' SOP. Established First Class Zongzi chain restaurants
1998	Chairman Dai is voted as a '21st Young Entrepreneur Paradigm'. Change strategy to focus on and sell National Steak, Mongolia Mutton Dinner Restaurant and First Class Zongzi chain restaurants
1999	Wowprime extends to 14 restaurants and revenue reached US$34,000,000
2000	Influence of recession; Wowprime reduces restaurants to 11–20% revenue decreased
2001	Promoting the 'awaking lions' project entrepreneurship plan. Tasty established to enter into middle price market Porterhouse Bistro Steak House established in Beverly Hills
2002	Established 'Taoban'. Each year has two new brand strategies
2003	Established Wang Steak in Shanghai (China) and broke even in two months
2004	Breakthrough of Group revenue to US$68,000,000
2005	Established 'Tasty' (Shanghai), 'Kiki' and 'Chamonix'. Implementing 'low price luxury' multi-store brand strategy
2006	Established as 'Fenghua' (China) and shut up 'Porterhouse'. Breakthrough of revenue to US$102 million. Strategy revised as one year one brand and one brand 50 restaurants and concepts of 'low price luxurious' and '2nd generation restaurant' become the main feature of stores
2007	Established first restaurant of 'Pintain' in Taipei to enter into low-price market
2008	Integrated stocks from eight brands to a joint-stock company to prepare for international franchise. Sales reached US$156 million
2009	Influenced by the global financial crisis, national economic growth drops to (2.9 but Wowprime has 14% growth, sales reached US$176 million)
2010	Taoban international franchise to Thailand. Restaurants expand to 161
2011	Sales reached US$324 million
2012	IPO (Initial Public Offering) with the highest stock price among all Taiwanese listed companies in the tourism/catering sector in Taiwan. Store number expands to 189

Source: The data from this research.

Episode 1: the family- and friends-owned stage: 1993–2000

Escape

Chairman S.Y. Dai entered into the family enterprise as vice president when he had just graduated from university. In order to avoid conflict among brothers in dividing up the family property, he decided to start his own business while he still had a good relationship with his brothers. He said:

> After that, I started borrowing money and my debt exceeded US$5.3 million. At that time, I founded Bi-Bi Paradise, Big Africa Zoo, etc. The fees of my scattered investments were higher than US$25 million. Once I founded Wang Steak restaurant in 1993, I changed my strategy from diversification to focus on restaurant businesses and then I sold the other unrelated businesses. (Dai, SY01_001[1])

Finding an opportunity

Chairman Dai started his restaurant business by finding an opportunity. He said:

> One day, I ate steak prepared for Y. Q. Wang, who is the president of Formosa Plastics Group and I found that this would be a great business for life, as it is a unique Chinese style steak.

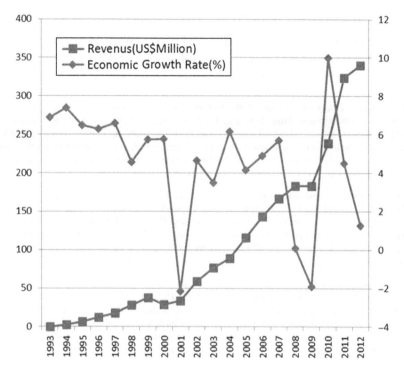

Figure 2.   Revenue compared to economic growth in Taiwan. *Sources*: This research.

The sauce is soy-based rather than western style and the meat is fresher than western style. Then, I asked the cooks to create even more delicious flavors, and advertised: 'one cow only six steaks'. This strategy made us famous. (Dai, SY01_003)

Resources (owned by employees)

The important point in starting a new venture is to raise capital and to find talent. At the very beginning, Dai's capital was from his savings and borrowing from four friends with professional backgrounds who were also invited to invest as partners. This was the foundation of the EOB. G.X.Wang, one of the partners, explained:

I was about 30 years old in 1994 and I had an easy job where I worked 5 days a week and earned US$50,000 annually, in contrast to Dai's offer,which was US$24,000 annually and I even needed to raise capital. So, friends thought I was insane. But, I believed in Dai. I finally decided to join Wang Steak, because I had a quarter of the decision authority. ... I set up 8 departments, ISO9001, directed meat purchasing from farms, and the development of the restaurant information system of Wang Steak. (Wang, GX01_005)

K.Z. Huang, one of the partners, said:

I worked at a university as a professor before I came to Wang Steak. ... I built the financial and computer framework infrustructure. (Huang, KZ01_002)

S.X. Chang, one of the partners, mentioned:

I worked for McDonalds as a training manager before I came to Wang Steak. ... I built the Standard Operating Procedures (S.O.P.) to normalize every procedure for Wang Steak and that is why Wang Steak can duplicate stores rapidly with consistently high quality. (Chang, SX01_003)

Innovative 'bonus share mechanism'

One important issue was how to keep capital and talent at Wang Steak to ensure continual growth. Chairman Dai implemented a bonus mechanism called the 'monthly bonus share' to keep them at Wang Steak. Dai explained:

> I went fishing with W. L. Xu one day. He asked us how many fish we would need to catch to make us happy. Everyone on board had different answers. Then he said, 'When everyone has got fish, it is the happiest thing. If you had the only fish and other people didn't, how long would happiness last'. He also told a story about how a monkey got candy from a jar. He said, 'There was a transparent jar filled with a lot of candies. A greedy monkey wanted more candies, so he grabbed lots of candies in his hand but he couldn't get it out of the jar because the neck of the bottle was too small'. (Dai, SY01_008)

> I went to his house and discovered how such a big businessman can live in a small place without a bodyguard. I asked, 'Aren't you afraid bad guys will rob you?' He said, 'I share all my money with all the employees. I donated my ChiMei Museum to the Tainan City Government. What can bad guys get from me?' I was inspired by him for making me realize that if a firm's achievements are all taken by the boss, how can employees identify with the company and how can an owner find peace of mind? (Dai, SY01_011)

> Another inspiration is from traveling. I traveled and watched dolphin performances as they jumped through flaming hoops at Hong Kong Ocean Park in 1992. I thought immediately that the encouragement of the dolphins from their animal trainer is the reason they are willing to jump again and again. If after one jump they do not have any encouragement or it is delayed, the dolphin will quit jumping. This is the nature of animals, so is it man's, and then I thought of the principle of investment of stocks and shares immediately. (Dai, SY01_015)

Team

The management team was established by the founder Chairman Dai, his family and friends. From past experience, even a very capable person will have blind spots, and autocratic decision-making makes for poor communication and execution. Hence, the founder and partners formed a Central Standing Committee (CSC) functioning as a family meeting since June 1994 to participate in the decision-making.

This episode, named the 'family and friend-owned' stage, illustrates how founder Dai found an opportunity from an imbalanced environment (very strong demand but weak supply) and acquired employees' resources by inviting capable friends to invest as co-owners and team members to contribute to growth. It was the foundation stage of the EOB and involved 10% employee ownership. Then, a team was built up to establish many innovative mechanisms to seize the opportunity as the foundation of Wowprime. This is the growth process from imbalance to a new balance.

Episode 2: the family–manager-owned stage: 2001–2005

Turning threat into opportunity

During the period from 1999 to 2001, environmental troubles assaulted Wang Steak and other restaurants. Disasters such as the 9-21-1999 earthquake which caused the greatest damage to Taiwan since World War II, a wave of emigration of the manufacturing industry to mainland China in 2000 and the biggest economic recession for the past 30 years in 2001 made Wang Steak downsize from 14 stores to 11 and sales decreased 20%. What did Wang Steak do to continue growing during this recession?

During economic recession, consumption demand is decreased. It becomes a good opportunity to develop lower-priced brands to fit the change in demand. Therefore, Wang

Steak started growing by duplicating its mechanism to the lower-priced market and gradually formed the Wowprime restaurant group. Dai explained:

> ... I and the C.S.C. thought, while the number of customers is down, that is a good opportunity to develop a lower-priced market. So I announced an offer for steak brand priced below US$10 (Wang Steak's average price is US$17). (Dai, SY01_025)

Resources (owned by employees)

Dai started looking for and recruiting external professional managers to join Wowprime as owners, and many professional managers joined Wowprime due to the 'Awaking Lions' project.

> ... in this situation, I announced an entrepreneurial project named 'Awaking Lions' to encourage managers to start venturing out with their own brands. This project created an incubation environment. ... I thought that Wowprime should have 'baby, child, young, and mature lions' in order to continue growing via venturing, so Wowprime needed many managers to start such venturing'. (Dai, SY01_028)

S.B. Lee, partner and founder of Gather, mentioned:

> I had graduated from the Department of Tourism. I met Chairman Dai, and he invited me to join Wang Steak, and then I established a brand called 'Gather'. (Lee, SB01_005)

Y.Z. Cao, partner and founder of Yuan-Shao Grills, mentioned:

> I spent my own US$34,000 to sample 303 restaurants around the world, and I finally found that grills which are free from the worry of whether there is a smoking restriction in place is a business niche. After that, I opened the first grill restaurant in Taipei, and this was the 7th business of Wowprime. (Cao, YZ01_003)

In addition, D.X. Koh, the Branding Vice General Manager, came from OGILVY. Other professional managers were invited to invest as new brand owners or functional directors. The entrepreneurial pattern was a duplication of Wang Steak.

Innovative entrepreneurial mechanism to satisfy the dream of being a boss

Dai explained why professional managers were willing to give up high salaries to start ventures at Wowprime. He mentioned:

> '... many Taiwanese have a dream of being a boss and that is why there are so many restaurants on just one small street. I satisfied that desire. It is human nature'. '... Wowprime's entrepreneurial mechanism allows managers to invest in their own business as family members. This mechanism created a personal venturing company with Wowprime's backup, and that is why Wowprime can attract talent and capital'. (Dai, SY01_028)

Team

The decision-making pattern was also duplicated to make a mechanism of innovation. Dai mentioned:

> Wang Steak is a mother brand and it not only duplicates into new brands, but also transfers traditional group decision making patterns from the first generation of the C.S.C. to the second generation of new brands. (Dai, SY01_035)

For the duration of venturing, group decision-making like the CSC is a very effective mechanism for quick response to environmental threats. Dai mentioned:

the group decision making pattern is very effective for rapid environmental change. In an economic recession, it can quickly respond to the change of environment and stablize sales. In addition, the pattern was good for breeding talent. (Dai, SY01_038)

This episode, named the 'family-manager-owned' stage, illustrates how founder Dai and the CSC turned a threat into a new opportunity from an imbalanced situation (changed demand), and acquired employees' resources by inviting external professional managers to invest as co-owners and team members to contribute to growth. It was the growth stage of the EOB, and involved 100% employee ownership. Then, new entrepreneurial teams were built up to establish and extend innovative mechanisms to make the most of the opportunity. This is another growth process from imbalance to a new balance.

Episode 3: the family–manager–staff-owned stage: 2005–2008

Growth opportunity from geographical expansion

While implementing brand duplication to the maximum, what could Wowprime do to keep on growing? It needed a new strategy to cope with this situation. Chairman Dai decided to develop brands with popular prices for store expansion. He mentioned:

Experience with the last multi-brand stage showed that brand quantity had reached its maximum. If Wowprime wanted more efficient expansion, it needed to move from multi-branding to a lower price level of multi-store-brands. (Dai, SY01_042)

Dai named the strategy 'low price luxury for 2nd generation stores'. Wowprime had developed stable businesses in first-level cities such as Taipei, Taoyuan, Hsinchu and Taichung. Thus, they started moving to the rim of the first-level cities or to second-level cities to expand their territory. They also entered into the mainland China market. Dai mentioned:

... We will have great opportunity if we choose the 'low price luxury for 2nd generation stores' strategy. For example, I told them to plan a 'one hundred stores celebration festival' last week. Twelve Chafing Dish will have such a celebration soon. We need to rely on such a 'low price luxury' strategy to promptly open stores .... For example, Pintina Farm adopted a '2nd generation store' strategy which focused on middle size cities and lower cost with more seats. Based on this strategy, Wowprime can enter into the big city rim and smaller sized cities. (Dai, SY01_048)

Resources (owned by employees)

Chairman Dai continued his organizational form and EOB mechanism to expand and attract capable and specialized workers such as store managers, chefs and staff to join Wowprime as owners for store expansion. Bonuses and shares were announced monthly on the internal website to every employee.

... Based on the 'monthly bonus share' principle, we allow store managers and chefs who are majorly skilled and knowledgeable investors to share bonuses every month once a store is opened. (Dai, SY01_055)

Based on the 'monthly bonus share' principle, the salary plus ratio of share is particularly high for a business owner (the bonus is usually higher than the salary). The restaurant manager's monthly income is above US$5000. A district manager is above US$10,000 monthly, while a brand general manager's annual income is above US$700,000. Besides executives, staff can also share significant bonuses.

Team

The managerial pattern based on group decision-making was also extended to stores. Dai mentioned:

> ... for geographical expansion, our decision making mechanism was also expanded to stores in second level cities. Therefore, the number of family members in the C.S.C. continues to grow. (Dai, SY01_058)

> Basically, I make 5% of the strategic decisions for major direction and the other 95% are made by all employees together. Except for the C.S.C. decision group, we also have a proposal system to allow every employee to participate in decision making. Store managers and chefs can draft resolutions every month ... such patterns formulate participation in the decision making culture. (Dai, SY01_065)

This episode, named the 'family-manager-staff-owned' stage, illustrates how founder Dai found an opportunity from an imbalanced situation (strong demand at the rim of a big city but weak supply) and acquired employees' resources by inviting store managers, chefs and staff to invest as co-owners and team members to contribute to growth. It was the extension stage of the EOB, and employee ownership was 100%. Then, new entrepreneurial teams were built up to establish and implement innovative mechanisms to fill the gaps. This is another growth process from imbalance to a new balance.

Episode 4: the family–manager–staff–franchisee-owned stage: 2008–2012

Growth opportunity from international franchise

The way to effectively and successfully expand overseas, since the domestic market is more and more crowded, has become a major strategic issue for Chairman Dai. He felt that an international franchise could conquer many problems such as cultural differences, and so decided that Wowprime could create a franchise with another famous international chain restaurant as a co-venture. His international entrepreneurial strategy needs solid preparation for negotiation and worldwide quality. Dai mentioned:

> I think that we will reach US$300 million in 2012, and then we can have franchise-rights. We will need a corporation, not a store, and we will also need to go public. What I am doing is for the future. (Dai, SY02_005)

Integration of ownership of all stores as a corporation based on different shares, performance and period of service is a big challenge. Dai mentioned:

> Oh! It is very complicated. I could spend a year describing it. Different stores have different ownership and performance. You have 10% share and I have 10% as well ... how can it be the same value? They also argue that my store has been open for only one year, but they have been open for 10 years, and they already got their money back and have even multiplied the initial capital ... how can we have the same share as one corporation? Many arguments like these. (Dai, SY02_011)

Due to the disparity of the period of service between old and new shareholders, Dai preferred to process this issue via referendum, rather than via the CSC. He explained:

> I did everything I could to make them agreeable ... I also agreed not to use the process of C.S.C. And then, I called a referendum in October. If the referendum could not be passed, we would cancel any integration. Then, 99.51% of employees agreed with integration. (Dai, SY02_018)

Resources (owned by employees)

After integration of ownership and management control, Wowprime launched the successful franchise 'Taoban' in Thailand in 2011 and the Initial Public Offering had the highest stock price among all Taiwanese listed companies in the tourism/catering sector in early 2012.

Chairman Dai defines the mechanism of shares to motivate all employees as the 'three principles of the people' where all the employees are treated as family. Dai mentioned:

> ... I believe in the three principles of the people: of the people, by the people, for the people. I released 80% of the shares to all employees (skilled workers), meaning that employees are the biggest shareholders of Wowprime, and so it is 'of the people'. It is also controlled by employees, and that is 'by the people'. I share bonuses monthly, and that is 'for the people'.
> ... Wowprime can be called a family-like business as all the employees treat each other as family. (Dai, SY02_025)

Team

Dai also defines Wowprime as a family in that all employees' interests are bound together. His management philosophy is familism so as to encourage all employees to be loyally dedicated to their business. He established a constitution for Wowprime to ensure that the employee-owned familism would be realized. The general meeting of shareholders is a family meeting. In addition, a new and integrated decision group with six members was formed for a more effective decision-making process. Dai mentioned:

> For the extension of brands and stores, the C.S.C. was also extended to the 3rd generation of 25 committees. For more efficient decision making, I gathered 6 people as a decision making group to replace the increasingly huge C.S.C. membership. The 6 members need to convey policy to the first generation C.S.C. and then, the first generation C.S.C. needs to convey policy to the second, and the second needs to convey it to the third, as well. I think this kind of transmitting is important for the will of the family. (Dai, SY02_031)

This episode, named the 'family-manager-staff-franchisee-owned' stage, illustrates how founder Dai found an opportunity from an imbalanced situation (strong overseas demand but weak supply) and acquired employees' resources by inviting international franchisees to invest as co-owners and team members to contribute to growth. It was the international extension stage of the EOB, and employees had about 90% ownership. Then, new entrepreneurial teams were set up and all employees were defined as members of the Wowprime family to bind their interest together and to make the most of the opportunities. This is another growth process from imbalance to a new balance.

Findings

From the above-mentioned episodes, this study found that this EOB had a dynamic growth pattern (Table 3). It is the growth circulation of recognizing opportunities, seeking needed resources from employees and building teams of employees via a mutual and cooperative venture of releasing ownership of Wowprime to all employees.

This growth pattern includes four stages. The first stage is the 'founder Dai-, his family- and friends-owned' stage. The second stage is the 'family- and (external professional) manager (brand general manager)-owned' stage. The third stage is the 'family-, (brand general and store) manager-, and staff-owned' stage. The fourth stage is the 'family-, manager-, staff- and franchisee-owned' stage.

These stages are also growth stages of the EOB and are stages of foundation, growth, extension and international extension. It can be described as the expanding processes of employee ownership from core to frontier relationships, and the advantages built from a family business (private ownership) to a manager mechanism (shareholder ownership) during the four stages.

The advantages of this pattern of development include loyalty, professional efficiency, scales of economy, scope of economy, information transparency, learning curve effect, innovation and cross-cultural management (see Figure 3). Moreover, the growth pattern avoids the disadvantages of private ownership and shareholder ownership. For example, Chairman Dai established a constitution for Wowprime to prohibit the possible disadvantages of family business (private ownership) and the manager mechanism (shareholder ownership), so such problems as nepotism, autocracy or agency will not influence its growth.

Contribution, implications, limitations and further research

Contribution

This research makes two contributions to the understanding of EOBs. First, this study advances the understanding of the growth pattern (model) of ownership from private (family), shareholder (manager) to employee. Second, previous studies related to EOBs mostly emphasize the content (of cause and result). This research fills the theoretical gap regarding the process of growth and the advantages gained.

Implications

This study generalizes a growth pattern of EOB which includes four stages: 'founder Dai-, his family- and friends-owned' stage, 'family- and (external professional) manager (brand general manager)-owned' stage, 'family-, (brand general and store) manager-, and staff-owned' stage and the 'family-, manager-, staff- and franchisee-owned' stage. Management practice also needs to follow such growth approach.

Therefore, the employment of the growth pattern should start from family members with a blood relationship, as it is the easiest way to collect capital with trust. It can then be extended to close friends (professional managers), then to staff and finally to overseas partners. It is an inside-out approach to management practice. It will not be easy to succeed if a firm takes the outside-in approach, as the establishment of trust from outside families is difficult in the short term.

The success of Wowprime is the result of the advantages of both family business and professional managers. That is, organizations that adopt the employee-owned growth pattern can avoid the limits of both private- and shareholder-owned businesses.

The pattern of EOB adopted by Wowprime may, however, also exhibit disadvantages, if decision-makers implicate the pattern of Wowprime but adopt the disadvantages of family businesses such as nepotism, autocracy, difficulties of delegation and so on, or adopt the disadvantages of the professional manager mechanism such as pursuing maximization of personal profit.

Limitations

This research is limited in that it only selected the company from food and beverage industry; thus, the growth pattern can only be elaborated in such settings. High-technology industries were not included in this study. In other words, businesses should recognize the industrial characteristics implied in the pattern. For example, the semi-conductor industry is a capital intensive industry, so the capital raised from private sources might not be sufficient to create new venture capital.

Table 3. Growth pattern of employee-owned business: Wowprime as an example.

Themes	Stage 1: the family (and friends)-owned 1993–2000	Stage 2: the family–manager-owned 2001–2005	Stage 3: the family–manager–staff-owned 2006–2009	Stage 4: the family–manager–staff–franchisee-owned 2010–2012
Business opportunities	World's first steak with Chinese soy-based sauce	Expanded from high- to middle- price brand via brand duplication	Expanded from city to suburbs via store development	Expanded via international franchise
Resource	Capital mainly from borrowing and capable friends' investment	Recruited external top professional managers to invest as owners for new ventures	Recruited and trained store managers, chefs and staff as owners to develop stores	Attracted franchisees to invest as owners to develop international market
Team	Founder–family–friends-controlled	Family–manager-controlled	Family–manager (chef)–staff-controlled	Family–manager (chef)–staff–franchisee-controlled
Growth path of opportunity-resource-organizational ownership	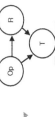 Op: founder Dai found that Chinese flavoured steak was a great opportunity	 Imbalance: economic recession causes lower consumption Op: economic recession is a good opportunity to develop lower-price brands	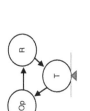 Imbalance: brand development reached its limit Op: store development is a new venture opportunity	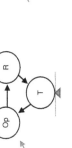 Imbalance: foreign restaurants hoped to join Wowprime Op: International franchise is a new opportunity. Wowprime needs to go public for better negotiation

| R: he borrowed money and invited friends to invest in the new venture | R: invited professional managers to develop their own brands as owners | R: invited store managers, chefs and staff to invest as owners | R: integrated brand- and store-based combined into one corporation to IPO for international franchise (not for raising money). It reserved 10% profit to buy stock from the market to give and motivate managers |
| T: founder, his family and friends established a management team and built foundation for Wang Steak to meet the opportunity with the advantage of loyalty and innovative mechanism | T: a new management team added nine brands; general managers were established to fit the gap with the advantages of professional efficiency and brand innovation | T: a new management team added; store man agers, chefs and staff were established to fit the gap with advantages of economies of scale and operational innovation | T: international franchises built advantage of cross-cultural management and innovation |

Note: This research. Remarks: 'Op' = opportunities. 'R' = resources. 'T' = team.

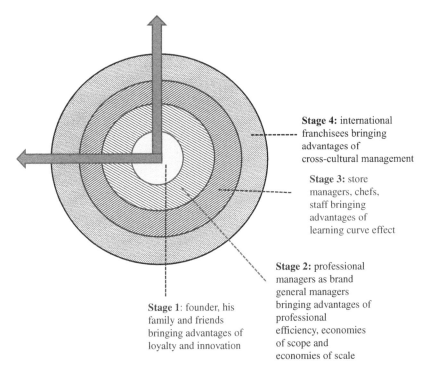

Stage 4: international franchisees bringing advantages of cross-cultural management

Stage 3: store managers, chefs, staff bringing advantages of learning curve effect

Stage 2: professional managers as brand general managers bringing advantages of professional efficiency, economies of scope and economies of scale

Stage 1: founder, his family and friends bringing advantages of loyalty and innovation

Figure 3. Ownership, advantages and the growth of employee-owned business. *Source*: This research.

Further research

Research has contributed to an understanding of the content and process of EOBs. Many aspects of the management of EOBs are still unknown. For example, private (family)-owned businesses emphasize the management of relationships, while shareholder-owned businesses emphasize the management of performance (effectiveness and efficiency). EOBs combine both emphases on relationship and performance. The first research question is: how do EOBs manage their vision, mission, strategy, planning, organizing, leadership, control and learning? The second question is: how do EOBs make policies concerning human resources, marketing, manufacturing, finance, and research and development? The final question is: what is the management pattern (model) of EOBs and how does it operate? All of these questions warrant further investigation.

Conclusions

This narrative inquiry explored the growth pattern of an EOB from its new venture creating nature to its source of advantages in order to explain why EOBs are becoming more and more important, when the EOB was started and how it is operating from the above-mentioned episodes and findings.

Through induction from these four stages, three conclusions are reached. First, this pattern of encouraging mutual ownership can turn environmental threats into new opportunities. Naturally, every employee (owner) wants to receive ample dividends while relying on mutual cooperation, so they will do their best to help each other (collective interest). Therefore, when the firm meets environmental threats, it will face them mutually,

136

and quickly find the solution that best protects their mutual interest. Mutual ownership can also avoid crises caused by pursuing maximized self-interest such as the 2008 financial crisis, because of participation in decision-making and information transparency. This pattern explains how EOBs such as Wowprime can grasp opportunities, turn environmental threats into new opportunities and grow with limited external negative impacts (see Figure 2).

Second, this pattern of allowing individual ownership by all employees can turn external resources such as professional managers, capital, etc., into intra-organization resources via fulfilling employees' dreams of being their own boss (self-interest). For the motivation of ownership, employees will try to do their best to improve their effectiveness and efficiency, so Wowprime can make improvements (innovations) and create new ventures continually with advantages such as loyalty and professional efficiency. This explains how EOBs such as Wowprime can continually grow and build on their advantages (see Figure 3).

Third, this pattern has advantages of both private and shareholder ownerships without the limits or disadvantages of either of them. It is a growth pattern based on both internal and external resources.

Acknowledgement

This study was funded by the Guangzhou Vocational College of Science and Technology (No. 2014JG02: transfer of social capital and absorptive capability: family business successors in Guangdong as examples).

Note

1. The interview code.

References

Arthurs, J. D., and L. W. Busenitz. 2006. "Dynamic Capabilities and Venture Performance: The Effects of Venture Capitalists." *Journal of Business Venturing* 21 (2): 195–215.
Bansal, P., and K. Corley. 2011. "The Coming of Age for Qualitative Research: Embracing the Diversity of Qualitative Methods." *Academy of Management Journal* 54 (2): 233–237.

Ben-Ner, A., and D. C. Jones. 1995. "Employee Participation, Ownership, and Productivity: A Theoretical Framework." *Industrial Relations: A Journal of Economy and Society* 34 (4): 532–554.

Bewayo, E. D. 2009. "Family Business in Africa: A Comparison with the U.S.-Western Model." *Journal of Global Business Issues* 3 (1): 171–181.

Block, Z., and I. C. MacMillan. 1985. "Milestones for Successful Venture Planning." *Harvard Business Review* 63 (5): 184–196.

Brush, C. G., P. Greene, and M. M. Hart. 2001. "From Initial Idea to Unique Advantage: The Entrepreneurial Challenge of Constructing a Resource Base." *Academy of Management Executive* 15 (1): 64–78.

Bruyat, C., and P. A. Julien. 2001. "Defining the Field of Research in Entrepreneurship." *Journal of Business Venturing* 16 (2): 165–180.

Cacioppe, R. L., and G. K. Kenny. 1987. "Work Attitudes in an Employee-Owned Company: Comparing Managers with Non-managers." *Journal of Managerial Psychology* 2 (3): 17–22.

Chandler, D. A. 1977. *The Visible Hand: The Managerial Revolution in American Business*. Cambridge, MA: Belknap Press.

Chang, Y. C., and M. N. Chen. 2010. "New Venture Growth Strategy: Co-Evolution between Opportunity, Resource and Organization." *Journal of Technology Management* 15 (2): 83–116, (in Chinese).

Chiu, W. C. K., C. H. Hui, and G. W. F. Lai. 2007. "Psychological Ownership and Organizational Optimism Amid China's Corporate Transformation: Effects of an Employee Ownership Scheme and a Management Dominated Board." *International Journal of Human Resource Management* 18 (2): 303–320.

Chiu, W. C. K., M. L. To, and J. Iun. 2006. "Measuring Climate of Organizational Optimism: Construct Development and Validation." Paper presented at the 5th Asian Academy of Management, Tokyo, Japan.

Clandinin, D. J., and F. M. Connell. 2000. *Narrative Inquiry: Experience and Story in Qualitative Research*. San Francisco, NC: Jossey-Bass.

Cohen, A., and M. Quarrey. 1986. "Performance of Employee-Owned Small Companies: A Prelim Study." *Journal of Small Business Management* 24 (2): 58–63.

Cope, J. 2005. "Researching Entrepreneurship through Phenomenological Inquiry: Philosophical and Methodological Issues." *International Small Business Journal* 23 (2): 163–189.

Czarniawska, B. 1997. *Narrating the Organization: Dramas of Institutional Identity*. Chicago, IL: University of Chicago Press.

Dawson, A., and D. Hjorth. 2012. "Advancing Family Business Research through Narrative Analysis." *Family Business Review* 25 (3): 339–355.

Dyer, G. 1989. "Integrating Professional Management into a Family-Owned Business." *Family Business Review* 11 (3): 221–235.

Eisenhardt, M. K. 1989. "Building Theories from Case Study Research." *Academy of Management Review* 14 (4): 532–550.

Gartner, W. B. 1985. "A Conceptual Framework for Describing the Phenomenon of New Venture Creation." *Academy of Management Review* 10 (4): 696–706.

Ginebra, J. 1999. [Family business: its management and continuity] *Las Empresas Familiares: Su Direccióny Su Continuidad*. México DF: Panorama.

Greenblatt, S. 1990. *Learning to Curse: Essays in Early Modern Culture*. New York: Routledge.

Holt, D. H. 1992. *Entrepreneurship: New Venture Creation*. Englewood Cliffs, NJ: Prentice Hall.

Ireland, R. D., M. A. Hitt, S. M. Camp, and D. L. Sexton. 2001. "Integrating Entrepreneurship and Strategic Management Actions to Create Firm Wealth." *Academy of Management Executive* 15 (1): 49–63.

James, H., and K. Kaye. 1999. "What Can the Family to Contribute to Business? Examining Contractual Relationships." *Family Business Review* 12: 61–75.

Jarillo, J. C. 1989. "Entrepreneurship and Growth: The Strategic Use of External Resources." *Journal of Business Venturing* 4: 133–147.

Kamm, J. B., J. C. Shuman, J. A. Seeger, and A. J. Nurick. 1990. "Entrepreneurial Teams in New Venture Creation: A Research Agenda." *Entrepreneurship: Theory and Practice* 11 (4): 7–17.

Kazanjian, R. K. 1988. "Relation of Dominant Problems of Stages of Growth in Technology-Based New Venture." *Academy of Management Journal* 31 (2): 257–279.

Kazanjian, R. K., and R. Drazin. 1990. "A Stage Contingent Model of Design and Growth for Technology Based New Ventures." *Journal of Business Venturing* 5 (3): 137–150.

Klein, H. K., and M. D. Myers. 1999. "A Set of Principles for Conducting and Evaluating Interpretive Field Studies in Information System." *MIS Quarterly* 23 (1): 67–94.

Larson, A. 1992. "Network Dyads in Entrepreneurial Settings: A Study of the Governance of Exchange Relationships." *Administrative Science Quarterly* 37 (1): 76–104.

Leadbeater, C. 1997. *A Piece of the Action: Employee Ownership, Equity Pay and the Rise of the knowledge Economy.* London: Demos.

Lechler, T. 2001. "Social Interaction: A Determinant of Entrepreneurial Team Venture Success." *Small Business Economics* 16 (4): 263–278.

Logue, J., W. Patton, A. Tevdosio, and K. Thomas. 1998. *Participatory Employee Ownership.* Worker Ownership Institute, Kent State University. Kent, OH: Kent Popular Press.

Maidique, M. A. 1980. "Entrepreneurs, Champions and Technological Innovation." *Sloan Management Review* 21 (2): 59–76.

McDougall, P. P., R. B. Robinson, and A. S. DeNisi. 1992. "Modeling New Venture Performance: An Analysis of New Venture Strategy, Industry Structure, and Venture Origin." *Journal of Business Venturing* 7 (4): 267–289.

Mygind, N. 2012. "Trends in Employee Ownership in Eastern Europe." *International Journal of Human Resource Management* 23 (8): 1611–1642.

Neubauer, F., and A. G. Lank. 1998. *The Family Business Its Governance for Sustainability.* Hampshire: Macmillan Press.

Park, S., and Z. T. Bae. 2004. "New Venture Strategies in a Developing Country: Identifying a Typology and Examining Growth Patterns through Case Studies." *Journal of Business Venturing* 19 (1): 81–105.

Pierce, J. L., and C. A. Furo. 1990. "Employee Ownership: Implications for Management." *Organizational Dynamics* 18 (3): 32–43.

Poutsma, E., W. D. Nijs, and M. Poole. 2003. "The Global Phenomenon of Employee Financial Participation." *The International Journal of Human Resource Management* 14 (6): 855–862.

Prashantham, S. 2008. "New Venture Internationalization as Strategic Renewal." *European Management Journal* 26 (6): 378–387.

Ridley-Duff, R. 2009. "Entrepreneurialism, Business Enterprise, Co-Operative Organizations, Equity Capital, Assets." *Social Enterprise Journal* 5 (1): 50–68.

Riessman, C. K. 1993. *Narrative Analysis: Sage Qualitative Research Methods Series Series.* Newbury Park, CA: Sage.

Romano, C. A., G. A. Tanewski, and K. X. Smyrnios. 2000. "Capital Structure Decision Making: A Model for Family Business." *Journal of Business Venturing* 16 (3): 285–310.

Sauser, W. I. 2009. "Sustaining Employee Owned Companies: Seven Recommendations." *Journal of Business Ethics* 84 (2): 151–164.

Sharma, P. 2004. "An Overview of the Field of Family Business Studies: Current Status and Directions for Future." *Family Business Review* 17 (1): 1–36.

Steier, L. 2001. "New Venture Firms, International Expansion and the Liabilities of Joint Venture Relationships." *Journal of High Technology Management Research* 12 (2): 295–321.

Timmons, J. A. 1999. *New Venture Creation.* Singapore: McGraw-Hill.

Timmons, J. A., and S. Spinelli. 2006. *New Venture Creation: Entrepreneurship for the 21st Century.* 6th ed. New York: McGraw-Hill.

Tsoukas, H., and R. Chia. 2002. "On Organizational Becoming: Rethinking Organizational Change." *Organization Science* 13 (5): 567–582.

Vesper, K. H. 1990. *New Venture Strategies.* Englewood Cliffs, NJ: Prentice Hall.

Wang, Z. H., and Y. H. Jiang. 2010. "The Impact of Family Relationship to Department Restaurants in Taiwan." Paper presented at the Conference of Enterprise History in Taiwan: Is family business still important?" National Chengchi University, Taipei, Taiwan (In Chinese).

Williams, M. 2000. "Interpretivism and Generalization." *Sociology* 34 (2): 209–224.

Wu, M. J. 1993. *Success of Family Business.* Taipei: Chinese Management Association (In Chinese).

Xiao, R. L. 2006. *Research without Numbers.* Taipei: Pearson Education (In Chinese).

Yin, K. R. 2009. *Case Study Research: Design and Methods.* London: Sage.

Appendix. List of interviewees

Names	Positions	Age	Job tenure	Length of interview
S.Y. Dai	Chairman	56	21 years	4 hours
G.X. Wang	Vice Chairman	53	20 years	1 hour
K.Z. Huang	Vice General Manager of Management Department	52	19 years	45 minutes
S.X. Chang	Vice General Manager of Training Department	52	18 years	45 minutes
S.B. Lee	Founder and General Manager of Gather Brand	53	12 years	45 minutes
Y.Z. Cao	Founder and General Manager of Yuan-Shao Grills	47	21 years	45 minutes
D.X. Koh	Vice General Manager of Branding Department	53	18 years	45 minutes

Sources: This research.

From corporate social responsibility to creating shared value with suppliers through mutual firm foundation in the Korean bakery industry: a case study of the SPC Group

Dongmin Lee[a], Junghoon Moon[a], Jongpyo Cho[a], Hyoung-Goo Kang[b] and Jaeseok Jeong[c]

[a]Program in Regional Information, Seoul National University, Gwanak-gu, Seoul, South Korea; [b]Hanyang University Business School, Hanyang University, Seongdong-gu, Seoul, South Korea; [c]Graduate School of Pan-Pacific International Studies, Kyung Hee University, Yongin-si, Gyeonggi-do, South Korea

This study introduces the transformation process of a company's non-market strategy from corporate social responsibility to creating shared value (CSV). The proposed framework depicts supplier relationship management (SRM) activity, through the case of a Korean bakery franchise, using non-market strategies as a tool for SRM. The analysis explains the backgrounds of the transformation and the ramifications of the changes on SRM actions, such as mutual firm foundations, long-term contracts, and temporal relations. A mutual firm is suggested as the representative form of CSV activity within a triple helix innovation that would create business and social value, ultimately achieving regional resilience.

Introduction

Over the past few decades, corporate social responsibility (CSR) has been receiving increased attention and has become a controversial issue in the field of business (Fukukawa, Balmer, and Gray 2007; Porter and Kramer 2011; Szmigin and Rutherford 2013). Recently, CSR and sustainability have converged to achieve a company's long-term success by considering both the natural and the social environment (Hildebrand, Sen, and Bhattacharya 2011). This movement has led corporations to take a more strategic perspective on CSR (Lantos 2001; Porter and Kramer 2002; Hildebrand, Sen, and Bhattacharya 2011) as an approach to non-market strategies (Baron and Diermeier 2007). This movement has led firms to benefit financially from the creation of social value, which is reinforced by the concept of creating shared value (CSV) that Porter and Kramer (2011) suggested.

Porter and Kramer (2011, 66) describe CSV as 'policies and operating practices that enhance the competitiveness of a company while simultaneously advancing the economic and social conditions in the communities in which it operates'. The differentiating point of CSV from CSR is that it 'expands the total pool of economic and social value' (65), rather than redistributing values already created by firms. Despite the active use of CSV in practical field, only a few studies have been conducted to investigate CSV (e.g., Moon

141

et al. 2011; Pirson 2012; Spitzeck and Chapman 2012; Szmigin and Rutherford 2013) in academia.

This study is exploratory in nature, since it aims to provide both theoretical and empirical backgrounds for the transformation process of a company's non-market strategy from CSR to CSV. In order to investigate the transformation, a study on shared values that has been created through supplier relationship management (SRM) was conducted. Specifically, this study demonstrates the effect and the outcome of non-market strategy transition on SRM such as temporal relations, long-term contracts, and mutual firm foundations. To accomplish the goal, a case study of a leading bakery franchise was conducted based on activity theory.

Literature review

CSR has always been an important topic both in academia and in the field (Fukukawa, Balmer, and Gray 2007; Porter and Kramer 2011; Szmigin and Rutherford 2013). The notion of CSR was initially considered to be merely support for charity by corporations (Bowen 1953; Barone, Miyazaki, and Taylor 2000; Maignan and Ferrell 2004). However, in recent times CSR has converged with the concept of 'sustainability' to attain long-term success, which requires meticulous supervision of its own performance within the natural and social environment (Hildebrand, Sen, and Bhattacharya 2011). This movement has led CSR to be more strategic (Lantos 2001; Porter and Kramer 2002; Hildebrand, Sen, and Bhattacharya 2011) through allowing a firm to benefit financially from both positive publicity and goodwill, as well as to create societal value (Lantos 2001, 2002). Several academic researchers consider this strategic use of CSR as the use of a non-market strategy (Baron and Diermeier 2007).

Porter and Kramer (2011) enhanced strategic CSR with CSV, resulting in a firm capitalizing on their core competitiveness rather than from their collateral competence. The decisive point of differentiation between CSV and CSR is that in the former activities are not only able to provide societal values by contributing to the communities they belong to, but also they are able to obtain substantial economic benefits that enhance their own competence and competiveness (Spitzeck and Chapman 2012). CSV negates the existing paradigm that there is no significant relationship between a firm's growth and the development of the community it is involved in. CSV argues that the absence of a link to the community can be attributed to the fact that companies only pursue short-term benefits without sincere intentions of innovation and strategy (Porter and Kramer 2011).

According to Porter and Kramer (2011), there are three distinct means of achieving CSV in order to enhance substantial competitiveness. The first method is through 'Reconceiving Products and Markets' (67). Companies have to pay close attention to the social demands related to their products or services. The second method is through 'Redefining Productivity in the Value Chain' (68). This can be done by minimizing externalities. Firms can reduce their internal operational costs by reducing the social cost of the whole community that they belong to. The last method of achieving CSV is through 'Enabling Local Cluster Development' (72). By making a local cluster that involves concentrating various assets and organizations related to the industry, productivity and competitiveness of the location increase. The process of achieving a resilient local cluster is sophisticated, since a resilient region is economically successful not only for the short term, but also for the long term (Christopherson, Michie, and Tyler 2010).

Despite the fact that several multinational companies (i.e. Nestlé, Unilever) are utilizing CSV robustly, only a few empirical and theoretical studies addressed CSV in academia. Prior studies tend to extend on the theoretical background of CSV, or attempt to develop a business strategy in a specific societal field. Some studies concentrated on extending the theory (e.g., Moon et al. 2011; Szmigin and Rutherford 2013), since CSV is a relatively recent term. Szmigin and Rutherford (2013) examined CSV to provide the demarcation between business and ethics based on Adam Smith's theory of moral sentiment. Moon et al. (2011) categorized four types of corporations, in terms of business and social value, by using a modified CSV framework based on Porter's diamond model.

In terms of developing a business strategy, previous studies focused on limited societal fields (e.g., environment, social entrepreneurs, and low-income market). Spitzeck and Chapman (2012) analysed the CSV activity of a collaboration of three Brazilian companies using the socio-eco-efficiency tool, focusing on creating value in the environmental fields. Pirson (2012) addresses the role of CSV for social entrepreneurs based on Porter and Kramer's (2011) assertion of social entrepreneurship as the basis of shared-value creation strategies. Based on the redefined relationship of CSV between business and society, Michelini (2012) identified ways in which to generate shared value in the low-income market. This was specified by Michelini and Fiorentino (2012) using two hybrid business models: the social and the inclusive business model.

Theoretical framework

This study intends to identify how a company transforms its CSR practices to CSV. What organizational components need to be changed to pursue CSV as a new business model, and what is the outcome of such a transformation? This study adopted the activity theory and the triple-helix theory to investigate such transformations in an organization.

Activity theory has been utilized as a useful explanation for elucidating different components of an activity and the relationship between them (Engeström, Miettinen, and Punamäki 1999; Uden, Aranda, and Pastor 2008). These components can influence the relationship between the subject and the object as well as the outcome of the activity. The triple-helix theory has been applied to explain the innovation process, in particular focusing on the interaction between the participating entities (Figure 1). This study postulates a transformation from CSR to CSV as an example of an 'activity' and understands the 'community', one of the components of the activity, using the triple-helix theory.

When considering the relationship among subjects, objects, and the surrounding circumstances of activity, activity theory is particularly prominent. It has been widely utilized in learning, education, human–computer interaction, and information system literature (Engeström 2001; Ditsa 2003; Wilson 2005). Bjørke (2004, 49) defined activity theory as one that 'emphasises goal-directed activities mediated by cultural tools and analysing contradictions and problems in activity systems'. Activity theory was also applied in a study to investigate the online community in digital life, and was used as a conceptual framework to explain combinations involving humans, technologies, and communities (Sam 2012).

Table 1 shows the components of the activity system. Engeström, Miettinen, and Punamäki (1999) visualized the relationship between the subject, object, and surrounding components using what is called an activity triangle. The constructs of this activity triangle are as follows. The subject in the activity is the main agent that performs the activity. The object is the purpose of the activity and it indicates the direction that the activity will take.

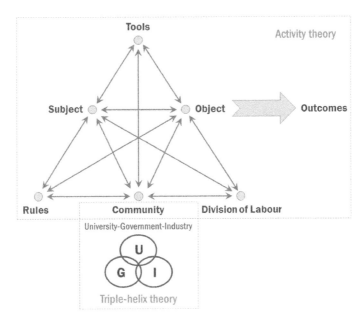

Figure 1. Theoretical framework.

Table 1. Components of the activity triangle.

Components	Definition
Subject	The principal agent that performs the activity in order to achieve the object
Object	The purpose of the activity suggesting the directions required to obtain the goal
Tools	The means by which the object is obtained
Community	The environment surrounding the activity triangle or the other participants within the activity system
Rules	The social norms or other norms that influence the components of the activity system
Division of labour	The specific division or divided tasks of the subject used to gain the object
Outcome	The obtained or projected consequences that result from the activity

Source: Modified from Engeström, Miettinen, and Punamäki (1999).

Tools can be used to interact with the object. The community is either the larger environment or the other activity systems that participate in the same activity. The rules influence the interactions between the subject, tools, community, and object. The division of labour is closely linked with the divided tasks of the subject as it attempts to achieve the object. The outcome is the desired result from the object.

Activity theory has been widely used in terms of the transformation process. When the relationship between the constructs in the activity system has to be changed, there are chances to reinterpret them (Blackler 1995). In his study, Louis (1980) contended that as the role of the constituents of an activity changes, a gap between the traditional role and a new one occurs. Thus, a new activity is required to fill in the gap. Jarzabkowski (2003, 50) also defined an activity theory to provide 'a dynamic view of strategic practices and their role in organizational continuity or change'.

Meanwhile, some previous studies address the transformation process in a societal or an organizational scope without an activity theory framework. These studies on societal transformation are mostly about the historical (e.g., Li 1992; Jürgens and Donaldson 2012), the political (e.g., Fletcher and Hurd 1998; Seeberg 2013), or the socially problematic issues (e.g., Hamilton and Flanagan 2007). Studies on organizational transformation are about the adoption of a new corporate strategy (e.g., Uys, Nleya, and Molelu 2004; Martincic 2010; Zakaria, Wan Yusoff, and Raja Madun 2012; Cil and Turkan 2013) or the identification of a suitable transformation framework (e.g., Nakhoda, Alidousti, and Fadaie 2011; Hewitt-Taylor 2013; Mitchell 2013). Most of the organizational studies mentioned above are mostly based on 'change management', defined as 'a structured approach for conducting a typical organization during its change process' (Nakhoda, Alidousti, and Fadaie 2011, 191), which emphasizes the instrumental and methodological view of transformation.

The activity theory, however, depicts the transformation process of each element that composes the transformed activity rather than the actual steps of transformation. As this study aims to identify the transformation process from CSR to CSV, it focuses on the elements of transformation such as the actors involved, the tools used, and the affected context; therefore, the activity theory framework by Engeström, Miettinen, and Punamäki (1999), who extended a study of Vygotsky (1978), was used to analyse the SRM activity in a food company.

In addition to activity theory, the triple-helix theory is also used to explain the transformation phenomena. The triple-helix theory explains the innovations among participating entities using a triple-helix spiral movement: industry, academia, and government. New roles and organizations are created at the intersection of the helixes, allowing for innovative knowledge production (Etzkowitz and Leydesdorff 2000). These intersections not only trigger the relationships between innovation entities, but also influence the environment surrounding the entities (Etzkowitz 2003). Particularly, the triple-helix model is a tool focused on the interaction between university and industry, and measures the level of network, which reflects governmental programmes, industrial innovative activities, and economic changes (Etzkowitz 2003; Inzelt 2004). Some studies refer to these levels of networks as 'regional innovation', and address the triple-helix theory as a model of analysis (e.g., Leydesdorff and Fritsch 2006; Lee, Lee, and Park 2010).

The framework of the triple-helix theory is used in this study to explain the transformation from the perspective of the community involved. Indeed, we posit the content of the SRM activity to be changed according to the role and scope of the community, such as a university, government, and industry.

Research questions

As suggested by previous studies, CSR activity has been transformed to CSV as a new practice. This study examines the effect of such transformations on the supplier–buyer relationship, which results in forming mutual firm foundations, long-term contracts, and temporal relations. Related case studies are rarely found, as suggested earlier in the literature review; therefore, discovering related case and conduct case studies regarding the transformation of a non-market strategy is critical. The aim of this study can be achieved by answering three research questions on the basis of the theoretical framework discussed earlier.

The previous studies investigated in the literature review point out the importance of sustainable CSR (e.g., Hildebrand, Sen, and Bhattacharya 2011). Nonetheless, due to the nature of CSR, which primarily aims to behave socially, there is the limitation to create business value; thus, the company transforms non-market strategy towards CSV, which pursues both social and business values, based on their core competencies or activities. The investigation into what makes a company's non-market strategy transform from CSR to CSV should be preceded to expand on the understanding of this phenomenon. To evaluate the influence of the transformed non-market strategy in a specific business activity, the activity classification (e.g., temporal relation, long-term contract, or mutual firm foundation) for each stage of transformation is needed. In this study, the SRM is selected as a unit of analysis due to the critical and enlarging role of suppliers in food companies (Van der Valk and Wynstra 2005). Moreover, the exploration of the outcome from classified SRM activity is needed.

- RQ1: What makes the SPC Group's non-market strategy transform from CSR to CSV?
- RQ2: What are the ramifications of this transformation, especially on the SRM actions of the SPC Group, such as mutual firm foundations, long-term contracts, and temporal relations?
- RQ3: What are the different outcomes produced by the various types of CSR/CSV-related SRM actions of SPC Group towards farmers?

In order to achieve the goal of this study, a case study method is used from one of the leading bakery companies in the Asia-Pacific area, the SPC Group, where the transformation from CSR to CSV occurred. While investigating the SPC Group's case, practices about the transformation from CSR to CSV were observed in their SRM activity. This activity was examined with a theoretical framework to solve the suggested research questions. The SPC Group's current business practices were explored earlier in order to detail investigation.

The SPC Group

The SPC Group is the largest, worldwide bakery franchise in Korea, with more than 5000 stores in the domestic and global market. The SPC Group has undergone a rapid growth in sales, reaching 3.4 billion USD in 2012 (Figure 2).

The SPC Group is a comprehensive food company relating to food and beverages, with 26 subsidiaries. There are bakery franchise brands (e.g., Paris Baguette, Paris Croissant),

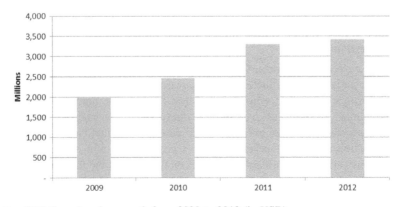

Figure 2. SPC Group's sales growth from 2009 to 2012 (in USD).

Table 2.   The state of Paris Baguette's domestic and overseas stores in 2012.

Area	Number of stores	Locations
Korea (domestic)	3215	Seoul, Pusan, Daegu, etc.
North America	24	Los Angeles, Santa Clara, Manhattan, Fort Lee, etc.
Asia-Pacific	112	Beijing, Shanghai, Nanjing, Ho Chi Minh City, Singapore, etc.

Table 3.   The state of SPC Group's Foodbank donations (in USD).

Year	2005	2006	2007	2008	2009	2010	2011	2012	Total
Amount	14,167	30,000	40,000	51,667	68,333	68,333	93,333	33,333	399,167

bakery production brands (e.g., Samlip, Shany), a coffee and doughnut brand (Licensed Dunkin Donuts), an ice cream brand (Licensed Baskin Robbins), restaurants (e.g., Lagrillia, Queens Park), and many other brands as well.

Moreover, the SPC Group has expanded its branches into the global market, including the USA, China, Singapore, and Vietnam. For instance, the main brand of the SPC Group, Paris Baguette, has expanded globally with 136 stores overseas (Table 2).

SPC, as a leading food company in Korea, has been under pressure to actively pursue its CSR programme for the benefit of society and its stakeholders. In order to meet those social demands, various types of CSR activities were conducted. For instance, in 2012, there were scholarship programmes for part-time workers who are students, baking education for disabled youths, donations through Foodbank, etc. The SPC Group's CSR activity expanded with time, as shown in Table 3, which is an example of the Foodbank donation. The detailed CSR activity conducted in 2012 is provided in Appendix 1.

Despite the initial success in CSR, the demands towards social responsibility continue to increase. Recently, the National Commission for Corporate Partnership (NCCP) of Korea has classified the bakery category as a 'SME-Suitable Business', which designates some businesses to be reserved for small and medium enterprises, and recommends that the major enterprises refrain from opening new stores. The objective of this administrative disposition is to protect minor enterprises from overheated competition by holding back large companies, which have a larger price power. Since the SPC Group is classified as a large company, they are prohibited from expanding their franchises and they are not allowed to open stores within 500 meters (1640 feet) of existing bakeries. In addition, the SPC Group's growth is limited to 2% of the total number of stores that they operated in the previous year.

It is evident that the SPC Group faces the challenge of social pressure while simultaneously pursuing an increase in business value. The SPC Group is confronted with transforming its existing non-market strategy to meet social demands.

Research model

Based on the employed theoretical framework (Figure 1), a research model (Figure 3) has been developed to propose changes in the outcomes when shifting a non-market strategy from CSR to CSV.

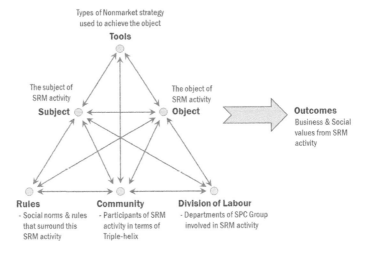

Figure 3.   Research model.

In particular, the SRM activity of the SPC Group is used as a unit in the analysis based on the activity theory and the triple-helix theory. The SPC Group, the subject of this SRM activity, manages its supplier relationship by encouraging suppliers to behave socially responsible (object) within a social norm and within the rules that surrounds this activity. This relationship between the subject and the object is mediated by tools, community, and the division of labour. Non-market strategy types, such as CSR and CSV, are used as a tool to encourage socially responsible behaviour. Other participants involved in SPC's SRM are referred to as the community. The community includes connections with the government, universities, or other industry entities. The division of labour is related to the departments that the SPC Group are involved with.

Methodology

An exploratory case study is conducted, since the current study aims to gain insights into the transformation of non-market strategy from CSR to CSV. Due to the novelty of the concept of 'CSV' both in academia and in the field, a case-based approach is used in this study. The case study is considered as a useful tool to explore a little known or poorly understood phenomenon (Kumar 2011) and is suitable to investigate changes over time as the result of certain circumstances or interventions (Leedy and Ormrod 2005).

This approach consists of two consecutive phases. The first phase aims to explore various SRM actions in the SPC Group; therefore, a focus group interview (FGI) with top management of the SPC Group was done twice from August to October 2012. An FGI is appropriate to expand on the existing knowledge in the field of study (Altintzoglou et al. 2012) and to gain multiple perspectives (Zikmund et al. 2012). To have a homogenous composition, only the top management personnel ($n = 6$) from the future strategy division and the divisions related to supplier management participated. Based on the results of the first FGI, which focused on a general discussion of the daily business activities, the second FGI addressed the details of each SRM action. Each focus-group session was moderated by one of the authors. The moderator asked open-ended questions about SRM activity in Korea and followed up with some probing questions. Each interview lasted about 100 minutes at the SPC Group's office in Seoul, and the interviews were digitally recorded with the consent of the interviewees. The recorded data were transcribed verbatim by a research assistant to extract quotes for selecting suitable SRM examples for each level of CSV.

The second phase includes the main interviews with the employees from the SPC Group. Each interviewee selected for this study met two criteria: (1) they had been in the business for more than 15 years and (2) they were involved in one of the SRM actions selected from the previous FGI. The purpose of these interviews was to gain richer and deeper information about each SRM action. Hence, an in-depth interview method was chosen, since it is advantageous for studying a unique basis or an unusual phenomenon, and it provides insight into a particular individual without any social effects (Zikmund et al. 2012). To attenuate the limitation of generalization and to minimize the personal bias, three or four employees from different departments (e.g., purchasing, social responsibility, marketing, strategic management, and a new business development department) were interviewed on a one-on-one basis for a case. Eight interviews were conducted in Korean at the SPC Group's office in Seoul. Each interview lasted 90–120 minutes, and the interviews were recorded with the interviewees' consent. After encouraging the respondents to speak freely about the background of each case, some open-ended questions were asked based on activity theory components, which took into account the 'tools' used to behave socially towards suppliers, the 'community', and the 'division labour' involved, and the 'outcome' of SRM was given. The reliability requirements were assured by using an identical protocol for each interview (Testa 2011). The protocol included an identical checklist of issues to cover all the components of the activity theory. The recorded data were transcribed verbatim by a research assistant to extract quotes. The detailed issues used in the in-depth interviews are explained as follows.

Subject, object and rules

The SPC Group (subject) manages supplier relationships in order to behave as socially responsible (object) within a specific social norm context (rules). The selected examples already address the SPC Group's SRM activity within the societal environment of the increase in demand on corporate strategies. Thus, factoring in the stakeholders, these three components are considered as constants in this research.

Tools

The non-market strategies used for SPC's SRM activity are considered as 'tools' to achieve the object of socially responsible behaviour. It is categorized with the CSR and CSV perspectives, positing four levels of shared value (Table 4). The CSR perspective, known as a representative non-market strategy (Baron and Diermeier 2007), is included as level 0 based on earlier literature on the movement of CSR towards CSV. Three levels of

Table 4.   Levels of shared value.

Levels of shared value	CSR/CSV	Definitions
0	CSR	Activities assuming and fulfilling social responsibilities
1	CSV	Reconceiving product and markets
2	CSV	Redefining productivity in the value chain
3	CSV	Enabling cluster development

the method to pursue shared value opportunities are included after Porter et al.'s (2012) definitions. To judge and assure the level of shared value is created for each case, an open-ended response query about the process of each case is asked: 'Explain the detailed process of this SRM action'. It is then followed by probing questions such as 'Is the relationship with the supplier temporal or long-term?' and 'What does the SPC Group do to improve the quality of supplied raw materials?'

Community

Communities that participate in SRM activity are asked: 'Other than the SPC Group, which entity participated?' The communities involved can be categorized based on the triple-helix theory, where universities or institutes are classified as 'University', government or a government-affiliated organization as 'Government', and private profit organizations as 'Industry'.

Division of labour

To accomplish socially responsible behaviour, the process is split into several steps. The relevant labours of the SPC group relating to each case are asked: 'Which departments are involved in this SRM action?' The labour was segmented into departments or the teams in the SPC group, such as marketing, purchasing, strategic management, and social responsibility departments.

Outcomes

The outcome of SRM activity is divided into two categories of social and business value, based on Porter's definition of CSV. To measure the outcomes, the triangulation approach is used, allowing for the increase in internal validity (Leedy and Ormrod 2005), in-depth interview, and survey method. Respondents are initially asked to answer questions on each outcome, and construct it in a form of open-ended questions through in-depth interviews. Then, a detailed survey in each prior open-ended question was given with a simple attitude scales of 'yes or no', since the concept of 'CSV' is only recently an emergent term in academia and in the field. Respondents were asked to check 'yes' when such outcome is revealed in a given SRM action; therefore, each outcome constructs were measured with the number of existing outcomes in the SPC Group. Constructs of the outcomes and their detailed questions were operationalized with the categorization of value chain (Porter and Millar 1985), and the levels of shared values (Porter and Kramer 2011) (Appendix 2). To verify if constructs (e.g., social outcome, business outcome) have equivalent concepts cross-culturally (English-Korean), the data were compared with Porter et al.'s (2012) study; the outcomes showed that the constructs have equivalent concepts.

To measure business outcome, some constructs from the value chain (i.e., margin and procurement) of the SPC Group were used. The 'margin' of the SPC Group was chosen to measure the direct effect of the transformation. The detailed items of 'procurement' were selected as its process in a food company is closely related to suppliers. Furthermore, the outcome items based on Porter and Kramer's (2011) three levels of CSV are developed. In terms of social outcomes, only the supplier and their community welfare were measured to focus on SRM action. Margin, infrastructure, R&D, logistics, and production related outcomes were questioned based on the value chain of the supplier. The questions relating to the margin of the supplier were constructed to measure the direct effect of the change.

Some of the support activities, infrastructure, and R&D are those that are mostly related to suppliers' competence. Similarly, logistics and production in primary activities were selected with detailed measures. Among the three levels of CSV, the 'local cluster' is selected due to its closeness with social outcomes of suppliers.

Data analysis

To explore the transformation process of non-market strategies, we examined the SPC Group's SRM actions. An activity can be achieved through a variety of actions (Uden, Aranda, and Pastor 2008). Three distinguishing actions are discovered from the SRM activity: temporal relationships, long-term contracts, and mutual firm foundations (Table 5). Operations that may contribute to a variety of actions are out of focus and are hence excluded from analysis.

In this section, we explored four actions of SRM in the SPC Group (subject) in which socially responsible behaviour (object) is accomplished within a constant norm (rule), in order to explore the transformation process of non-market strategies. After describing the components of each actions of the SRM activity (Table 6), the specific SRM actions are used and its outcomes are discovered from each case (Table 7).

Donation to the local community

To maintain its place in the bakery franchise industry in Korea, the SPC Group diversified its product lines using various types of raw materials. The purchase of mini-apple from the Young-Cheon district, as one example, started in 2012. The marketing team emphasized the name of district when they promoted new products using mini-apple. It is enhanced by CSR activity, where the donation to the district's scholarship committee was accumulated from the 10% of profit margin of selling mini-apple-used bakery products.

Since this donation is part of the reverting of wealth to society, it does not directly influence a firm's revenue, but it is perceived as CSR. The SPC Group obtains a temporal relationship with the supplier, mainly expecting social outcomes. Government organizations, such as the Young-Cheon district's scholarship committee, are involved in terms of community. From the SPC Group, only the marketing team attends this activity in order to promote products.

S-Dairy Foods Foundation

The baking industry, the core competences of the SPC Group, is considered as being paired with the dairy industry. The social needs for high-quality dairy products and internal corporate demands for diversification have increased. Since the SPC Group had no prior experience in the dairy products business, they decided to establish a joint venture named 'S-Dairy Foods' in 2011 with the College of Agriculture and Life Sciences in Seoul National University (SNU), where R&D competency is accumulated. So as to be supplied

Table 5. Three levels of SRM activity.

Activity	Supplier relationship management (SRM)		
Action	Temporal relation	Long-term contract	Mutual firm foundation
Operation		N/A	

Table 6. Activity components of the four supplier relationship management actions.

Case	Subject	Object	Norm	Tools	Community	Division of labour
Donation to the local community	SPC Group	Socially responsible behaviour	Increase in preference on local agricultural products	CSR (Level 0)	G	Marketing division
S-Dairy Foods Foundation				CSV (Level 1)	I–U	Purchase division Marketing Division New business development team
Local wheat purchase			Increase in demand on corporate strategy considering its stakeholders	CSV (Level 2)	I – G	Purchase division Marketing division Mildawon (milling factory)
S-Farm Foundation				CSV (Level 3)	I–U–G	Purchase division Marketing division Future strategy division New business development team

Note: G – government, I – industry, U – university.

Table 7. Outcomes of four SRM actions.

Supplier relationship management actions in the SPC group	Date started	Types of supplier relationship management actions	Business value					Social value			
			Profit (5)	Proc (3)	Prod/market (5)	Efficiency (5)	Local cluster (2)	Profit (4)	Infra/R&D (5)	Logis/prod (4)	Local cluster (5)
Donation to the local community	2012	Temporal relations						3	2 Increased local welfare	0	2
S-Dairy Foods Foundation	2011	Long-term contract	5 Increased brand equity Increased revenue Pioneered new product lines High-quality milk products (milk, yogurt)	2	4	0	2	4 Improved farmer incomes Improved production skills Increased productivity	4	2	1
Local wheat purchase	2008	Long-term contract	5 Increased brand equity Increased revenue Pioneered new product lines (local wheat made bakery) Secured supply structure (local wheat) Increased efficiency in procurement	3	3	5	2	4 Improved farmer incomes Improved production skills Increased productivity Reduced cost of production and logistics	5	4	4
S-Farm Foundation	2012	Mutual firm	N/A Increased brand equity Increased revenue Secured supply of optimized raw materials Increased efficiency in procurement	N/A	N/A	N/A	N/A	N/A Improved farmer incomes Improved production skills Increased productivity Reduced cost of production and logistics Increased local welfare	N/A	N/A	N/A

with higher quality raw milk, S-Dairy Foods contracted Cargill AgriPurina to develop a customized stock feed product that is based on SNU's consultation on the feed management system. Local dairy farmers produce raw milk with SNU's technical support and optimize the stock feed product. The entire quantity of raw milk supplied to the SPC Group under the yearly contract is with S-Dairy Foods.

They create shared values by launching new dairy products, which reconceive the market and satisfy customer needs following the CSV level 1. The university (SNU) and industry (Cargill AgriPurina and local dairy farmers) participated in terms of community. Since SPC is concerned with new business product development, SPC's new business development team involves the division of labour with the marketing and purchasing divisions.

Local wheat purchase business

In 2008, the SPC Group paid attention to the country of origin of major raw material, wheat. Existing bread products were entirely made from imported wheat due to the low self-sufficiency rate of wheat in Korea. Moreover, the social demands increased for local wheat products, which were perceived as healthy food. Initially, the group pursued business value through the launch of new products using local wheat, and social value through revitalization of the local wheat industry. To stabilize the supply chain of local wheat, a yearly contract was made between Mildawon, a milling factory owned by the SPC Group, and local wheat farmers. With produced flour, the R&D team in the SPC Group developed compatible flour for baking. The consistent quality of wheat can be supplied, since the cooperation with Rural Development Administration of Korea, a government agency, is developing new breeds of wheat that are appropriate for making baked products.

The group started to purchase local wheat, and moved to level 2 of CSV. The shared value is created by obtaining economies of scale in the local wheat procurement process. As a community, the government participates to develop a new breed of wheat, and local farmers are involved in wheat production. Labour is composed of the purchasing, marketing divisions, R&D team, and Mildawon.

S-Farm Foundation

The firm confronted the increased need for stably priced and customized raw materials for their bakery products. Thus, the SPC Group founded a mutual firm named 'S-Farm' with the local agricultural cooperation and SNU. The critical point of a 'mutual firm' is the actual ownership of investors: SPC Group, the local agricultural cooperation, and SNU. Local farmers who are affiliated with the agricultural cooperation produce customized raw materials for the SPC Group under the yearly contract with S-Farm. In order to maintain a stabilized production, SNU supports technical issues and certificate agricultural products of the S-Farm. The SPC Group takes charge of the purchasing, processing, and distribution of products. Although the local government does not have the ownership of S-farm, it supports with tax benefits or land rent.

Since it was founded in December 2012, it is difficult to measure the outcomes. The SPC Group expects to create a shared value of level 3 through developing local clusters, especially by collaborating with communities such as the local government, the agricultural cooperation, and SNU. In terms of the division of labour, the future strategy division's involvement is critical, which presents a long-term oriented business model that is relative to other SRM actions.

Summary of the SPC Group's supplier relationship management activity

Since the SRM actions develop from temporal relationships into long-term contracts or a mutual firm foundation, the non-market strategy's level increases from CSR to a higher level of CSV. Also, the scope of the community enlarges. In the case of temporal relationships, only the government participates, but within the long-term contracts, suppliers (I) and other organizations such as the university (U) or the government (G) get involved. In a mutual firm foundation, industry, the university, and the local government (I–U–G) participate in creating backgrounds for the triple-helix innovation. Labour is increasingly divided into several segments involving more departments of the SPC group. Only the marketing division is involved in temporal relationship actions. However, as the relationships become deeper, the participation scope enlarges to the purchasing division, the new business development team, or the future strategic team.

The outcomes are divided into two values based on CSV (Table 7). Since temporal relationships use CSR as a tool, only an increase in local welfare of social value is observed. Nevertheless, a long-term contract with suppliers creates value in both business and society. In terms of social value, there is an improvement in the supply structure, the farmer's income, etc. Concerning business value, the change in tools from CSR to CSV indicates an obvious difference. When CSR is used, there is no direct business value created, since it is mainly used as a source of marketing. Nonetheless, when CSV is used, business value is created, such as increased revenues or brand equity.

The S-Farm case's outcome is hard to measure since it was established in late 2012; however, an increase in value creation can be expected. Level 3 of CSV was used by establishing a mutual firm to develop a local cluster. The SPC Group, university, and local farmers have mutually invested and have 'ownership' of the S-farm. Local farmers, especially, participate as an agricultural cooperative federation, which enables more equivalent governance. This firm is a result of the collaboration of SPC–SNU–local farmers in a triple-helix perspective and is expected to trigger regional resilience. After Christopherson, Michie, and Tyler (2010), a resilient region is not just about short-term economic success, but also about maintaining values over the long term in a rapidly changing environment, which is related to the mutual firm foundation.

Discussion

Summary of findings

Three research questions summarize the findings in this study. The first question, 'What makes a company's non-market strategy transform from CSR to CSV?' can be related to social backgrounds relating to 'rules' of activity theory. In Korean society, there is an increased demand to implement corporate strategies considering stakeholders. Despite several CSR activities (Appendix 1) to cope with, society's demands gradually increase. For instance, in early 2013, the NCCP of Korea designated the bakery franchise as 'a business reserved for small and medium enterprises' and recommended larger companies to refrain from opening new stores. Since the SPC Group has a strong will to overcome these difficulties, they tried to launch a new business model that creates value within the company's value chain in order to enhance the sustainability of socially responsible behaviour. In other words, the SPC realized the initial limitation of CSR strategy, in which only the social demands are met, and gradually changed its non-market strategies to CSV. One of their approaches was seizing upon the customer demand for local agricultural products and focused on managing the 'suppliers'.

The detailed circumstances of each case are as follows. The donation to the local community begun as part of their philanthropic actions, which is a CSR approach, and the donation was used as a source of marketing the SPC Group. The CSV approach concentrates on finding the intersection between social and business needs. First, the S-Dairy Foods was founded due to the increase in social demands for high-quality dairy foods and the increase in business demands for product diversification. Second, local wheat purchase action was started within the increasing social demands. The self-sufficiency rate of wheat was only about 1–2%, and local wheat was considered as a healthy food ingredient. Also, the SPC Group needed to stabilize the wheat supply chain, which was all imported. Lastly, the S-Farm was founded using the supplier's demands for the stable sales network and also the SPC Group's demands for optimized food ingredients.

Here the question arises: why and what happens to 'SRM'? This is related to the second research question: 'What are the ramifications of the non-market strategy transformation on SRM?' The SRM sector is addressed based on the importance of suppliers in the food industry. The role of the supplier became critical as their involvement in the food industry enlarges, such as consulting new product development (Van der Valk and Wynstra 2005). Since suppliers are major stakeholders of priority control for the food industry, this study focuses on the SRM activity. Thus, the SRM actions in the SPC Group that purposes to behave as socially responsible are investigated using activity theory in order to find variations. As a result, there are variations in the three components of SRM activity: the tools used, the surrounding community, and the divisions of labour. Moreover, there were changes in the types of SRM activity itself, such as temporal relationships, long-term contracts, and mutual firm foundation.

The higher the level of the non-market strategies pursued, the greater the depth of the relationships between the SPC Group and its suppliers. Moreover, the scope of the involved community or the involved internal departments of the SPC Group increases. The temporal relationship is generally found in the SPC Groups' CSR actions, such as donations to the local community. Since it is a temporal relationship, fewer external communities and internal departments are involved. Long-term contracts involve a deeper relationship between the supplier and buyer, which were found in the CSV approach. Thus, more external and internal actors are involved. A mutual firm foundation was also found in the CSV approach, but the level of involvement differed; suppliers actually have 'ownership' of the mutual firm. The result shows larger community involvement, such as from the university, industry, and the government. Also, in terms of internal actors, purchase, marketing, future strategy, and new business development divisions were also involved.

The last research question is 'What are the different outcomes produced from various types of CSR/CSV-related SRM actions?' As explained earlier, the deeper relationship actions, such as a mutual firm, allow for the increase in involvement of participants, and the increase in business and social values. There is also an increase in business value, such as company revenue, efficiency, and product lines. Also, an increase in social values exists with improvements in local welfare, incomes, skills, and productivity. Moreover, the larger community involves the SRM case, where longer relationships exist. Especially, the last case about the mutual firm foundation is expected to increase business and social outcomes when compared to other forms of SRM. The mutual firm leads to the longer relationship between the suppliers and the firm, stabilizing the creation of business and social values. Suppliers, the food company, university, and the local government mutually cooperate to form a triple-helix network. Hence, a mutual firm can be considered as the typical form of SRM action that enhances CSV level 3, developing a local cluster, with triple-helix innovations and ultimately allowing regional resilience.

Theoretical contributions

First of all, this study is one of the first investigations that examine CSV-related SRM activity. In the prevalent literature, studies on CSV are rarely conducted, and their covered areas are limited to those of environment (e.g., Spitzeck and Chapman 2012), social entrepreneurship (e.g., Pirson 2012), or the low-income market (e.g., Michelini 2012; Michelini and Fiorentino 2012). This study especially examines the relationship between buyer and supplier, focusing on the food industry where the supplier plays a major role.

Then, this study identified the different organizational components between CSR and CSV, from the perspective of the relationship management. These differences explain the transformation process from CSR to CSV. There was no study addressing the transformation of the non-market strategy, particularly with the perspective of elements of activity (i.e., subject, object, community). This study especially addresses the components that constitute the CSV and also the outcome of the CSV. Four actions of SRM activity indicate that there are different components involved, in terms of the tools used, the community, and the departments of the SPC Group involved.

The second aspect is the focus on identifying components of a CSR/CSV related to SRM by using activity theory. Since activity theory is a framework used to examine continuity and a change in the patterns of activity (Jarzabkowski 2003), it is appropriate to explain the transformation process of SRM actions. This study especially addresses the components that constitute the CSV and also the outcome of CSV. The four actions of SRM activity indicate that there are different components involved, in the terms of tools used, community, and the departments of the SPC Group involved.

The third aspect is about the use of activity theory for the organizational transformation process. It has been mainly used in learning, education, human–computer interaction, and information system field (e.g., Engeström 2001; Ditsa 2003; Wilson 2005). This study extends the scope of its use to the examination of the transformation process in the corporate non-market strategy to the CSV. As a result, it was found that the activity theory is a relevant framework in explaining the transformation or change phenomena.

The measures of the CSV outcome from the SRM activity were primarily developed in this study for the first time. Even though Porter et al. (2012) suggested that the conceptual measuring process is based on three levels to create shared value, there is no study on measuring CSV directly. The measures that this study has developed include both social and business value related items that are associated with the value chain (Porter and Millar 1985) and the three levels of CSV (Porter and Kramer 2011).

Managerial implication

Porter's third level of CSV, and enabling local cluster development, is closely related to the context of Christopherson, Michie, and Tyler's (2010) achievement of regional resilience. Hence, the simultaneous creation of business and social value contributes to the achievement in regional resilience.

Many of the findings offer guidance to top management and SRM practitioners, establishing a new SRM activity that can enhance their bottom line and social outputs by using the CSV framework. This study can also be relevant to policy-makers interested in regional resilience through developing region/local clusters. Detailed descriptions are given, as a manual, on three actions representing the three ways of CSVs. In particular, this study provides detailed advice about which community or department in the company should participate as well as the types of relationships that should be developed with suppliers. This study concretely suggests an approach to obtain regional resilience from the perspective of the CSV by using the case study method. For example, if an organization plans to stabilize the supply chain or increase the overall quality of the raw material, there are long-term contract and mutual firm foundation options.

Furthermore, using the measure developed by this study, practitioners can evaluate their own businesses from the perspective of CSV. They can diagnose their current or new business models in order to identify the shared value created by them, for both business and society. The measures developed are especially appropriate to practitioners who try to produce the desired outcomes through collaboration with their suppliers. The measure can be modified for their own business forms. This self-evaluation enables an organization to assess the contribution and the performance of their CSV-related business model and enables them to make decisions on whether to increase the input resources. Assessments should be conducted regularly so that the company can monitor the balance in the CSV-related business model between social and business value.

From the perspective of a transformation process from CSR to CSV, this study provides a guideline on where to start. The findings show that while the transformation from CSR to a higher level of CSV occurs in an organization, proper change in management is needed. When designing an organization to transform, the misalignments of organizational components lead to a decrease in organizational performance (Burton, DeSanctis, and Obel 2006). Therefore, a proper phased transformation to reduce the risk is needed. Based on the activity theory framework, the elements of an SRM activity should be previously aligned in order to minimize the risk and the cost. For instance, the companies aiming to extend their non-market strategies to CSV level 2 by redefining productivity in the value chain should expand on the scope of the community (i.e., the university) or the internal divisions (i.e., R&D, production) involved, and should also enhance the relations with a supplier from the temporal relation to a long-term contract or a mutual firm foundation. This alignment process enables the minimization of risk and cost.

Limitations and future research directions

Some limitations and related future research directions are enumerated as follows. The generalization of this study is limited, due to the nature of the case study method being used and the novelty of the CSV concept. To attenuate the limitation, each of the actions is thoroughly investigated by interviewing three to four employees from various departments, allowing for the increase of external validity. A follow-up study would be to enlarge the samples from food companies that have implemented a non-market strategy relating to their core competencies concerning suppliers. The results can be tested empirically with a larger number of samples to justify the generalization.

Moreover, the actions about the SRM of the food industry limit the generalization of the findings. Even though suppliers in food industry are enlarging their roles and responsibilities (Van der Valk and Wynstra 2005), the food industry is widely known as a relative low-tech industry (Hulme 2005), which has largely differed aspects from the high-tech industry. Future study should widen the scope to cover other industries, such as the high-tech industry.

Lastly, the outcomes of CSV-related actions are measured within a subjective perspective. The questionnaire was developed and modified with a value chain process of suppliers and corporations, which can limit the scope of 'social value'. As addressed in the discussion, a sophisticated SRM action, such as a mutual firm foundation, leads to local cluster development, resulting in regional resilience (Christopherson, Michie, and Tyler 2010), which means more than just a supplier's value. Therefore, a follow-up study should include factors enabling 'regional resilience', such as a modern productive infrastructure, a skilled workforce, and a supportive financial system.

Conclusion

CSV is suggested as a new paradigm, which enables the creation of social and business values simultaneously. Differing with CSR, CSV enhances and uses the corporation's core competencies to create shared value. Focusing on the food industry, where the supplier plays an important role, this study proposed a theoretical framework, considering SRM as a unit of activity using activity theory to observe the transformation of non-market strategy from CSR to CSV. Four SRM actions from a leading bakery franchise were addressed to see the changes of components that constitute SRM activity.

The third level of CSV by enabling local cluster development is compatible with the emerging issue of regional resilience achievement. This study proposes that regional resilience can be accomplished through CSV, where CSV can in turn be developed effectively within the triple helix framework. Thus, the policy roadmap from the triple helix to CSV and to regional resilience can be clarified. A mutual firm is suggested as a representative form of CSV activity with a triple-helix innovation structure that accomplishes regional resilience.

In addition, this finding presents the immense opportunity for firms to discover competitive advantages. Friendly business ecosystems and platforms have been regarded as the core source and capability about the competitive advantage of firms (Moore 2006). Firms can build powerful and legitimate ecosystems by combining and seeking regional resilience and the triple helix. More specifically, ecosystems can apparently be built by contributing regional resilience through CSV designed upon the triple helix, such as a mutual firm foundation. Thus, firms should no longer regard regional resilience, CSV, and the triple helix as separate, and integrated strategies are required.

References

Altintzoglou, Themistoklis, Helen Nøstvold Bjørg, Mats Carlehög, Morten Heide, Jens Østli, and Finn-Arne Egeness. 2012. "The Influence of Labelling on Consumers' Evaluations of Fresh and Thawed Cod Fillets in England." *British Food Journal* 114 (11): 1558–1570.

Baron, David P., and Daniel Diermeier. 2007. "Introduction to the Special Issue on Nonmarket Strategy and Social Responsibility." *Journal of Economics and Management Strategy* 16 (3): 539–545.

Barone, Michael J., Anthony D. Miyazaki, and Kimberly A. Taylor. 2000. "The Influence of Cause-Related Marketing on Consumer Choice: Does One Good Turn Deserve Another?" *Journal of the Academy of Marketing Science* 28 (2): 248–262.

Bjørke, SvenÅke. 2004. "The Concepts of Communities of Practice, Activity Theory and Implications for Distributed Learning." *Artikler om høgskolepedagogikk* 49.

Blackler, Frank. 1995. "Knowledge and the Theory of Organizations: Organizations as Activity Systems and the Reframing of Management." *Journal of Management Studies* 30 (6): 864–884.

Bowen, Howard Rothmann. 1953. *Social Responsibilities of the Businessman*. New York: Harper.

Burton, Richard M., Gerardine DeSanctis, and Borge Obel. 2006. *Organizational Design: A Step-by-Step Approach*. New York: Cambridge University Press.

Christopherson, Susan, Michie Jonathan, and Peter Tyler. 2010. "Regional Resilience: Theoretical and Empirical Perspectives." *Cambridge Journal of Regions, Economy and Society* 3 (1): 3–10.

Cil, Ibrahim, and Yusuf S. Turkan. 2013. "An ANP-Based Assessment Model for Lean Enterprise Transformation." *The International Journal of Advanced Manufacturing Technology* 64 (5–8): 1113–1130.

Ditsa, George, ed. 2003. "Activity Theory as a Theoretical Foundation for Information Systems Research." In *Activity Theory as a Theoretical Foundation for Information Systems Research*, 192–231. Wollongong: University of Wollongong.

Engeström, Yrjö. 2001. "Expansive Learning at Work: Toward an Activity Theoretical Reconceptualization." *Journal of Education and Work* 14 (1): 133–156.

Engeström, Yrjö, Reijo Miettinen, and Raija-Leena Punamäki. 1999. *Perspectives on Activity Theory*. Cambridge: Cambridge University Press.

Etzkowitz, Henry. 2003. "Innovation in Innovation: The Triple Helix of University-Industry-Government Relations." *Social Science Information* 42 (3): 293–337.

Etzkowitz, Henry, and Loet Leydesdorff. 2000. "The Dynamics of Innovation: From National Systems and 'Mode 2' to a Triple Helix of University–Industry–Government Relations." *Research Policy* 29 (2): 109–123.

Fletcher, Bill, and Richard W. Hurd. 1998. "Beyond the Organizing Model: The Transformation Process in Local Unions [Electronic Version]." In *Organizing to Win: New Research on Union Strategies*, http://digitalcommons.ilr.cornell.edu/articles/322/ edited by K. Bronfenbrenner, S. Friedman, R. W. Hurd, R. A. Oswald, and R. L. Seeber, 37–53. Ithaca, NY: ILR Press.

Fukukawa, Kyoko, John M. T. Balmer, and Edmund R. Gray. 2007. "Mapping the Interface between Corporate Identity, Ethics and Corporate Social Responsibility." *Journal of Business Ethics* 76 (1): 1–5.

Hamilton, Carmen, and Constance Flanagan. 2007. "Reframing Social Responsibility within a Technology-Based Youth Activist Program." *American Behavioral Scientist* 51 (3): 444–464.

Hewitt-Taylor, Jaqui. 2013. "Planning Successful Change Incorporating Processes and People." *Nursing Standard* 27 (38): 35–40.

Hildebrand, Diogo, Sankar Sen, and C. B. Bhattacharya. 2011. "Corporate Social Responsibility: A Corporate Marketing Perspective." *European Journal of Marketing* 45 (9–10): 1353–1364.

Hulme, George V. 2005. "Food Chain's Fear Factor." *InformationWeek* 1040: 39–41.

Inzelt, Annamária. 2004. "The Evolution of University–Industry–Government Relationships during Transition." *Research Policy* 33 (6): 975–995.

Jarzabkowski, Paula. 2003. "Strategic Practices: An Activity Theory Perspective on Continuity and Change." *Journal of Management Studies* 40 (1): 23–55.

Jürgens, Ulrich, and Ronnie Donaldson. 2012. "A Review of Literature on Transformation Processes in South African Townships." *Urban Forum* 23 (2): 153–163.

Kumar, R. 2011. *Research Methodology: A Step-by-Step Guide for Beginners*. Thousand Oaks, CA: Sage.

Lantos, Geoffrey P. 2001. "The Boundaries of Strategic Corporate Social Responsibility." *Journal of Consumer Marketing* 18 (7): 595–632.

Lantos, Geoffrey P. 2002. "The Ethicality of Altruistic Corporate Social Responsibility." *Journal of Consumer Marketing* 19 (3): 205–232.

Lee, Chul Woo, Jong Ho Lee, and Kyung Sook Park. 2010. "An Inquiry into the Triple Helix as a New Regional Innovation Model." *Journal of the Economic Geographical Society of Korea* 13 (3): 335–353.

Leedy, Paul D., and Jeanne Ellis Ormrod. 2005. *Practical Research: Planning and Design.* Upper Saddle River, NJ: Pearson Education.

Leydesdorff, Loet, and Michael Fritsch. 2006. "Measuring the Knowledge Base of Regional Innovation Systems in Germany in terms of a Triple Helix Dynamics." *Research Policy* 35 (10): 1538–1553.

Li, Peilin. 1992. "China in a Period of Social Transformation." *International Social Science Journal* 44 (3): 433–443.

Louis, Meryl Reis. 1980. "Surprise and Sense Making: What Newcomers Experience in Entering Unfamiliar Organizational Settings." *Administrative Science Quarterly* 25 (2): 226–251.

Maignan, Isabelle, and O. C. Ferrell. 2004. "Corporate Social Responsibility and Marketing: An Integrative Framework." *Journal of the Academy of Marketing Science* 32 (1): 3–19.

Martincic, Romana. 2010. "Change Management in Adult Educational Organizations: A Slovenian Case Study." *Managing Global Transitions* 8 (1): 79–96.

Michelini, Laura. 2012. *Social Innovation and New Business Models Creating Shared Value in Low-Income Markets.* Berlin: Springer.

Michelini, L., and D. Fiorentino. 2012. "New Business Models for Creating Shared Value." *Social Responsibility Journal* 8 (4): 561–577.

Mitchell, G. 2013. "Selecting the Best Theory to Implement Planned Change." *Nursing Management* 20 (1): 32–37.

Moon, Hwy-Chang, Jimmyn Parc, So Hyun Yim, and Nari Park. 2011. "An Extension of Porter and Kramer's Creating Shared Value (CSV): Reorienting Strategies and Seeking International Cooperation." *Journal of International and Area Studies* 18 (2): 49–64.

Moore, James F. 2006. "Business Ecosystems and the View from the Firm." *Antitrust Bulletin* 51: 31.

Nakhoda, Maryam, Sirous Alidousti, and Gholam Reza Fadaie. 2011. "Selecting an Appropriate Change Management Model for Iranian Academic Libraries Using MADM Methods." *Libri* 61 (3): 190–204.

Pirson, Michael. 2012. "Social Entrepreneurs as the Paragons of Shared Value Creation? A Critical Perspective." *Social Enterprise Journal* 8 (1): 31–48.

Porter, Michael E., Hills Greg, Marc Pfitzer, Sonja Patscheke, and Elizabeth Hawkins. 2012. *Measuring Shared Value: How to Unlock Value by Lining Social and Business Results*, FSG Report.

Porter, Michael E., and Mark R. Kramer. 2002. "The Competitive Advantage of Corporate Philanthropy." *Harvard Business Review* 80 (12): 56–68.

Porter, M. E., and M. R. Kramer. 2011. "Creating Shared Value." *Harvard Business Review* 89 (February): 62–77.

Porter, Michael E., and Victor E. Millar. 1985. "How Information Gives You Competitive Advantage." *Harvard Business Review* 63 (4): 149–160.

Sam, Cecile. 2012. "Activity Theory and Qualitative Research in Digital Domains." *Theory Into Practice* 51 (2): 83–90.

Seeberg, Peter. 2013. "The EU and Constitutionalism in Egypt: EU Foreign and Security Policy Challenges with a Special Focus on the Changing Political Setting in the MENA-region." *European Foreign Affairs Review* 18 (3): 411–428.

Spitzeck, Heiko, and Sonia Chapman. 2012. "Creating Shared Value as a Differentiation Strategy – The Example of BASF in Brazil." *Corporate Governance* 12 (4): 499–513. doi:10.1108/14720701211267838.

Szmigin, Isabelle, and Robert Rutherford. 2013. "Shared Value and the Impartial Spectator Test." *Journal of Business Ethics* 114 (1): 171–182.

Testa, Stefania. 2011. "Internationalization Patterns among Speciality Food Companies: Some Italian Case Study Evidence." *British Food Journal* 113 (11): 1406–1426.

Uden, Lorna, Pedro Jose Valderas Aranda, and Oscar Pastor. 2008. "An Activity-Theory-Based Model to Analyse Web Application Requirements." *Information Research* 13 (2): 1.

Uys, Philip M., Paul Nleya, and G. B. Molelu. 2004. "Technological Innovation and Management Strategies for Higher Education in Africa: Harmonizing Reality and Idealism." *Educational Media International* 41 (1): 67–80.

Van der Valk, Wendy, and Finn Wynstra. 2005. "Supplier Involvement in New Product Development in the Food Industry." *Industrial Marketing Management* 34 (7): 681–694.

Vygotsky, Lev. 1978. *Mind in Society*. Cambridge, MA: Harvard University Press.

Wilson, Tom D. 2005. "A Re-examination of Information Seeking Behaviour in the Context of Activity Theory." *Information Research* 11 (4): 1.

Zakaria, Sabarudin, W. Wan Yusoff, and R. Raja Madun. 2012. "Leadership Challenges during Change Transformation Process." *International Journal of Interdisciplinary Social Sciences* 6 (6): 223–232.

Zikmund, William G., Barry J. Babin, Jon C. Carr, and Mitch Griffin. 2012. *Business Research Methods*. Mason, OH: South-Western.

Appendix 1.   The SPC Group's CSR activities in 2012.

Name of CSR activity	Characteristics and outcomes
SPC & SOUL Happy bakery class	Cooperate with SOUL bakery factory run by disabled people, and aids with a bakery class with technical support
Happy Bakery & Cafe	Opens a bakery for trainees in SPC & SOUL Happy bakery class
Happy bread share car	Donate bakery products through Food Bank
Happy fund	Volunteer donation of SPC employees of 1000 KRW every month
Happy scholarship	Support 50% of tuitions of some students who work part-time in SPC franchise stores
Yeong-Cheon district's learning centre	Support construction of a learning centre for adolescent in Yeong-Cheon district
SPC happy Friday	Set every fourth Friday as a volunteer day
Happy pastiche academy	Run a bakery training programme for North Korean refugee adolescents or multicultural family adolescents
SPC & DAUM Happy birthday party	Support birthday parties of community child centres in remote areas

Appendix 2.   Questionnaire to measure social and business value.

Shared value	Value evaluation criteria	Questions
Business value	Margin	The sales increased
		The market shares increased
		Customer trust is obtained
		New customers are attracted
	Procurement	Supply uncertainty of raw materials is reduced
		Customized materials for company are supplied
		Risk is reduced through diversification of raw materials
	Redefine product/market	Discriminative/new product or service is launched
		New market is pioneered
		Price competitiveness is acquired
		New intellectual property is obtained
		Product quality is improved

(Continued)

Appendix 2 – (*Continued*)

Shared value	Value evaluation criteria	Questions
	Increase efficiency	Time/cost is saved
		Production cost is reduced
		Delivery cost is reduced
		Quality control efficiency is increased
		Manufacture/production efficiency is increased
	Developing local cluster	Distribution/storage/transportation infrastructure is constructed
		Brand value in local area is increased
Social value	Margin	Annual income is increased
		Delivery profit is relatively high
		Bargaining power of supplier is increased
		Stable selling channel is created
	Infrastructure/R&D	Technical education (cultivation, post-harvest management) accessibility is improved
		Market information accessibility is improved
		Production technology is enhanced
		Technical development cost is reduced
		Managerial capability is improved
	Logistics/production	Productivity is increased
		Quality level of products is enhanced
		Production cost is reduced
		Distribution/disposal cost is reduced
	Developing local cluster	Regional employment is created
		Inter-producer conflict in region is decreased
		Living/cultural amenity is increased
		Regional socio-economic status is advanced
		Regional socio-economic field of activity is broadening

Assessing the performance of co-operatives in Malaysia: an analysis of co-operative groups using a data envelopment analysis approach

Azmah Othman[a1], Norma Mansor[b] and Fatimah Kari[c2]

[a]Department of Development Studies, Faculty of Economics and Administration, University of Malaya, Kuala Lumpur, Malaysia; [b]Department of Administrative Studies and Politics, Faculty of Economics and Administration, University of Malaya, Kuala Lumpur, Malaysia; [c]Department of Economics, Faculty of Economics and Administration, University of Malaya, Kuala Lumpur, Malaysia

This study assesses the performance of co-operatives in Malaysia by evaluating 56 out of the 70 co-operative groups. The productivity and efficiency of the groups were evaluated in the first- and second-stage analysis by employing the data envelopment analysis and Tobit regression model. Despite the financial and non-financial support by the federal government and perceived significant role played by the co-operatives in the country's development, the findings indicate that the performance of co-operatives have not been satisfactory. Only 19.6% of the groups under study were found to be efficient and the 'big co-operatives' that comprise less than 2% of total co-operatives in the country dominated among the successful ones. The results endorse the general perception that co-operatives in Malaysia are facing challenges necessitating immediate attention.

1. Introduction

Although co-operatives were first introduced to Malaysia by the British colonial administration 90 years ago, they were not considered as a significant vehicle of economic growth in the national development plans. The primary objective of co-operatives then was to assist people in the rural areas to combat pervasive rural and urban indebtedness (Fredericks 1986). While the economic policies are dominated by neo-Keynesian philosophy, Malaysia believes in free market, focusing on private sector enterprise and since the mid-1980s on foreign direct investment to propel economic growth. Despite greater state involvement in the economy through the introduction of the New Economic Policy (1970–1990) with the twin objectives of eradicating poverty and restructuring of society with very strong identification of race with economic activities, social enterprises such as co-operatives were hardly viewed as one of the mechanisms to spur growth. However, in the Fourth Malaysia Plan (1981–1985), the role of the co-operative movement was recognized by the government as a third sector besides government and the private sector in contributing to the economy (Malaysia 1981). Nonetheless, no serious effort was made to the development of the co-operative sector per se. Post-1997 Asian Financial Crisis (AFC), when private investments plunged (National Economic Advisory Council 2010), the government began to consider co-operatives. However, it took a decade for the government to reform the institutional support for co-operatives by establishing a commission, the Malaysia Co-operative Societies Commission (MCSC), in 2008. The objective of the Commission is to ensure the stability and soundness of financial and management operations of co-operatives. However, the following questions remain. How sustainable are the co-operatives? Is the co-operative a suitable institution for development?

Hence, the objective of this paper is essentially to assess the performance of co-operatives in Malaysia. In keeping this objective in perspective, this paper aims to answer the following questions. How efficient are the co-operatives? Which co-operative is the most efficient and productive? What are the factors that influence the performance of co-operatives? The paper is organized as follows. The first section is the introduction, followed by the review of the literature. The third section provides an overview of the co-operative movement in Malaysia, the fourth part discusses the methodology employed in this study, followed by the deliberations on findings in part five; in part six are the discussions, and the final section highlights some theoretical and policy implications.

2. Literature review

Co-operatives are a user-owned, user-controlled enterprise that benefits its members on the basis of use (Zeuli and Cropp 2004). Past research on co-operatives by Birchall and Simmons (2004) had incorporated mutual incentive theory (MIT) in the study of members' participation. MIT stressed on the two social-psychological theories of motivation, namely individualistic and collectivistic values. A member's decision whether to participate or not in the co-operatives is influenced and motivated by considering both the positive (benefits and habits) incentives and the negative aspects (costs and satiation). An interaction between rewards (positive) and risks (costs), depending on the stronger (positive or negative) influence, would determine the member's final decision. Similarly, a member's participation in the co-operatives is driven by (collectivistic values) three variables: shared goals, shared values and sense of community. Birchall and Simmons (2004) conducted the study after a failed attempt in 1997 to demutualize the Co-operatives Wholesale Societies (CWS). Instead, it has led to the merger of the CWS and the Co-operatives Retail Services that formed the CWS Ltd in 2002 and currently is the biggest co-operatives with food retailing, department stores, banking, insurance, automotive sales and building services in Britain. Hence, co-operatives differ from other enterprises in their concept, organizational structure, governance and equity management (Frederick 1997; Zeuli and Cropp 2004).

There are more than 800 million people who are members of co-operatives around the world (International Co-operative Alliance 2010), thus indicating that co-operatives are relevant to the economic and social development of many countries. Various studies on the role of co-operatives in promoting community development and eradicating poverty confirm the importance of co-operatives (Birchall 2003, 2004; Birchall and Ketilson 2009; Birchall and Simmons 2008; Frederick 1997; Zeuli and Cropp 2004). Birchall highlighted the enormous potential of co-operatives in assisting the poor, especially in developed countries, but points out that successes in the developing countries were less evident with the exception of countries that had promoted the co-operative movement intensively.

Opinions regarding supportive public policies, efficiency and performance of co-operatives, however, have been mixed. Porter and Scully (1987) discuss the inefficiencies arising from public resources allocated to co-operatives in the USA. They noted that dairy co-operatives incurred costs (as an economic agent) and created control problems resulting in efficiency losses. Weak property rights structure was observed to be the cause of inefficiencies in co-operatives compared to non-co-operative firms. Cain, Toensmeyer, and Ramsey (1989), however, held the view that farmers' co-operatives were more beneficial in providing services than ordinary firms. Sexton and Iskow (1993), on the other hand, established that there is no conclusive evidence to fully support the notion that co-operatives are better organizations than investor-owned firms. However, they were convinced that as voluntary organizations, co-operatives played an important role in the development of the agricultural sector in the USA.

Efficiency measurement of firms based on production frontier with a non-parametric framework could be traced to the work of Farrell in 1957. Since then, data envelopment analysis (DEA) has been utilized successfully to appraise the performances of profit as well as non-profit organizations (Ramanathan 2003). Numerous studies apply DEA to examine the technical, cost and profit efficiency of financial institutions (Berger and Humphrey 1997; Emrouznejad, Parker, and Tavares 2008). Although there are studies on co-operatives, comparatively these are scarce. Lang and Welzel (1996), in conducting the analysis of 757 German co-operative banks from 1989–1992 data, discovered that smaller banks enjoy higher total factor productivity (TFP) growth in relation to bigger banks. Mergers of small inefficient banks were proposed to reap economies of scale and eliminate inefficiencies. However, their research on bigger German banks does not indicate any evidence of economies of scale. It was the external factors that influenced significantly the cost differences between high- and low-cost banks. It was noted that smaller banks were more responsive to input prices (Lang and Welzel 1998).

Two other investigations into efficiency of co-operatives that employed DEA were conducted by Fukuyama, Guerra, and Weber (1999) and Pasiouras, Sifodaskalakis, and Zopounidis (2007). Fukuyama's (1996) analysis of the Japanese Shinkin banks indicates that overall technical inefficiency was due to pure technical inefficiency and it improved as asset size of credit co-operatives increased. Fukuyama, Guerra, and Weber (1999) studied efficiency and productivity growth of Japan credit co-operatives from 1992 to 1996 with respect to types of ownership. The work by Pasiouras, Sifodaskalakis, and Zopounidis (2007) analysed the cost efficiency of the Greek co-operative banks by applying the two-stage DEA. It concluded that cost inefficiency was due to allocative and not technical inefficiency. Factors such as gross domestic product (GDP) per capita, unemployment rate and disposal income influenced the efficiency of banks. They noticed that the TFP experienced a small decrease and the relationship between size differences and productivity was not statistically significant (Pasiouras and Sifodaskalakis 2007).

Most of the DEA research on co-operatives has been conducted in the Western developed countries which have benefited the co-operative movement in developed and developing countries as lessons were drawn and good practices were replicated in different national settings. Malaysian researchers and academics are not attracted towards research on co-operatives. Although considerable amount of studies were done on other enterprises, organizations, financial institutions and banking industry in Malaysia, the interest in co-operatives is still lacking. Research on the Malaysian banks by Katib (1999), Dogan and Fausten (2003), Krishnasamy, Ridzwa, and Perumal (2003), Sufian (2004, 2006, 2007), Sufian and Ibrahim (2005) and Sufian and Abdul Majid (2007) highlighted the challenges faced by the banks but their analysis excluded co-operative banks and credit co-operatives. However, there were two other studies that included co-operative banks in their studies. One is by Othman (2010), which examined co-operative and conventional banks, using Malmquist productivity index, DEA. The study noted that the TFP of the co-operative bank (*Bank Kerjasama Rakyat* [Bank Rakyat]) improved by 28.2%. *Bank Rakyat* led in terms of improvement in productivity among all the 10 banks within the tenure of study. *Bank Rakyat* was able to utilize and capitalize on the improvements in technology.

The other study was by Islam (2012) who studied *Bank Rakyat* and National Savings Bank by employing financial ratios to compare the performance of both the banks in relation to the achievement of socio-economic development objectives of the country. The findings indicate that *Bank Rakyat* was more effective and efficient in the management of expenses and assets, and in generating income.

However, other studies on Malaysian co-operatives highlighted the challenges faced by co-operatives in Malaysia. First, most agricultural co-operatives in Malaysia do not work on their own co-operative farms but rely solely on government land development agencies such as the Federal Land Development Authority (FELDA) and the Federal Land Consolidation and Rehabilitation Authority (FELCRA) for contract work (such as harvesting, transporting harvest, irrigation and others) to generate income (Idris and Abdullah 2011). The work contracted out by FELDA involves large tracks of land which formed part of the land development scheme introduced by the government to address the plight of landless farmers. It provided a steady stream of income for the co-operatives as it involved the government. However, this study noted that co-operative sales were affected by insufficient supply of labour due to lack of interest among the younger generation in the agricultural co-operatives. The younger generation seems to be less interested in the community-type of work and prefer to be employed or pursue individual-oriented ventures (Idris and Abdullah 2011).

Another challenge is the lack of managerial capacity. A study by Ismail and Mohd Sarif (2010) discovered that there was knowledge gap with regard to global competition and suggested that co-operative managers be equipped with global managerial skills to face international challenges successfully. A study by Kaur et al. (2005) on co-operatives' workforce in Malaysia found that 61% of co-operatives do not have executive staff. Over 80% of these workers do not receive any co-operative training and lagged behind the employees of other organizations in career planning and development. Din (2006) analysed the efficiency of the Fishermen's Associations in Malaysia by applying DEA and concluded that co-operatives are beneficial as they provided both economic and social benefits to their members.

3. Co-operative development in Malaysia

Malaysian law defines co-operative as an organization consisting of individual persons with the objective of promoting the economic interest of its members in accordance with co-operative principles (Laws of Malaysia 2008).

The co-operative movement was introduced by the British colonial administration into Malaysia to address credit and indebtedness in the rural areas (Fredericks 1986). While employed as a tool to overcome the problem of indebtedness especially to middlemen, the co-operative movement was also viewed as self-help and became part of an integrated rural development by the indigenous government. Hence, co-operatives were encouraged among the peasants, farmers and fishermen. Similarly, in the urban areas, it started with the lower-level government servants and later among consumer societies. The direction of local co-operative movement appears to be in parallel with other international co-operatives' focus, which is the revitalization of the communitarian tradition (Borgaza and Spear 2004).

However, co-operatives have often been viewed as weak due to indebtedness and inefficient due to lack of managerial capacity as participation was voluntary. It was the Fourth Development Plan, 1981–1985, that recognized the co-operative movement as a vehicle for development. The launch of the National Co-operative Policy (NCP) in 2002 provided the movement a further boost. Among others, the policy includes the tightening of the co-operative's legislation to ensure better governance and management.

Co-operatives were given financial and non-financial support (related to management, audit and education) to enhance their development (Othman and Kari 2008). The government allocated RM 114.2 million[3] (2.23%) for co-operative development out of its total development expenditure of RM 51.3 billion in 2010 (MCSC 2010). In fact, Malaysia's favourable public policy towards co-operatives resembled the accommodative public policy in the USA and Western European countries (Sexton and Iskow 1993). The types of assistance provided by the government are as follows:

(1) Basic support (maximum RM 30,000.00) which includes:
   (i) Physical sub-assistance: This assistance involves the provision of basic infrastructure to the shop/business premises of co-operatives; and
   (ii) New co-operative sub-assistance: This assistance is provided to start business activities.
(2) Strengthening/stabilization assistance (maximum RM 300,000.00):
   (i) Co-operatives were given this assistance in the form of matching grant for the purpose of providing basic infrastructure, facilities and/or capital contributions in order to enhance or expand the existing activities.
   (ii) This assistance includes business premise renovations, purchase of business equipment, machinery and other facilities in line with the activities conducted according to respective sectors.
(3) Marketing assistance (maximum RM 300,000.00):
   (i) Co-operatives are given assistance to promote or advertise co-operative products or goods, collection and marketing of products in a systematic manner through branding, packaging, halal certification and also image building to enable co-operatives to penetrate a wider market.
(4) Research and development aid (maximum RM 300,000.00):
   (i) Co-operatives were given this assistance to conduct research and development activities on their products and services as recommended by Malaysian Agricultural Research and Development Institute and universities act as consultants.
(5) Strengthening the knowledge and skills of human capital among co-operative members. Co-operative's members and leaders undergo training and courses to learn co-operative principles, concepts and management.
(6) Promotion of co-operatives' activities and business through expos, exhibitions and carnivals.
(7) All grants or soft loans are charged at a low interest of 1–6% per annum depending on the activities and size of the loan.

Figures 1–4 show the development over the last two decades. There has been a continuous increase in the establishment of co-operatives in Malaysia. When the nation experienced economic growth in the 1990s, the co-operative movement grew at 3.5% a year, while membership, share capital and asset growth expanded at 3.2%, 9.93% and 11.42%, respectively. The movement was adversely affected by the 1997 AFC that hit Malaysia and other countries in the region. This was indicated by the decrease in growth rate compared to the previous period in terms of number of co-operatives, membership, share capital and assets. The total asset value fell by more than 4% to a mere 7% as compared to 11.42% in the earlier period. Co-operatives with investments in shares were also affected by the unanticipated financial bubble burst and were left financially

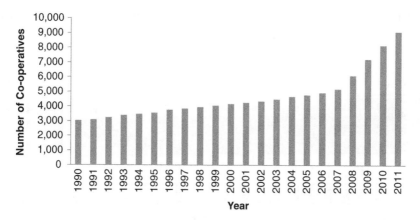

Figure 1. Number of co-operatives. *Source*: Monitoring Division, Malaysia Co-operative Societies Commission (MCSC), various years.

vulnerable with liquidity problems (Md. Salleh et al. 2008). Co-operatives that invested in shares and trust funds especially with borrowings from the private financial institutions suffered severely from the crisis. They faced liquidity problems but received assistance from the government to ease their financial problems. However, the improvements in the economy and the capital market have led to the recovery of the co-operatives.

The recovery years of the Malaysian economy from the AFC had witnessed growth in the movement. The movement started to record positive growth in terms of numbers, membership, shares and assets. The NCP (2002–2010) focused on co-operatives playing a bigger role in the economy especially towards poverty eradication, employment creation and business expansion. The development of co-operatives was further strengthened when the Department of Co-operative Development was upgraded into a commission, MCSC, in 2008. The second NCP (2011–2020) was launched and it focused on increasing co-operatives' participation in the wealth creation by strengthening co-operatives' capacity and capabilities, especially the managerial capabilities. The second NCP is in line with the new direction in Malaysia's development as envisaged in the New Economic Model,

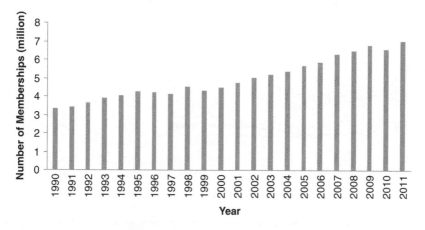

Figure 2. Number of memberships. *Source*: Monitoring Division, Malaysia Co-operative Societies Commission (MCSC), various years.

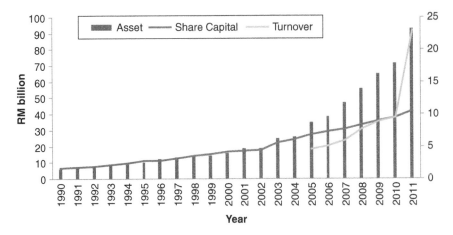

Figure 3. Share capital, asset and turnover. *Source*: Monitoring Division, Malaysia Co-operative Societies Commission (MCSC), various years. Note: Turnover data are not available before 2005.

introduced in 2010, which outlined specific strategic reform initiatives for Malaysia to progress to the next level of development as a high-income nation from its current middle-income status (National Economic Advisory Council 2010; Rodrigo and Mansor 2013). Although the NCP had been important in spurring rapid co-operative development, its effectiveness was limited, as despite the increase in number of co-operatives, the growth of membership, share capital and assets had decreased. Figure 1 indicates that in 2011 there were 9074 registered co-operatives. The movement had 7.04 million members, about 26% of the population, share capital amounting to RM 10.49 billion, total assets worth about RM 92.8 billion, turnover of RM 23.09 billion and profits of RM 2.62 billion (MCSC 2012).

Although Figure 4 shows that growth of co-operative turnover had decreased from 18% (2005–2009) to 11% (2009–2010) due to the global economic downturn but the rapid increase in 2011 was due to the change in the computation of the movement's assets

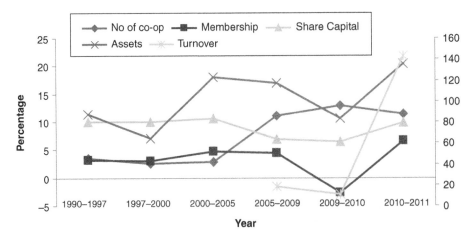

Figure 4. Growth trend of the co-operative movement in percentage. *Source*: Monitoring Division, Malaysia Co-operative Societies Commission (MCSC), various years. Note: Growth percentages calculated by author. Turnover data are not available before 2005.

and turnover as these assets and turnover included that of co-operatives' subsidiaries. Prior to 2011, subsidiaries were excluded from the statistics, hence resulting in the big percentage increase in assets and turnover for the period 2010–2011.

The number of co-operatives dispersed across the 14 states in Malaysia is shown in Figure 5. This figure shows that Selangor, Perak and Johor have the three highest numbers of registered co-operatives. Taking turnover as an indicator of financial performance as a measure of success of co-operatives, the co-operatives with the highest percentage turnover are: *Bank Rakyat*, the National Co-operative Organization of Malaysia (ANGKASA), Pahang, Wilayah Persekutuan, Johor and Terengganu. In general, all the states portrayed positive co-operative performances as more than 60% of the co-operatives were generating profits from their business activities. Co-operatives in Negeri Sembilan registered the highest percentage in terms of profit turnover. With regard to the performance, both *Bank Rakyat* and ANGKASA achieved turnover of above RM 800,000. These two entities played a significant role in the performance and development of the movement.

Generally, the co-operative movement could be categorized into urban and rural segments. Rural category includes various types of agro-based co-operatives, fishermen's co-operatives and co-operatives under the Farmers' Organization Authority (*Lembaga Pertubuhan Peladang*), Malaysia Fishery Development Authority *(Lembaga Kemajuan Ikan Malaysia, LKIM)* and government land development agencies such as FELDA, FELCRA and Rubber Industry Smallholders Development Authority (RISDA). Credit and banking co-operatives formed the backbone of the co-operative movement in the urban areas, and these two types of co-operative contributed the highest percentage of turnover to the movement. In 2010, the credit and banking percentage of share capital in the movement was 72%, while assets of the banking co-operatives alone were 90.3% (MCSC 2010). Other primary societies include consumer, housing societies, land development and school co-operatives.

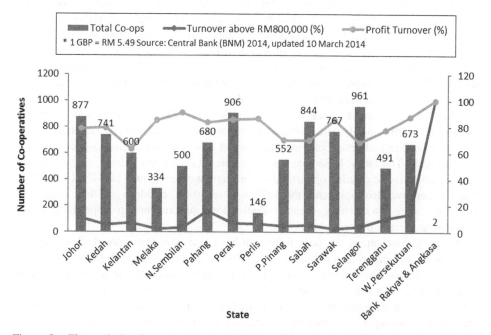

Figure 5.   The analysis of co-operatives' performance by turnover and states in 2011. *Source*: Monitoring Division, Malaysia Co-operative Societies Commission (MCSC), 2011.

It has been widely acknowledged that co-operatives played an important role in providing services to the rural community. Among their main functions are contractual work, transport services (lorries, buses and tankers), retail stores and mini-markets, the supply of electrical appliances, motorcycles and furniture. In the land development schemes, co-operatives are important as they became agents for their members to cater to the needs of settlers, thus ensuring the provision of quality goods at reasonable prices and at the same time undertake collective marketing of their produce including fruits, vegetables, chickens, goats and others.

The data show that 92.8% of co-operatives (6695 co-ops) are in the small (with annual sales between RM 200,000 and less than RM 1 million) and micro-clusters (with annual sales less than RM 200,000) and contributed only 4.5% and 3.4%, respectivel,y to the movement's turnover in 2009 (MCSC 2009). In contrast, the big cluster co-operatives (only 2.2% with annual sales above RM 5 million) were responsible for 83.1% of total co-operative movement's turnover. These comprise the banking and credit co-operatives. The medium-size cluster co-operatives (with annual sales of above RM 1 million but less than RM 5 million) contributed 9% of the movement's turnover. Therefore, the success, strength and performance of co-operatives are skewed towards the biggest cluster which is dominated by the banking and credit co-operatives.

Evidently, co-operatives by membership target groups show that the adoption co-operatives are present in various occupations among Malaysians. Co-operatives data in 2011 were further categorized by MCSC into 70 various sub-target membership groups. The groups are based on members' occupation, land development scheme, special needs criteria, educational institutions and activities performed. The special needs criteria group is related to single mothers, the disabled, the poor, pensioners and indigenous people. Co-operative memberships are also from various types of occupations such as government agencies, private sector, sports, banking, youth, land development schemes, doctors, teachers, small industries, insurance, lawyers, imam, factory and estate workers. To encourage a multi-ethnic co-operation, the government has launched 1 Malaysia. In line with the concept, the MCSC launched the 1 Community 1 Co-operative in 2010 (MCSC 2010). In 2011, there were 25 co-operatives among the estates workers with 9660 members. These co-operatives have an asset worth RM 14,575,744 and share capital of RM 4,579,913. On average, however, share holdings of an individual member in co-operatives amounts to only RM 474 per member.

The National Land Finance Co-operative Society Ltd (NLFCS) is a co-operative established in 1960 to solve the problems among retrenched and homeless estates workers arising from sale and resale of European-owned rubber estates. This co-operative was established by Tun Dr. V.T. Sambanthan, a prominent Malaysian Indian Congress leader, with the objective of creating opportunities for estate workers to own land (NLFCS 2012). The co-operative also looks after the welfare of members' children and their education, promotes house ownerships, creates small-scale entrepreneurship opportunities and provides financial aid to members.

Co-operatives among the poor fishermen have also been encouraged. However, the progress of fishermen co-operatives is relatively slower compared to others in the agriculture sector. Fishermen co-operatives were formerly under the surveillance of LKIM in accordance with the 1971 Fisheries Development Authority Act (Law of Malaysia 2006). However, with the new mandate of the MCSC in 2008, the fisheries co-operatives are currently managed by themselves to function within the fishing community to support the fishing industry. However, only 53% of these co-operatives are active, while 26% have been identified as potential to be effective (MCSC 2008). Another 26% which are deemed to have some possibilities would be revived. Their activities include marketing, transportation of fish, ice production and supply, leasing of licenses of boats and sale of diesel. MCSC is also entrusted with the responsibility to empower fishermen (upgrading the traditional coastal/inshore fishermen to become deep-sea fisherman) by providing technical training to the fishermen to enhance their skills and transforming the fishing industry into a commercialized business.

Some of the co-operatives such as the fishermen's and farmer's co-operatives are steered by government entities to achieve development measures as mentioned earlier. In some cases, co-operatives become a focal point for political mobilization at the local level especially at the state level. Hence, the reason for the escalation in the number of co-operatives, albeit, small and micro in size.

4. Research methodology

DEA was employed to estimate the relative efficiencies of co-operatives based on membership target groups (groups are made by MCSC). Data provided by MCSC are for the year 2011. Out of the 70 groups, only 56 profitable groups were selected for analysis as the DEA model is non-negative. The 56 profitable groups comprise 8944 co-operatives or 98.6% of the total registered co-operatives. DEA method was chosen for its ability to overcome problems of evaluating firm with multiple inputs and outputs and complex performance (Cooper, Seiford, and Zhu 2004; Zhu 2003). DEA could be performed even when conventional cost and profit functions (that depend on optimizing reactions to prices) could not be justified. Furthermore, DEA was developed by Charnes, Cooper, and Rhodes (1978) for applications in the public sector and not-for-profit organizations where typical economic behavioural objectives, such as cost minimization and profit maximization, may not be relevant.

The decision-making units (DMUs) in this study comprise 56 membership target groups. Following Coelli et al. (2005), variable returns to scale (VRS) input-oriented approach model was employed to measure technical efficiency of these groups as VRS calculates technical efficiency without being confounded by scale efficiency. Furthermore, constant returns to scale (CRS) assumption is only appropriate when all firms are operating at optimal scale and with perfect competition without constraints or influence from government or other factors. VRS model was chosen as it would indicate whether the DMUs are operating at constant, increasing or decreasing returns to scale. Input-oriented approach would measure how much of the inputs could be proportionally reduced without changing the outputs.

Table 1 shows the details of membership target group such as turnover, profit, members, assets and share equity. The choice of outputs in this analysis follows the study

Table 1. Descriptive statistics of output and inputs in the DEA membership groups analysis 2011.

Variables	Minimum	Maximum	Mean	SD
Outputs				
Turnover (RM)	43,452.00	13,690,540,598.00	328,606,602.61	1,825,328,291.85
Profit (RM)	11,219.00	153,6724,691.00	46,774,041.7679	213,565,107.77
Inputs				
Members (person)	317.00	2,087,254.00	125,077.78	341,625.78
Asset (RM)	119,192.00	73,389,316,753.00	1,656,712,859.46	9,801,047,084.73
Equity (RM)	38,723.00	2,599,264,172.00	187,145,985.392,9	502,383,391.975,13

done on the performance of Fortune 500 companies by Zhu (2003). Zhu studied the performance of the top 20 companies by considering revenue and profit as outputs, while assets, employees, equity, market value, earnings per share and return to equity were regarded as inputs.

In this case, turnover and profits constitute one of the three criteria, besides average ratio and non-financial aspects that are considered by the MCSC in ranking the performance to determine the best 100 co-operatives (MCSC 2012). It is imperative for co-operatives to be profitable to achieve their socio-economic goals. Members are considered as inputs because in co-operatives, besides being users of goods and services, they are also the owners of the co-operative enterprise. They have a very important role in management decision-making and they are required to contribute in terms of manpower, support and collective financial contributions towards their co-operative activities.

The discussion on DEA follows consideration of a set of n observations on the DMUs. Each observation, DMU_j ($j = 1, \ldots, n$), uses m inputs x_{ij} ($i = 1, 2, \ldots, m$) to produce s outputs y_{rj} ($r = 1, 2, \ldots, s$). The efficient frontier is determined by these n observations as in Equation (1) (Zhu 2003). θ^* represents the input-oriented efficiency score of DMU_j under evaluation. If $\theta^* = 1$, this indicate that DMU_j is on the efficient frontier:

$$\theta^* = \min \theta,$$

subject to

$$\sum_{j=1}^{n} \lambda_j x_{ij} \leq \theta x_{io}, \quad i = 1, 2, \ldots, m;$$

$$\sum_{j=1}^{n} \lambda_i y_{rj} \geq y_{ro}, \quad r = 1, 2, \ldots, s;$$

$$\sum_{j=1}^{n} \lambda = 1,$$

$$\lambda_j \geq 0, \quad j = 1, 2, \ldots, n.$$

(1)

The DEA process involves the following model:

$$\min \theta - \varepsilon \left(\sum_{i=1}^{m} s_i^- + \sum_{r=1}^{s} s_r^+ \right),$$

subject to

$$\sum_{j=1}^{n} \lambda_j x_{ij} + s_i^- = \theta x_{io}, \quad i = 1, 2, \ldots, m;$$

$$\sum_{j=1}^{n} \lambda_j y_{rj} - s_r^+ = y_{ro}, \quad r = 1, 2, \ldots, s;$$

$$\sum_{j=1}^{n} \lambda_j = 1,$$

$$\lambda_j \geq 0, \quad j = 1, 2, \ldots, n.$$

(2)

The frontier determined by Equation (2) (Zhu 2003) exhibits VRS, and the model is input-oriented VRS envelopment model. $\lambda_j = 1$ is the convexity constraint to account for VRS model. The VRS envelopment model identifies the VRS frontier with DMUs exhibiting increasing return to scale (IRS), CRS and decreasing return to scale (DRS) (Zhu 2003). Scale efficiency measures could be obtained for each DMU by conducting both CRS and VRS DEA, and then decomposing the technical efficiency (TE) scores obtained from the CRS DEA into two components, one due to scale inefficiency and one due to 'pure' technical inefficiency (i.e. VRS TE). The appearance of difference in the CRS and VRS TE scores for DMU is an indication that the DMU has scale inefficiency.

This research employs a two-stage method where the efficiency scores in the first stage are regressed upon the environmental variables (Coelli et al. 2005). This analysis would determine which of the inputs have significant influence on efficiency scores. Work by Simar and Wilson (2011) was considered as cross-sectional data were used, which means that homoscedasticity assumption would be violated. The use of ordinary least squares as proposed by Banker and Natarajan (2008; cited in Simar and Wilson 2011) is with the assumption that bounded noise at constant would be violated as well. Therefore, the DEA efficiency estimates from first-stage analysis are regressed on co-operative variables (turnover, member, equity) using non-linear Tobit regression.

The standard Tobit model is as follows for observation (co-operative group) i:

$$y_i^* = \beta x_i + \varepsilon_i,$$
$$y_i = y_i^* \quad \text{if } y_i^* \geq 0, \tag{3}$$
$$\text{and} \quad y_i = 0, \quad \text{otherwise,}$$

where $\varepsilon_i \sim N(0, \sigma^2)$, x_i and β are vectors of explanatory variables and unknown parameters, respectively, while y_i^* is a latent variable and y_i is the DEA score. Tobit regression was run using Gretl software version 1.1. Tobit regression equations are as follows:

$$\theta_i = \alpha_0 + \beta_1 * \text{Tover} + \beta_2 * \text{Pro} + \beta_3 * \text{Equity} + \beta_4 * \text{member} + \varepsilon_i, \tag{4}$$

where dependent variables are

θ_i: technical efficiency score (TE); scale efficiency (SE) and pure technical efficiency score at time t extracted from the DEA first stage.

The independent variables are as follows:

Tover: membership groups' turnover;
Pro: membership groups' profit;
Equity: membership groups' equity;
Member: membership groups' members;
ε is the random error term.

5. Empirical findings

5.1. DEA first-stage analysis findings

Sensitivity checking was conducted to ensure that there were no errors in measurement that would affect results. A test was run by omitting one output while repeating the DEA analysis (Ramanathan 2003). Results from several runs showed no significant change in the efficiency pattern. Analysis of peer result also confirm the result's robustness as all the efficient DMUs are similar in all the analysis and have formed peers of inefficient DMUs. The groups that have been found to be most efficient by DEA are with the efficiency measure of 1. Table 2 shows the efficiency scores from the analysis. The efficient groups are operating at the most productive scale size. The results reveal that based on CRS, only 10.7% of the co-operatives groups are efficient, while with VRS 19.6% are efficient. The difference between the percentages of efficient groups between CRS and VRS is quite significant. However, as discussed by Ramanathan (2003), this is because the assumption of CRS is relaxed as VRS variables are assumed. The percentage is higher under the VRS method as some groups which are not efficient under the CRS model had become efficient when the assumption of CRS (convexity constraint) is relaxed. The top 11 most efficient groups are banking, doctors, FELDA, affiliated co-operative (secondary co-operatives), single mothers, surveyors, welfare (co-operatives performing welfare activities), South Kelantan Development Authority (KESEDAR), Matriculation College, village development and schools.

Referring to Table 2, the mean score of CRS technical efficiency is 0.438. This score implies that the co-operatives on the whole should reduce their consumption of all inputs by 56.2% to be efficient. As for VRS (mean score 0.527), the co-operatives' consumption of all inputs should be reduced to 47.3% to become efficient. Following the study done by Bader et al. (2008), this finding could also be interpreted to consider the inefficiency of co-operatives. The results suggest that co-operatives have slacks where the resources are not utilized efficiently to produce the same outputs. Taking the mean score of VRS, this implies that co-operatives on the whole are having inefficiency level of 89.8% in producing their outputs.

Table 3 presents the distribution of efficiency results according to four categories. The results are ranked according to four different categories from highest, upper and lower intermediate to the least efficient. Only 11 membership target groups have the most efficient score (DMU 2, 5, 7, 8, 10, 13, 16, 20, 23, 27 and 50), while 10 groups are moderately efficient (DMU 6, 11, 22, 25, 26, 29, 47, 48, 52 and 55) and 21 groups are in lower efficiency group (DMU 12, 14, 17, 21, 24, 30, 31, 32, 33, 34, 36, 38, 39, 41, 42, 44, 45, 49, 51, 53 and 54). The least efficient groups are DMU 1, 3, 4, 9, 15, 18, 19, 28, 35, 37, 40, 43, 46 and 56.

The scale of efficiency of the DMU is computed as the ratio of CRS efficiency (technical [TE] and scale efficiency [SE]) to its VRS efficiency (pure technical efficiency [PTE]). As in many studies, the TE from CRS DEA is decomposed to one due to scale inefficiency and pure technical inefficiency. The results show 86% of the groups are with scale inefficiency.

This investigation found that 46.4% (26 groups) of the co-operative operating at the IRS. This means that they are currently operating at a lower scale sizes by operating under IRS, utilization of resources whereby they can achieve greater economies of scale if the level of operations are increased. Results indicate that 32.1% of the co-operatives (18 groups) are operating at DRS that is at a higher scale size than it should be.

5.2. Second-stage Tobit regression findings

The second-stage analysis attempts to investigate if any of the co-operative group characteristics (turnover, profits, members' equity and membership) have any influence on the efficiency scores. The goodness of fit of the models was assessed based on the test for normality of residuals. The results had indicated that all models had a good fit as all the

Table 2.   Efficiencies of co-operatives by membership target group.

DMUs (membership groups)	TE	PTE	SE	RTS
1. Gov. agencies	0.180	0.181	0.999	–
2. Banks	0.227	1.000	0.227	DRS
3. Youth land scheme	0.131	0.132	0.996	DRS
4. Fire brigade	0.014	0.112	0.121	IRS
5. Doctors	1.000	1.000	1.000	–
6. FELCRA settlers	0.621	0.709	0.876	DRS
7. FELDA settlers	1.000	1.000	1.000	–
8. Affiliated co-operative (secondary co-ops)	1.000	1.000	1.000	–
9. Teachers	0.159	0.246	0.647	DRS
10. Single mothers	0.527	1.000	0.527	IRS
11. Imam/bilal (mosque staff)	0.839	0.897	0.935	IRS
12. KIK (village industry co-ops)	0.075	0.347	0.216	IRS
13. Surveyors	0.183	1.000	0.183	IRS
14. Mosque members	0.477	0.493	0.969	IRS
15. Customs	0.039	0.131	0.301	IRS
16. Welfare activities	1.000	1.000	1.000	–
17. Family	0.530	0.532	0.997	DRS
18. KEMAS community development	0.067	0.070	0.953	IRS
19. Association	0.135	0.138	0.977	IRS
20. KESEDAR	1.000	1.000	1.000	–
21. KOBERA (co-operatives of the poor)	0.296	0.311	0.954	IRS
22. Community college	0.777	0.795	0.977	IRS
23. Matriculation college	1.000	1.000	1.000	–
24. Private college	0.553	0.5564	0.980	IRS
25. Landownership	0.632	0.637	0.993	IRS
26. KPK/KEDA (village development)	0.811	0.812	0.999	–
27. Rural development	0.412	1.000	0.412	IRS
28. Uniformed personnel	0.059	0.096	0.613	DRS
29. Teachers college	0.758	0.769	0.985	IRS
30. Fishermen	0.444	0.445	0.997	DRS
31. OKU (co-ops of the disabled)	0.394	0.440	0.897	IRS
32. General public	0.204	0.598	0.341	DRS
33. Government servants	0.202	0.352	0.575	DRS
34. Statutory agency workers	0.220	0.305	0.723	DRS
35. Factory workers	0.273	0.287	0.952	DRS
36. Estate workers	0.374	0.375	0.996	IRS
37. Stevedoring	0.203	0.205	0.989	IRS
38. Private co. workers	0.211	0.308	0.685	DRS
39. KPP (worker's investment co-ops)	0.387	0.390	0.992	IRS
40. Drivers	0.152	0.157	0.968	IRS
41. KPD (district development co-ops)	0.358	0.370	0.968	DRS
42. District officers	0.129	0.344	0.376	IRS
43. Small business	0.066	0.067	0.984	DRS
44. Pensioners	0.505	0.507	0.996	IRS
45. Farmers	0.315	0.315	0.999	–
46. Police	0.180	0.181	0.997	IRS
47. Technical workers	0.671	0.672	0.999	DRS
48. MARA Training Institute (IKM)	0.728	0.738	0.986	IRS
49. RISDA	0.318	0.470	0.676	DRS
50. Schools	1.000	1.000	1.000	–
51. Graduates	0.332	0.451	0.737	IRS
52. Housing estate	0.655	0.836	0.782	DRS
53. IPT (higher learning institute)	0.348	0.348	1.000	–

(Continued)

Table 2 – *continued*

DMUs (membership groups)	TE	PTE	SE	RTS
54. IPTS (private higher learning institute)	0.504	0.508	0.992	IRS
55. Entrepreneurs	0.699	0.699	0.999	DRS
56. Women	0.173	0.173	0.997	DRS
Mean	0.438	0.527	0.826	

Note: TE = technical efficiency based on CRS; PTE = pure technical efficiency based on VRS; SE = scale efficiency = CRS TE/VRS TE. E is efficiency. To calculate Inefficiency (IE), IE = (1 − E)/E. E.g. when $E = 0.527$, (1 − 0.527)/0.527 = 0.898 or 89.8% inefficiency.

errors exhibited were normally distributed with very small *p*-value. Table 4 portrays the co-operative group's Tobit regression results.

Tobit regression's results in Table 4 reveal that turnover, profit and equity are statistically significant at 1% alpha in influencing TE. Profits, members and share equity are statistically significant in influencing PTE of the groups, while only turnover and equity are statistically significant in influencing SE. Equity and members are found to be negatively correlated to TE and PTE. However, turnover and profits are positively correlated.

Co-operative turnover, profit and equity are representative of co-operative size; thus, it could be stated that the group size is statistically significant in influencing and determining the efficiency of the membership groups. This finding is consistent with the study by Jaforullah and Devlin (1996) on New Zealand's dairy industry that confirmed that co-operative farm size had an influence on the industry's efficiency. The findings demonstrate that the bigger the co-operatives' turnover and profit, the higher the co-operative efficiency scores.

Membership as an independent variable, however, is found to be statistically significant in explaining PTE but not statistically significant in explaining SE and TE. As reported by Fulton and Giannakas (2001), co-operative membership size has a negative impact on co-operative success; therefore, this result is also consistent with their findings as increased membership has an impact of decreasing both TE and PTE of co-operatives.

6. Discussion

The annual increase in the number of co-operatives indicates the relevance of co-operative movement in the Malaysian economy. The NCP and the creation of the Commission have further spurred the growth. The financial and management support by the government has enabled the co-operatives to sustain their activities. The spillover effect of the country's buoyant economic growth has also contributed to the co-operatives' moderate but steady growth for the past 90 years. These two factors are very important as they have ensured the

Table 3. Efficiencies scores of membership target group by various range.

Efficiency scores (VRS)	No. of co-operative (%)
1 (highest)	11 (19.6)
0.61–0.99 (upper intermediate)	10 (17.9)
0.3–0.6 (lower intermediate)	21 (37.5)
<0.3 (least efficient)	14 (25)
Total	56 (100)

Table 4.   Co-operative groups Tobit regression results.

Variables	TE	PTE	SE
Constant	0.653708	0.76286	0.741822
LNTurnover	0.0717038	0.030437	0.0782241
	(0.00272)**	(0.29159)	(0.00944)**
LNProfit	0.119534	0.149293	0.026824
	(<0.00001)**	(<0.00001)**	(0.38131)
LNMembers	− 0.023376	− 0.0505148	0.00694829
	(0.22555)	(0.02999)*	(0.77496)
LNEquity	− 0.179797	− 0.149251	− 0.1.3356
	(<0.00001)**	(<0.00001)**	(−0.00001)**

Note: Results obtained from data analysed using Gretl Version 1.1.
**Significant at 1%; **significant at 5%.

survival of the co-operatives. Apart from the 'big' co-operatives (which is only slightly over 2% of the total co-operatives), over 90% of co-operatives (micro and small) grew, developed and survived as mentioned earlier with very heavy government financial and management support.

Although, in general co-operatives have been perceived as important and beneficial to the country's development, DEA results indicate that the performances of co-operatives membership target groups are not satisfactory. This estimation by VRS revealed only 19.6% of the groups performed efficiently, while 55.4% of the groups are between upper and intermediate efficiency, and although they are underperforming, they still may be able to survive as profits are being made (not optimal) which could help sustain their operations. About 25% of the groups are with very low efficiency scores and should be considered as vulnerable groups which may face the risk of making losses if situation does not improve. The weak groups are predominantly among the government agency workers, youth land development scheme, small business, KEMAS (workers in department of community development), Koperasi Bela Rakyat (KOBERA) (co-operative of the very poor), the general public, factory workers, fire brigade, uniform personnel, teachers, customs, drivers and women. Equally relevant is the fact that 46.4% of the groups are operating at a lower scale size and 32.1% operating at a much higher scale size resulting in unattainable economies of scale.

Tobit regression had demonstrated that turnover, profit, equity and members are important variables that influence efficiency scores of the membership groups under study. Turnover, profit and equity are pertinent and statistically significant in influencing the technical efficiency. Scale efficiency scores are influenced only by equity and turnover. Turnover is positively correlated to all three scores which postulate that the higher the turnover of co-operative groups, the greater the efficiency scores. The negative relationship between equity and members with the efficiency scores, however, became a challenge to co-operative performance because as equity and members increased, all three efficiency scores decrease. This outcome suggested that co-operatives are less efficient when membership size and equity gets bigger. The result further reinforced the perception that co-operatives are facing members' apathy and free rider problem (Department of Co-operative Development 2003). As memberships became larger and equity increased, the co-operatives could encounter problems in retaining members' loyalty and support towards their co-operatives. It appears that co-operative members are not active members but they became members just to cash on the dividends distributed by their co-operative and subsequently not motivated to participate in the co-operatives any longer. This finding seems to concur with the MIT. As evident from other research mentioned earlier, poor management skills among the co-operatives have been identified as one of the main challenges. The issues include financial mismanagement and fraud as highlighted in cases such as the Deposit Taking Co-operatives in 1986, Co-operative Central Bank (CCB) 1986 and ANGKASA in 2008 (Consumers Association of Penang 2013).

7. Theoretical and policy implications

7.1. Theoretical implications

As pointed out earlier, co-operatives are voluntary in concept and user-based in nature, and hence, the members' loyalty and active participation in the activities of their co-operatives are crucial for success. They have a role to play to ensure that their co-operatives' are efficiently managed. The findings of this study conclude that there is a relationship between members' active participation and efficient performance of co-operatives.

The other theoretical implication of this study is on the methodology. The advantage of this method is on its objectivity. DEA efficiency rating is based on the numerical data and not on the subjective opinions of respondents. Building upon the strength of this method, future analysis would have to consider the performances of co-operatives by their functions such as credit and finance, consumer, housing and services as this information is critical to benchmark co-operatives against their competitors in the market.

7.2. Policy implications

The co-operative movement's sustainability and progress are dependent on the improvement of co-operatives' performance. The high percentage of inefficient co-operatives should be monitored closely and addressed effectively to ensure the success and achievement of the National Co-operative Plan. Public perception on the role of co-operatives in the nation's economic and social development should be improved. Improvement of the movement's efficiency will directly enhance public perception of co-operatives.

Also, the government should review its policy to establish co-operatives in every community in Malaysia. It is not the number of co-operatives that matters but the quality of these co-operatives. Efforts have to be geared towards driving the existing co-operatives to be efficient and profitable. As the current co-operatives have not achieved their full potentials, inefficiencies could be costly not only to the relevant co-operatives but also for the government.

7.3. Governance and managerial implications

Only with efficient management will there be a strong co-operative movement which is truly a self-help and independent business enterprise. Members that fail to uphold their responsibilities to their co-operatives will destroy the organization. As evident from the analysis, it is critical for the members to participate to ensure a vibrant co-operative. Members need to be educated to perform their role and understand the governance structure of co-operatives.

Although the co-operative movement was an option to assist the government to accomplish national development goals, the co-operative movement needs to be re-examined, especially with regard to its membership, governance and management. Serious consideration has to go into improving the governance and management of co-operatives. Strict enforcement of co-operative law to ensure co-operative compliance towards co-operative principles and law could further improve co-operative businesses, increase sustainability and enhance the possibility of success and achievement of any government plan for the development of co-operatives.

This study found that that there is a relationship between professional managers and profitable co-operatives. The successful co-operatives are big co-operatives and these co-operatives are managed by professional managers. Hence, the remuneration for the management personnel of co-operatives has to be reviewed and upgraded to a performance-based compensation and attractive promotion packages.

7.4. Limitations

Determining the relevant inputs and outputs to be considered in the analysis was a challenge as data were limited. Despite the limitations, this study provides empirical evidence on co-operatives. Social output data, number of co-operative workers, wages and operating costs are important considerations but, unfortunately, were unavailable at the point of research. Due to this limitation, results on efficiency ratings should be interpreted with caution. Such information would further enhance the development of co-operative movement. Further analysis on the efficiencies would also include the external factors such as the GDP per capita, inflation rate and unemployment rate.

8. Conclusion

Overall assessment of the co-operative performance indicated positive growth in the number of co-operatives, memberships, share capital, assets and turnover within the Malaysian co-operative movement. This achievement was possible due to the strong financial and non-financial support by the federal government and the perceived significant role that co-operatives played in the country's development. DEA evaluation on the efficiencies of 56 co-operative groups in the movement, however, had revealed an unsatisfactory performance. Only 19.6% of the groups achieved the highest efficiency scores. These results thus revealed that the co-operative groups are not operating at their most productive scale or optimal scale.

The management capacity of co-operatives is a key factor in determining their performances. Building strong managerial and executive team is paramount and this could be achieved by enhancing the understanding of the members, board of directors and management on the principles and concept of co-operatives through effective communications, education and training which would improve members' motivation to participate and support their own co-operative business. Groups that are efficient are likely to be groups with active membership and effective leadership.

The high percentage of inefficient groups in this study indicates wasted resources in co-operatives' operations which could be the result of poor governance or management problems. The problem is more acute among the poor and rural dwellers' (e.g. farmers and fishermen) co-operatives. As a result of the inefficiencies, it became a disincentive among the existing members which led to apathy towards their co-operatives. Tobit regression results further confirmed that group size is important in influencing the efficiency of co-operative groups and reinforced the issue of members' apathy and free rider problem in the movement. The results endorse the general perception that co-operatives in Malaysia are facing challenges which require immediate attention.

Notes

1. Email: g3azmah@um.edu.my
2. Email: fatimah_kari@um.edu.my
3. GBP = RM 5.49. Source: Central Bank (BNM) 2014, updated 10 March 2014.

References

Bader, M. K. I., S. Mohamad, M. Ariff, and T. Hassan. 2008. "Cost, Revenue and Profit Efficiency of Islamic versus Conventional Banks: International Evidence Using Data Envelopment Analysis." *Islamic Economic Studies* 15 (2): 23–76.

Berger, A. N., and D. B. Humphrey. 1997. "Efficiency of Financial Institutions: International Survey and Directions for Future Research." *European Journal of Operational Research* 98 (2): 175–212.

Birchall, J. 2003. *Rediscovering the Cooperative Advantage: Poverty Reduction through Self-Help*. Geneva: International Labour Organization. Accessed October 24, 2008. http://www.acdivocacoopex.org/acdivoca/CoopLib.nsf/d40b394e0533f5b285256d96004f1ad4/e23f0c803fc6060485256ef400575ed8/$FILE/Rediscovering%20the%20Cooperative%20Advantage.pdf

Birchall, J. 2004. *Co-operatives and the Millennium Development Goals*. Geneva: International Labour Organization. Accessed December 15, 2007. http://www.ilo.org/public/english/support/lib/resource/subject/coop/birchallbook_2004.pdf

Birchall, J., and L. H. Ketilson. 2009. *Resilience of the Cooperative Business Model in Times of Crisis*. International Labour Office, Sustainable Enterprise Programme. Geneva: ILO. http://www.copac.coop/publications/2009-ilo-coop-resilience.pdf

Birchall, J., and R. Simmons. 2004, January. *What Motivates Members to Participate in the Governance of Consumer Co-operatives? A Study of the Co-operative Group* (Research Report No. 2), Accessed May 30, 2012. http://www.uwcc.wisc.edu/info/consumer/rr2.pdf

Birchall, J., and R. Simmons. 2008. "The Role of Cooperatives in Poverty Reduction: Network Perspectives." *The Journal of Socio-Economics* 37: 2131–2140. www.elsevier.com/locate/soceco

Borgaza, C., and R. Spear, eds. 2004. *Trends and Challenges for Co-operatives and Social Enterprises in Developed and Transition Countries*. Trento: Edizioni 31.

Cain, J. L., U. C. Toensmeyer, and S. Ramsey. 1989. "Cooperatives and Proprietary Firm Performance as Viewed by Their Customers." *Journal of Cooperatives* 4: 81–88.

Charnes, A., W. W. Cooper, and E. Rhodes. 1978. "Measuring Efficiency of Decision-making Units." *European Journal of Operational Research* 2: 429–444.

Coelli, T. J., D. S. P. Rao, C. J. O'Donnell, and G. E. Battese. 2005. *An Introduction to Efficiency and Production Analysis*. 2nd ed. New York: Springer Science + Business Media.

Consumers Association of Penang. 2013. "History of Co-operative Scandals." Accessed December 2. http://www.consumer.org.my/index.php/focus/cooperative-scandals/391-history-of-cooperative-scandals

Cooper, W. W., L. M. Seiford, and J. Zhu. 2004. *Handbook on Data Envelopment Analysis*. Boston, MA: Springer.

Department of Co-operative Development. 2003. *Dasar Koperasi Negara dan Pelan Tindakan 2002–2010* [The National Co-operative Policy and Action Plan]. Kuala Lumpur: Malaysia Department of Co-operative Development.

Din, J. 2006. "Applying Data Envelopment Analysis to Evaluate the Efficiency of Fishermen Associations in Malaysia." PhD thesis, University Putra Malaysia, Selangor, Malaysia.

Dogan, E., and D. K. Fausten. 2003. "Productivity and Technical Change in Malaysian Banking: 1989–1998." *Asia-Pacific Financial Markets* 10 (2–3): 205–237.

Emrouznejad, A., B. Parker, and G. Tavares. 2008. "Evaluation of Research in Efficiency and Productivity: A Survey and Analysis of the First 30 Years of Scholarly Literature in DEA." *Journal of Socio-Economics Planning Science* 42 (3): 151–157.

Frederick, D. A. 1997. *Co-ops 101: An Introduction to Cooperatives* (Cooperative Information Report 55, Rural Business-Cooperative Service), US Department of Agriculture. www.rurdev.usda.gov/rbs/pub/cir55/cir55rpt.htm

Fredericks, L. J. 1986. *The Co-operative Movement in West Malaysia: Policy, Structure and Institutional Growth*. Kuala Lumpur: Department of Publications, University of Malaya.

Fukuyama, H. 1996. "Returns to Scale and Efficiency of Credit Associations in Japan: A Non-Parametric Frontier Approach." *Japan and the World Economy* 81: 259–277.

Fukuyama, H., R. Guerra, and W. L. Weber. 1999. "Efficiency and Ownership: Evidence from Japanese Credit Cooperatives." *Journal of Economics and Business* 51 (6): 473–487.

Fulton, M., and K. Giannakas. 2001. "Organizational Commitment in a Mixed Oligopoly: Agricultural Cooperatives and Investor-Owned Firms." *American Journal of Agricultural Economies* 83 (5): 1258–1265. http://www.jstor.org/stable/1244817

Idris, N., and A. M. Abdullah. 2011. "Evaluation of Factors Affecting Agricultural Cooperative Performance in Malaysia." Proceedings of the 2nd International Conference on Business and Economics, Holiday Villa Beach Resort and Spa, Langkawi, Kedah, March 14–16, 2354–2361.

International Co-operative Alliance. 2010. "International Cooperative Alliance Statistical Information on the Co-operative Movement." Accessed February 8, 2010. http://www.ica.coop/coop/statistics.html

Islam, M. A. 2012. "An Appraisal of the Performance of Two (2) Development Financial Institutions (DFIS) in Malaysia." *International Journal of Economics and Management Sciences* 1 (70): 64–74.

Ismail, Y., and S. Mohd Sarif. 2010. "Convergence of Global and Traditional Managers' Characteristics: A Case of Senior Management of Cooperatives in Malaysia." *Journal of International Business and Entrepreneurship Development* 5 (1): 28–47.

Jaforullah, M., and N. J. Devlin. 1996. "Technical Efficiency in the New Zealand Dairy Industry: A Frontier Production Function Approach." *New Zealand Economic Papers* 30: 1–17.

Katib, M. 1999. "Technical Efficiency of Commercial Banks in Malaysia." *Banker's Journal Malaysia* 111: 40–53.

Kaur, I., S. Devi, R. Omar, R. Abd, and R. Samad. 2005. *Kajian Kedudukan Tenaga Kerjadan Kepuasan Kerjadalam Kalangan Kakitangan Gerakan Koperasi di Malaysia* (Research Monograph). Cooperative College of Malaysia.

Krishnasamy, G., A. H. Ridzwa, and V. Perumal. 2003. "Malaysian Post Merger Banks' Productivity: Application of Malmquist Productivity Index." *Managerial Finance* 30 (40): 63–74.

Lang, G., and P. Welzel. 1996. "Efficiency and Technical Progress in Banking. Empirical Results for a Panel of German Cooperatives Banks." *Journal of Banking and Finance* 20: 1003–1023.

Lang, G., and P. Welzel. 1998. "Technology and Cost Efficiency in Universal Banking: A 'Thick Frontier'- Analysis of the German Banking Industry." *Journal of Productivity Analysis* 10: 68–84.

Laws of Malaysia. 2006. *Lembaga Kemajuan Ikan Malaysia Act 1971*. Kuala Lumpur: National Printing Department.

Laws of Malaysia. 2008. *Cooperative Societies Act 1993 (Act 502) and Regulations*. Kuala Lumpur: MDC Publishers Printers.

Malaysia. 1981. *Fourth Malaysia Plan (1981–1985)*. Kuala Lumpur: National Printing Department.

Malaysia Co-operative Societies Commission. 2008. *Suruhanjaya Koperasi Malaysia: Peneraju Kecemerlangan Koperasi*. Kuala Lumpur: SKM.

Malaysia Co-operative Societies Commission. 2009. "Co-operative Movement Annual Statistics." MCSC Official Portal. Accessed February 8, 2010. http://www.skm.gov.my/web/guest/perangkaan-am-koperasi-mengikut-fungsi1

Malaysia Co-operative Societies Commission. 2010. "Economic Reports Co-operative Sector 2010." Accessed September 7, 2012. http://www.skm.gov.my/getmedia/d2bc3d2b-5682-4cad-8070-9b595abe5e22/Economic-Report.pdf.aspx

Malaysia Co-operative Societies Commission. 2012. "Malaysia Co-operative Societies Commission Official Portal, Indeks 100 Koperasi Terbaik Malaysia." Accessed November 26, 2012. http://www.skm.gov.my/getmedia/d673a4fb-4815-4c9f-aace-b215313b36bf/DIREKTORI-INDEKS-100-KOPERASI-TERBAIK-MALAYSIA-2012-updated.pdf.aspx

Md. Salleh, H., A. Arshad, A. F. Shaarani, and N. Kasmuri. 2008. *Gerakan Koperasi Di Malaysia*. Selangor: Co-operative College of Malaysia.

National Economic Advisory Council. 2010. *New Economic Model for Malaysia*. Kuala Lumpur: Percetakan Nasional Malaysia Berhad.

National Land Finance Co-operative Society Ltd. 2012. "Official Portal." Accessed May 5, 2013. http://www.nlfcs.com.my/

Othman, A. 2010. "Estimating the Productivity Change of Bank Kerjasama Rakyat Malaysia Berhad and Malaysia Nine Commercial Banks: A Malmquist Productivity Index Approach." Paper presented at the Euricse Conference 2010: Financial Co-operative approaches to Local Development through Sustainable Innovation, Trento, Italy.

Othman, A., and F. Kari. 2008. "Enhancing Co-operative Movement to Achieve Malaysia's Development Goals." Paper presented at the ICA Research Conference 2008: The Role of Co-operatives in Sustaining Development and Fostering Social Responsibility, Trento, Italy.

Pasiouras, F., and E. Sifodaskalakis. 2007. *Total Factor Productivity Change of Greek Cooperative Banks* (Working Paper), University of Bath, School of Management.

Pasiouras, F., E. Sifodaskalakis, and C. Zopounidis. 2007. *Estimating and Analyzing the Cost Efficiency of Greek Cooperative Banks: An Application of Two-Stage Data Envelopment Analysis* (Working Paper), University of Bath, School of Management.

Porter, P. K., and G. W. Scully. 1987. "Economic Efficiency in Cooperatives." *The Journal of Law and Economics* 30: 489–512.

Ramanathan, R. 2003. *An Introduction to Data Envelopment Analysis: A Tool for Performance Measurement*. New Delhi: Sage.

Rodrigo, Shamsulbahriah K. A., and N. Mansor. 2013. "Narrowing Disparities via the New Economic Model (NEM): Is Malaysia Set to Excel Beyond Its MDGs Targets MDGs." In *Millennium Development Goals and Community Initiatives in the Asia Pacific*, edited by A. Singh, E. T. Gonzalez, and S. B. Thomson, 11–33. New Delhi: Springer.

Sexton, R. J., and J. Iskow. 1993. "What Do We Know about the Economic Efficiency of Cooperatives: An Evaluative Survey." *Journal of Agricultural Cooperatives* 8: 15–27.

Simar, L., and P. W. Wilson. 2011. "Two-Stage DEA: Caveat Emptor." *Journal of Productivity Analysis* 36 (2): 205–218.

Sufian, F. 2004. "The Efficiency Effects of Bank Mergers and Acquisitions in Developing Economy: Evidence from Malaysia." *International Journal of Applied Econometrics and Quantitative Studies* 1 (4): 53–74.

Sufian, F. 2006. "Size and Returns to Scale of the Islamic Banking Industry in Malaysia: Foreign versus Domestic Banks." *IIUM Journal of Economics and Management* 14 (2): 147–175.

Sufian, F. 2007. "What Explains Differences in the Efficiency of Non-Commercial Bank Financial Intermediaries? Empirical Evidence from Malaysia." *Asian Academy of Management Journal of Accounting and Finance* 3 (1): 37–57.

Sufian, F., and M. Z. Abdul Majid. 2007. "Bank Ownership, Characteristics and Performance: A Comparative Analysis of Domestic and Foreign Islamic Banks in Malaysia." *Munich Personal RePEc Archive (MPRA)*. http://mpra.ub.uni-muenchen.de/12131/

Sufian, F., and S. Ibrahim. 2005. "An Analysis of the Relevance of Off-Balance Sheet Items in Explaining Productivity Change in Post-Merger Bank Performance: Evidence from Malaysia." *Management Research News* 28 (4): 74–92.

Zeuli, K. A., and R. Cropp. 2004. *Cooperatives: Principles and Practices in the 21st Century*. http://learningstore.uwex.edu/assets/pdfs/A1457.PDF

Zhu, J. 2003. *Quantitative Models for Performance Evaluation and Benchmarking: Data Envelopment Analysis with Spreadsheet and DEA Excel Solver 2005*. Boston, MA: Kluwer Academic.

Conclusion: Mutuality in the Asia Pacific region

Jonathan Michie[a] and Chris Rowley[b,c]

[a]Department for Continuing Education, University of Oxford, Oxford, UK; [b]Centre for Research on Asian Management, City University, London, UK; [c]HEAD Foundation, Singapore Department for Continuing Education, University of Oxford, Oxford, UK

Co-operatives, mutuals and employee-owned businesses play an important role in the economies and societies of a number of Asia Pacific countries. They have a long history, and an evolving and interesting future. The case of China is perhaps particularly significant, as the co-operatives there are operating still within the context of state control, and it is not clear how they might develop in the future. Were China to decide that the co-operative and mutual corporate form had an important role to play alongside state, personal and shareholder-ownership models, then given the significant role of China in the global economy, this could have a major impact on the type of corporate diversity the world's economy enjoys in future years. These 'alternative' corporate forms include consumer co-operatives and producer co-operatives, as well as financial mutuals and employee ownership. There have been calls for this broadly defined mutual sector to become the most dynamic part of the global economy by the end of this decade. In the context of the Asia Pacific, this looks an attractive proposition in terms of promoting corporate diversity and delivering sustainable development and regional resilience.

1. The landscape

The research reported in this collection has revealed a rich diversity of co-operative and mutual businesses across the Asia Pacific region, with many longstanding co-operative and mutual organizations – most obviously in the agricultural and food retail sectors – being joined by new mutuals, in some cases responding to the dissatisfaction with the Western 'shareholder value' approach to business. The collection reports research from a range of sectors of the economy, across a number of countries. Many of the case studies include important insights regarding the particular organizations or national contexts being researched, but they also suggest various common themes and areas for future research and policy work that this concluding contribution draws together and develops, pointing to an important emerging agenda that does indeed deserve further consideration, analysis and policy action.

2. Key research findings

We present five key research findings from our collection.

2.1 The role of mutuals in China, and the role of China for mutuals

The 'The long march of Chinese co-operatives: towards market economy, participation, and sustainable development' considers the development of co-operative firms in China from their origins in the early twentieth century. The key conclusions are that the contemporary Chinese economic transition would benefit from the presence of a strong, Western style, co-operative sector, but that the contribution of the co-operative sector towards sustainability requires civil society to develop as well. We return to this thought, but first it is worth considering the related findings from the research on 'Old and new rural co-operative medical schemes in China' which compares the health cooperatives fêted in Maoist China in the 1960s to the New Rural Medical Co-operative Scheme (NRCMS) that has been operating in China since 2002. Organizational and ideological similarities between the old and new co-operative medical schemes are described, and by mapping continuities and discontinuities in the way the co-operative organizational model has been deployed under different contexts, it argues for the usefulness of blending historical method and organizational analysis as a means of understanding some of the challenges of contemporary Chinese social policies. It concludes that the new incarnation of the scheme is closer now to Western models of mutual insurance, that political emphasis has shifted and in turn so has consumer expectations, and that China is now no longer inward looking – as the second largest economy and a key player in the modern world stage, it is attempting to apply broadly western models of insurance to tackle its population challenges.

The paper on 'The role and characteristics of social entrepreneurs in contemporary rural cooperative development in China' describes how rural communities in China have experienced rapid changes in recent years under the government's policy of 'new countryside development'. It is found that there has been an increase in social entrepreneurship led by village leaders and capable individuals with an entrepreneurial spirit. This research is based on in-depth interviews with several of these social entrepreneurs. It aims to explore the key issues related to the role of social entrepreneurship and leadership in developing rural co-operatives. The findings suggest that there are multiple key characteristics of social entrepreneurship in the process of rural co-operative development. The research findings have implications for rural community development in transitional economies in terms of developing social entrepreneurship capabilities.

A key conclusion from these three studies of China is that the co-operative and mutual model could well have an important role to play not only in the country's continued economic development, but also in the related development of social services (or a welfare state) and civil society, and also for the country's regional development. Further, the global significance of the Chinese economy gives the potential for corporate forms developed by China to help shape the future development of corporate forms globally. The current, Western-based 'shareholder value' model will not necessarily endure as the globally dominant one, and what replaces it could well be influenced by the sort of alternatives explored in this special issue – with stakeholders other than shareholders playing a crucial role.

2.2 Producer co-operatives

The piece on 'Governmental influences on the evolution of agricultural cooperatives in Vietnam' examines the evolution of Vietnamese agricultural co-operatives over the last six decades through four distinct phases – the voluntary collectivization period of 1954–1975, the compulsory collectivization period of 1975–1981, the de-collectivization period of 1981–1997 and the neo-collectivization period since 1997. It argues that a stable legal environment and appropriate government support are important for the successful development of co-operatives. Thus, the Cooperative Law 1997 and its revisions in 2003 and 2012 established a legal framework to encourage the formation and development of commercialized agricultural co-operatives at the national level. Most of these agricultural co-operatives have been able to provide valuable services to their members, especially input supply, marketing and selling of agricultural outputs. Some co-operatives have diversified their services by mobilizing investment capital, developing production planning, building market share, creating jobs and achieving high returns. This model of agricultural co-operatives could work well, it argues, in the context of transitioning economies more generally. And as argued above, what economies in the global economy will transition to is no longer as clear as it might have appeared 10 years ago. It now appears more likely that models other than the 'shareholder value' one may hold sway.

In Papua New Guinea (PNG), co-operatives have a long and dynamic history, and since 2000 they have been promoted by the government as a vehicle for economic and social development. There have been few studies on co-operatives in PNG and no prior research into cocoa co-operatives. 'Development and challenges of Cocoa Cooperatives in Papua New Guinea: the case of Manus Province' explores the development and challenges of cocoa co-operatives, formed mainly in response to governmental initiatives, to provide access to processing facilities, overcome market difficulties, reduce unemployment and improve living conditions. Co-operatives and collectives among farmers and growers have proved important mechanisms in fostering social and economic development in PNG. Problems associated with land tenure insecurity, small land holdings, lack of access to capital and poor rural infrastructure, among others, have been reduced with farmer collectives and co-operatives across the Pacific countries. Again, there appear to be lessons for future developments internationally.

2.3 Employee ownership as an answer to the problem of succession planning

The growth pattern of a major employee-owned business in Taiwan, finding four growth stages: the 'family-owned', the 'family- and manager-owned', the 'family-, manager-, and staff-owned' and the 'family-, manager-, staff- and franchisee-owned' is proposed in 'Growth pattern of an employee-owned business: a narrative inquiry concerning the new venture creation experience of wowprime in Taiwan'. This suggests that such a pattern could become an important part of the business environment around the world, especially as they find that mutual ownership had enabled the enterprise to grasp opportunities and turn environmental threats into new opportunities. This study contributes to advancing the understanding of the ownership pattern from private (family), to shareholder (manager), to employee-ownership. Certainly such succession planning, beyond family ownership, is one that faces family owned firms across the world. In the UK, such owners will be advised by their banks or other financial advisors that the options are to sell to an established firm, or float on a stock exchange. The alternative, of selling to the existing employees – most likely by selling the business to an employee-ownership trust that will borrow funds to purchase the shares, and then hold the shares on behalf of the employees, paying off the loan from future profits – is unlikely to be mentioned. And other stakeholders in addition to employees – such as customers or suppliers – can be incorporated in such a trust ownership model. Were this option to be promoted, publicized, supported and understood, then such a corporate model, with a significant ownership stake held by the employees – and/or by other stakeholders – would no doubt come to play a far greater role than is the case today, growing over time.

2.4   Alternative business models

Co-operatives and mutuals are owned by their members (customers, producers or employees), in contrast to shareholder-owned (or privately owned) companies. Their alternative corporate forms are generally associated with alternative aims, objectives, missions and purposes, with concomitantly different behaviours, policies, practices and outcomes. One of these differences is often a greater concern for societal impact and the local community. However, shareholder-owned companies have over the past 20 years or so also been adopting 'corporate social responsibility (CSR)' policies and strategies. The nature and significance of such approaches have of course varied hugely. In some cases, it is no more than a 'box ticking' exercise and PR opportunity; in other cases, the approach is taken more seriously. The objective basis for such policies and practices to become embedded in shareholder-owned companies is where they can be shown to make good business sense. This is the basis of the concept of creating shared value (CSV) that Porter and Kramer (2011, 66) describe as 'policies and operating practices that enhance the competitiveness of a company while simultaneously advancing the economic and social conditions in the communities in which it operates'. The differentiating point of CSV from CSR is that it 'expands the total pool of economic and social value' (65), rather than redistributing values already created by firms. To the extent that the local communities become genuine stakeholders in these firms, they may be seen as at least a parallel to mutuality. The contribution 'From corporate social responsibility to creating shared value with suppliers through mutual firm foundation in the Korean bakery industry: a case study of the SPC Group' analyses the process of a company's strategy developing from CSR to CSV using a case study of a leading bakery franchise in Korea. It concludes that this process has enabled local cluster development, which they see as being closely related to 'regional resilience' (as described by Christopherson, Michie, and Tyler 2010), with the simultaneous creation of business and social value contributing to the achievement of this regional resilience. In an era when regional economies, competitiveness and resilience appear to be taking centre stage, this is an important argument, and links back to the importance noted above of alternative corporate forms playing a potentially significant role in China's regional development.

2.5   Efficiency and economic competitiveness

So, co-operatives and mutuals have been found to play an important role in the economies and societies of the Asia Pacific region. Yet, the importance of their future role will no doubt depend on how competitive and resilient these corporate forms prove to be, not only in delivering on the agendas for which they are particularly well suited, but also in competing more generally with shareholder-owned companies, which globally remain dominant.

Analysing the performance of co-operatives in Malaysia in 'Assessing the performance of co-operatives in Malaysia: an analysis of co-operative groups using a data envelopment analysis approach' suggests that there is huge potential for the sector, provided the existing co-operatives can be made to raise their game to match the performance of the 'best in class'. Evaluating 56 out of Malaysia's 70 co-operative groups, productivity and efficiency were evaluated. Despite the financial and non-financial support by the federal government – and the perceived significant role played by the co-operatives in the country's development – the performance of the majority of co-operatives was found not to have been satisfactory. However, around 20% of the groups under study were found to be efficient. Interestingly, the 'big co-operatives' (that comprise less than 2% of co-operatives in the country) dominated among the successful ones. This is interesting, given that it is often thought that the co-operative model can work well at small scale, but is not so suited to large-scale operations. It concludes that co-operatives in Malaysia are facing challenges necessitating immediate attention. The point about scale might be born in mind in this regard, perhaps looking at how economies of scale and scope could be better developed and exploited, including through the development of 'shared services' and joint 'back office' operations that could be owned and operated by consortiums of co-operatives, using this as a mechanism to raise performance to match the levels of efficiency enjoyed by many of the large co-operatives.

3. The future research and policy agenda

Several important conclusions thus emerge from this collection of diverse and original research into a number of Asia Pacific countries reported here. First, the co-operative and mutual sector is found to play in important role in a number of these countries – important economically and socially.

Second, such corporate forms appear particularly well suited to certain sectors, such as agriculture where producer co-operatives can provide shared services to the individual producers who are the co-operative's members. Such collaboration can provide the economies of scale and scope necessary to be efficient.

Third, though, the significance of co-operatives and mutuals is most certainly not limited either to the past or to certain sectors only: quite the contrary, new developments in the global economy, such as 'CSV', and the role of social entrepreneurship, lend themselves far more naturally and effectively to co-operative and mutual corporate forms than to 'shareholder value' constructs.

Fourth, all economies are faced with the issue of succession from family ownership when for whatever reason those families are no longer able or willing to continue to lead those firms. At present, the dominance of shareholder ownership as a corporate form is fed by such successions invariably being into a shareholder-owned model – either through flotation on a stock exchange or through sale to an existing shareholder-owned company. If the 'employee trust' model came to be seen as the – or at least a – natural form of succession, then that in itself would feed what would likely come to be a growing sector of the economy along co-operative, mutual and employee-ownership lines.

Fifth, whether this will be the future of the Asia Pacific – and global – economies will depend in part on public policy; the fact that the co-operative and mutual sector has proved more resilient than the shareholder model since the global financial crisis of 2008 may lead public policy to become more supportive of such developments – but this is unlikely to happen automatically. There are powerful voices and forces promoting the orthodox 'shareholder value' model, so for an alternative to be promoted will require policy activism, and powerful countervailing pressure to overcome the orthodox pro-business lobby.

Sixth, co-operatives and mutuals can play important local and regional roles, promoting local and regional resilience: as regional competitiveness is seen to be an increasingly important goal of public policy, this may provide a route to public policy recognizing the benefits of a stronger co-operative and mutual sector.

Seventh, the findings cast further doubt on the ideas behind universal theories such as convergence (Rowley and Benson 2004). The diversity of organizational structures and practices as well as the continuing and differential role of the state, all need to be taken on board and considered in more contextually sensitive theory building.

4. Conclusion

The 2008 global financial crisis also led to a growing recognition that a degree of corporate diversity is useful and important to economic success and resilience, including by the 2010–2015 coalition government in the UK (see Michie 2011). Promoting co-operatives and mutuals is one way of achieving and sustaining such diversity, in face of the strong and continual counter-pressures in favour of the 'shareholder value' model. Of course, committing to greater diversity is not sufficient unless the degree of diversity is actually measured and reported – something that the UK government has failed to do, but which is being undertaken by the Oxford Centre for Mutual and Employee-owned Business (see www.kellogg.ox.ac.uk).[1] Achieving government commitments to promoting corporate diversity, including through the promotion of co-operatives and mutuals would be an important and historic step towards strengthening the economies of the Asia Pacific region.

In this, the International Co-operative Alliance has taken an important lead, with an ambitious *Blueprint* to make the co-operative and mutual sector the most dynamic sector of the global economy by the end of this decade (see Davies and Mills 2012). The research published in this special issue suggests that such a goal is indeed relevant, important and achievable.

In this final contribution to this collection on the important alternative organizational forms of mutuals and co-operatives in the Asia Pacific region, we have reiterated the key findings thematically. We have also set out a future research and policy agenda for this important area. We hope this comes to fruition in the near future.

Note

1. See Michie and Oughton (2013) for details of the 'Michie-Oughton' Index of Corporate Diversity, which demonstrates that the degree of corporate diversity in the UK economy since 2010 has actually deteriorated, rather than improved.

References

Christopherson, Susan, Jonathan Michie, and Peter Tyler. 2010. "Regional Resilience: Theoretical and Empirical Perspectives." *Cambridge Journal of Regions, Economy and Society* 3 (1): 3–10.

Davies, Will, and Cliff Mills. 2012. *Blueprint for a Cooperative Decade*. Brussels: International Co-operative Alliance.

Michie, Jonathan. 2011. "Promoting Corporate Diversity in the Financial Services Sector." *Policy Studies* 32 (4): 309–323.

Michie, Jonathan, and Christine Oughton. 2013. "Measuring Diversity in Financial Services Markets: A Diversity Index." Centre for Financial & Management Economics Discussion Paper No. 113, SOAS, London.

Porter, M. E., and M. R. Kramer. 2011. "Creating Shared Value." *Harvard Business Review* 89 (February): 62–77.

Rowley, C., and J. Benson, eds. 2004. *The Management of Human Resources in the Asia Pacific Region: Convergence Reconsidered*. London: Frank Cass.

Index

For Product Safety Concerns and Information please contact our EU
representative GPSR@taylorandfrancis.com Taylor & Francis Verlag GmbH,
Kaufingerstraße 24, 80331 München, Germany

Printed and bound by CPI Group (UK) Ltd, Croydon, CR0 4YY
08/05/2025
01864357-0005